The Penguin Dictionary of South African Quotations

Jennifer Crwys-Williams

THE PENGUIN DICTIONARY OF SOUTH AFRICAN QUOTATIONS

PENGUIN BOOKS

PENGUIN BOOKS
Published by the Penguin Group
27 Wrights Lane, London W8 5TZ, England
Viking Penguin, a division of Penguin Books USA Inc, 375 Hudson Street, New York, New York 10014, USA
Penguin Books Australia Ltd, Ringwood, Victoria, Australia
Penguin Books Canada Ltd, 10 Alcorn Avenue, Toronto, Ontario, Canada M4V 3B2
Penguin Books (NZ) Ltd, 182-190 Wairau Road, Auckland 10, New Zealand
Penguin Books, Amethyst Street, Theta Ext 1, Johannesburg, South Africa

Penguin Books Ltd, Registered Offices: Harmondsworth, Middlesex, England

First published by Penguin Books 1994

ISBN 0 140 51311 6

Typeset by Iskova Image Setting
Printed and bound by Creda Press
Cover design by Hadaway Illustration & Design

Contents

Acknowledgements

Sincere thanks to Michelle Leon, Chief Librarian, Times Media, and to Sheila Watts, Chief Librarian, *The Star*. Damian Hardy's help was both enthusiastic and invaluable. Professor Alf Stadler of the University of the Witwatersrand found a long-elusive quote for me.

It is customary to thank one's editor – out of politeness and custom. But my thanks to Pam Thornley, whose editing was meticulous, thoughtful and, on occasion, deliciously quirky, are both sincere and appreciative.

But the biggest vote of thanks must go to the numerous South Africans who opened their mouths, sometimes rashly, allowing their words to be captured for posterity in this book. It goes without saying that *The Penguin Dictionary of South African Quotations* would not have been possible without the journalists, past and present, who faithfully (and sometimes with obvious glee) reported the statements of both the mighty and the ordinary man and woman in the streets of South Africa.

Acknowledgements

Abortion

If conceived in derelict poverty and squalor, the foetus has no rights – better not to have been born.
Anonymous doctor

If South Africa is to survive, let alone thrive, abortion laws will have to be liberated from their current patriarchal, conservative origin.
Anonymous doctor

We deplore the Holocaust after 50 years, yet ignore the slaughter of unborn babies.
Wendy Busby

Abortion will never be a part of the South African way of life.
Department of Health & Population Development

It is important to realise that doctors have never been in the forefront of the issue. It is a women's issue.
Marge Dyer, doctor

If you go to the dongas there are abandoned children there.
Nomboniso Gasa, activist

Every abortion stops a beating heart.
Peter Hammond, cleric

Our hormones ensure that even when an abortion or a miscarriage is a blessed relief, our minds and bodies go on mourning long after our wombs have returned to normal.
Jane Raphaely, editor, publisher

When pro-lifers push pictures of tiny bodies into the faces of women whose feelings about abortion are already complex and far too deep for words, they are not being cruel to be kind. They are being stupid.
Jane Raphaely

It's not just your body; that's a person you're carrying.
Dene Smuts, politician

The next step might be euthanasia, where people who are a burden to society, like the elderly or even persons with Aids, will simply be removed.
Albu van Eeden, doctor

Given the conservatism of South Africans, a party that fights an election on an abortion ticket can probably flush its future down the loo.
Andrea Vinassa, journalist

Advertising

Societally, advertising's major role is the presentation of a better standard of living through the persuasive communication of newer, better products or services.
Graham de Villiers, businessman

Advertising is merely the tool of business.
Derrick Dissel, businessman

Advertising should sell, not tell.
Derrick Dissel

Whenever advertising begins to pall the ad industry finds a 'new' sub-species of mankind.
John Farquhar, editor

There isn't an editor in the world who isn't aware every minute of the day that he needs advertising like a drowning man needs air.
Marilyn Hattingh, editor

To say advertising is at the cutting edge of various art forms is bullshit.
John Hunt, creative director

Advertising people use great music, they take lines of great poetry and distort them – if they could get away with it, they would use the crucifixion to advertise nails.
Robert Kirby, satirist

Great advertising is an idea that's just one nano-second ahead of the wave.
Mike Lipkin, marketer

The Johannesburg advertising game is a Gucci streetfight.
Chris Marais, editor

Life's a pitch and then you die.
Style

Any advertising campaign, no matter how brilliant the creative content, is only as good as the people who see or hear it.
Len van Zyl, businessman

In advertising it is undoubtedly true that a rifle is better than a shotgun.
Len van Zyl

The use in advertising of so-called pornographic representation of women is much more pernicious than your common or garden blue movie simply because the 'short stories' in ads are presented as if they are normal and natural.
Andrea Vinassa, journalist

We believe that the best advertising talks to individuals, not to target markets.
Graham Warsop, businessman

Affirmative Action

For every token hired, there's always work for a consultant.
Anonymous

Here we have not a mere fashion but an ethic and a strategy concerned both with compensating for past wrongs towards the disadvantaged and ensuring a more equitable and secure future for the whole society.
Lionel Abrahams, poet, novelist

A particular bridgehead for the assault on social institutions in South Africa today is that of 'affirmative action', a conveniently woolly term which in the guise of upliftment is prone to stray from the necessary provision of extra training and development into group-based schemes inimical to individual merit.
Jack Bloom, politician

Heaven help the white boy because the new constitution won't – especially if the poor sap is trying to get a job.
Andrew Donaldson, journalist

Affirmative action is not about handouts, it's about working.
Andrew Donaldson

Affirmative action programmes that do not address white insecurities are doomed to failure.
David Lapin, rabbi, academic

As a white youth with your spoilt little yuppie ethos, you're marginalised from jobs with social relevance.
Lianne Mazzulo, a 20-something

Affirmative action is not in conflict with equality.
Etienne Mureinik, academic

Affirmative action will mean an explosion of black yuppies followed by a flood of Rolexes on the market.
Hilary Prendini Toffoli & Carolyn Sacks, journalists

Affirmative action: the revenge of tokenism.
Hilary Prendini Toffoli & Carolyn Sacks

We're going into social engineering in the market place just as we had social engineering in the past and the results will be disastrous – not only for individuals but for business.
Johann Redlinghuys, businessman

I have seen affirmative action programmes designed to advance black people which are excluding many black people because they aren't considered black enough.
Barry Ronge, journalist

A necessary process of bending over blackwards.
Pieter-Dirk Uys, satirist

One of the unspoken tenets of affirmative action is that white women are about to be squeezed.
Janet Wilhelm, journalist

African National Congress (ANC)

They can't control their own people – they will never control us.
Anonymous Zulu

The Nats have succeeded through the media in painting the ANC black, literally and metaphorically.
Neville Alexander, intellectual

The message must have got through to the ANC by now that, as tools for Soviet purposes, they are obsolete.
Pik Botha, politician (1989)

It has been a favourite conversational gambit of mine for some time to put it to white South Africans that they should be on their knees every morning giving thanks to God for the fact that the African National Congress is the dominant force in black politics.
John Carlin, correspondent, The Independent (UK)

Round its neck, like an albatross, hangs Winnie Mandela.
FW de Klerk, State President, 1989-94; Deputy President, 1994-

It's almost an extinct species.
FW de Klerk

Those who make a living reporting political activities must surely have heard ANC anthems, which have been a standard part of peace marches and in which, even if you can't understand the language, the rat-tat-tat of automatic rifle fire

in the chorus and the firing position taken up by the singers, are unmistakable.
Wessel Ebersohn, journalist

They are a threat to public safety.
Jannie Geldenhuys, soldier

The ANC is a destructive organisation which uses violence as a method and is ideologically dominated by the communists.
Chris Heunis, politician (1988)

The ANC is what our forefathers bequeathed to us, to win back the freedom of this, our vast and lovely country.
Patrick 'Terror' Lekota, politician

We of the ANC do not wish to dominate others by virtue of our numerical superiority.
Albert Luthuli, ANC President General, Nobel Peace Prize

We are fighters for freedom, in a manner of course that demands no bloodshed, yet fighting on the political platform.
Albert Luthuli

I have joined my people in the new spirit that moves them today, the spirit that revolts openly and boldly against injustice, and expresses itself in a determined and non-violent manner.
Albert Luthuli

Ask me anything, but don't ask me to kill the ANC.
Samora Machel, President (Mozambique), to Pik Botha

The ANC was in no mood to be stymied by a lack of solid facts.
Rian Malan, writer

You must decide whether you are for a political or a military solution in South Africa because the ANC is for a political solution.
Nelson Mandela, President, May 1994-

The ANC wants peace, but we are not pacifists... We are militants in the struggle for freedom.
Nelson Mandela

The ANC will not compromise on a matter of principle or policy.
Nelson Mandela

Nobody who hears our policy can fault it.
Nelson Mandela

The ANC couldn't run a bath let alone a country.
Hugh Murray, publisher

A somnolent body of professional men.
New York Times (1952)

The ANC acknowledges that Afrikaners were never the sole implementers and benefactors of apartheid; and that Afrikaners are not inherently racist; and that there is a long Afrikaner history of anti-colonialism and freedom fighting.
Carl Niehaus, politician

We prefer not to have people with a non-political record but I would hesitate to call it a strict code.
Carl Niehaus

Afrikaans

As long as people like Eugene Terre'Blanche and Ferdi Hartzenberg are out there associating Afrikaans with their raucous style of racist nationalism, the language is under threat.
Achmat Davids, historian

If it is recognised that Afrikaans has so many varieties, that even fly-taal or tsotsi-taal is part of the language, then Afrikaans has a future.
Achmat Davids

Most Afrikaans people are like jibbing horses, they won't believe that we have a language of our own.
Stephanus du Toit, cleric, founder of Afrikaans language movement

The language the Afrikaner is so proud of was in fact not started by only them, but also by slaves amongst whom were our Khoikhoi, Abathwa and Xhosa forebears.
Patrick 'Terror' Lekota, politician

Afrikaans is the product of South African conditions – a cultural treasure which is an intrinsic part of our country's history.
Patrick 'Terror' Lekota

We are going to transform Afrikaans from being the language of the oppressor into the language of freedom, of liberation.
Nelson Mandela, President, May 1994-

Afrikaans as a language might not be the rich language it is today if the English had not oppressed them.
Thandi Modise, politician

Afrikaans is a language invented by and for the settlers in South Africa.
Gaddi Ngirane, academic

Most Afrikaners have always known that the majority of those that speak the language are black, and yet they have tried to project a special character for Afrikaans as the language of white Afrikaners.
Carl Niehaus, politician

Afrikaans is the most beautiful language in the world to have been made up in 10 minutes.
Pieter-Dirk Uys, satirist

A language of great words to use in rude jokes or to describe an unforgettable sunset in the Karoo.
Pieter-Dirk Uys

If ordered under threat of death not to speak it at all, I shall quietly pray in Afrikaans.
At van Wyk, academic

Afrikaners

An Afrikaner is a person of Dutch extraction who believes in the expansion of the brandy market, the promotion of the corn market and suppression of the native.
Anonymous official (19th century)

They like to kick up a lot of dust, then do a cost-benefit analysis.
Anonymous

We need to get back to our roots to feed the plant of our culture.
Anieta Armand, broadcaster

There is nothing the blacks can offer that the Afrikaner wants.
Carel Boshoff, secessionist; chairman, Afrikaner Volkswag

Because he had to fight for his survival he was inclined to isolate himself in such a way that he could maintain his own way of life.
PW Botha, Prime Minister/State President, 1978-89

The idea of an Afrikaner people as a cultural entity and religious group with a special language will be retained in South Africa as long as civilisation stands.
PW Botha

The security and happiness of all minority groups in South Africa depends on the Afrikaner.
PW Botha

There is only one element that can break the Afrikaner in this country, and that is the Afrikaner himself. It is when the Afrikaner, like a baboon shot in the stomach, pulls out his own intestines. We must guard against that.
PW Botha

If you leave Afrikaners alone they are not such bad bastards.
Breyten Breytenbach, poet, writer

The Afrikaner has been undergoing a slow, more or less private change of heart and mind for a long time; and it has proved decisive.
William Deedes (Lord Deedes of Aldington), politician, editor (UK)

Their religion, setting them apart from the unelected pagans about them, bred in them a sense of special destiny as a people.
CW de Kiewiet, author, academic

As long as there is a commitment among Afrikaners to cherish their language and their culture and traditions, the Afrikaner nation will continue to exist.
FW de Klerk, State President, 1989-94; Deputy President, 1994-

The Afrikaner is bursting out of his definitions of himself as well as those of others.
Willem de Klerk, businessman, academic

One must not expect that the Afrikaner will break away from his philosophy of separateness, and the idea of majority rule will remain unacceptable to the greater number, even were it forced upon them.
Willem de Klerk

The Afrikaner started off as a rural entrepreneur.
JP de Lange, academic

The real Afrikaner is a man who longs to be accepted, a man who longs to be wanted, and to be loved.
René de Villiers, editor, politician

The Afrikaners look upon anyone who talks of leaving as a traitor, almost exclusively because they have nowhere else to go.
Chris Gibbons, broadcaster

In an attempt to match history to present realities, suddenly they've started discovering coloureds in Voortrekker laagers.
Hermann Giliomee, academic

Nothing which can affect the well-being of the Afrikaners escapes the notice of the Broeders.
David Harrison, documentary film maker, author

We cannot be the slaves of others.
Ferdi Hartzenberg, CP leader

God is our most powerful weapon, our spiritual atomic bomb.
Ferdi Hartzenberg

From the Afrikaner's history it may be deduced that he wants to live, and if survival means recasting political ideology he will do so.
Johan Heyns, theologian

Hidden by the simplifications of the mass media are the stoic majority who work hard and obey their God.
Fergal Keane, correspondent, BBC Radio

I have observed instances in which the children of Afrikaner families were running around as naked as kaffirs in Congoland.
DF Malan, Prime Minister, 1948-54

The right wing does not have the copyright on Afrikaners.
Madelein Malan, lawyer

We shit on the altars of Western enlightenment and defy the high priests who would have us behave in accordance with its moral tenets.
Rian Malan, writer

They had come to believe that only the strong survived, that a white man had to hold his ground, gun in hand, or else go under.
Rian Malan

One does not become less of an Afrikaner because of what other people think.
Wynand Malan, politician

Decent people who have been misled by their leaders.
Nelson Mandela, President, May 1994-

We have to acknowledge and confess a history where Afrikaners, once having gained power, held on to it at all costs, and committed terrible crimes against humanity in the process.
Carl Niehaus, politician

Afrikaners are the children of an uncertain frontier, born into enduring insecurity on the open veld.
Ken Owen, editor

The Christian rulers of Afrikanerdom began to observe the un-Christian precept that the end justified the means.
Alan Paton, writer

One of the many tragic ironies I see here is the spectre of a ruling people who survived the concentration camps of the Anglo-Boer War, yet inflict forced removals upon others, and after a long struggle for educational liberation, imposed Bantu education upon people striving for better opportunities.
Edward J Perkins, ambassador (USA)

The Afrikaners might fight dirty in politics, like politicians everywhere, but in my opinion it is not in their nature to stoop to assassination.
Eschel Rhoodie, propagandist

Afrikaners hardly read books, never mind showing admiration for people who write them.
Karel Schoeman, writer

Liberalism, communism, Mohammedanism threaten to rob the Afrikaner of the legacy of Blood River.
Eugene Terre'Blanche, AWB leader

Finally to be condemned to be a footnote in the history books: a white tribe of basically decent people who went mad on the southern tip of Africa and had to eventually be put to sleep in the most humane way, democratically of course.
Pieter-Dirk Uys, satirist

No one should underestimate Afrikanerdom's capacity to slough off the old skin of white superiority and re-emerge with non-racialism written all over its smiling face.
Stanley Uys, journalist

The Afrikaner has always been divided, although there is an underlying bond in a common state.
Piet van der Schyff, historian

White Afrikaners are not exactly a protected species in darkest Africa.
Dries van Heerden, journalist

I don't think that our roots as Afrikaners are planted in the soil of justice.
Wilhelm Verwoerd, academic

We are not colonialists, we carry the name of this continent in the denomination of our people.
Constand Viljoen, soldier, politician

So long as we honour God we will survive as a volk.
Constand Viljoen

Nobody can be a good South African if he is not first an Afrikaner.
Koot Vorster, dominee

Without doubt they understand Africa better than any other whites have ever done, for the simple reason that for much of their tortuous history they have lived like Africans, close to the land, risking all its hazards, its harshness, and its caprice.
Peter Younghusband, foreign correspondent

Afrikaners know that in Africa power is respected and compassion is often mistaken for weakness.
Peter Younghusband

Afrikaner Weerstandsbeweging (AWB)

The AWB, like the National Socialist German Workers Party, is run on the *führerprinzip*.
Wessel Ebersohn, journalist

The AWB and their cronies are more noise than anything.
Hernus Kriel, politician

Those in the northern suburbs have decided the AWB is their only salvation.
Japie Oelofse, AWB

Despite misconceptions associated with the coincidental similarity between the movement's emblem and three Luger pistols joined at the lips, the AWB has no plans to seize the country by force, and will settle for an independent Volkstaat consisting of the Transvaal, the Orange Free State, and a small slice of northern Natal with access to the Indian Ocean, but not vice versa.
Gus Silber, journalist

From far away you can recognise us as the bearers of God's light in Africa.
Eugene Terre'Blanche, AWB leader

A minor grouping of eccentric, overweight, old-fashioned former Nationalists who have found the easy way to free publicity on CNN and in other media by wearing funny hats, growing dirty beards, falling off angry horses and waving a Nazi salute at the world.
Pieter-Dirk Uys, satirist

The kindergarten cops.
Weekly Mail & Guardian

Age

I worship youth. Getting old is a tragedy.
Chris Barnard, surgeon

The older you grow, the more you are inclined to reach back to the things of your youth.
PW Botha, Prime Minister/State President, 1978-89

At my age I don't have much patience.
Mangosuthu Buthelezi, IFP leader, politician

With my hands like I've always done.
Danie Craven, SA Rugby Board President (on being asked how he felt on his 75th birthday)

I don't mind the lines and wrinkles, it's the cross-hatching that irritates me.
Bruce Fordyce, sportsman

I can't say that all of a sudden, wow, I'm a grand and wise old man.
Sol Kerzner, entrepreneur (on turning 50)

Only an enduring sense of humour sculpts those laughter lines.
Reg Lascaris, businessman

When you reach a certain age, herbaceous borders begin to hold more interest.
Prue Leith, cook

A woman who will tell her age will tell everything.
Olga Levinson, writer

In the economy of the poor, every man over 65 and woman over 60 is worth maybe R400 a month – and, therefore, better be treated right.
Mike Muller, academic, writer

I find it much better than I feared.
Harry Oppenheimer, businessman (on turning 84)

No matter how old you are you can always find a young cucumber.
Sharon Rohrbeck, journalist

What use is a disappointed mind in a body which may fleetingly look like a thirty-something?
Clem Sunter, businessman, scenario strategist

We only become aware of our mortality – and in so doing enter the realm of adulthood – when we begin to recognise the fundamental facts of life: growing old and death.
Marianne Thamm, journalist

Longevity in this country can mean staying out of the firing line of an R1 or an AK-47.
Andrea Vinassa, journalist

When my CV is read out I feel like a piece of Africana.
John Vorster, Prime Minister, 1966-78 (1963)

Aids

All agree that workplace discrimination – for instance, dismissal, demotion or transfer – merely on the grounds of Aids or HIV is unwarranted and will constitute an unfair labour practice.
Edwin Cameron, lawyer

It is a tragic historical irony that just when South Africa is on the brink of a new political dispensation, it should also be facing the onslaught of the most devastating plague of modern times.
Sholto Cross & Alan Whiteside, academics

It is inconceivable that the course of the epidemic will not add fuel to an already fiery political debate.
Sholto Cross & Alan Whiteside

The legacy of Afrikaner Calvinism still means that government interventions are, at worst, prudish and, at best, elliptical.
Mark Gevisser, journalist

Aids sends the Hippocratic oath scurrying for cover.
Georgina Hamilton, journalist

Nature's truth is that unless we guide the youth towards safer sex, the alternative is playing into the hands of a killer disease.
Nelson Mandela, President, May 1994-

With Aids as the prison warder, sex has ceased to be something you do.
Barry Ronge, journalist

The way any mention of condoms is banned by some local organisations – the SABC, for instance – you'd think they gave people Aids, not helped prevent it.
Sunday Times

Aids simply cannot play second fiddle to political and economic upheaval in South Africa.
Tracy Webster, actress

Ambition

Without a mixture of good human emotions and a sense of priorities, ambition can be changed from an asset of virtue to a monster.
Jack Penn, surgeon, philosopher, artist

If you are too ambitious you will lose everything.
Constand Viljoen, soldier, politician

Angling

Morality has little to do with angling *per se,* except in the wider context of human behaviour and motivation.
Wolf Avni, ranger

Casting for trout is like ballet, nè?
Evita Bezuidenhout, ambassador

I have always been under the impression that for trout fishing one had to be decked out top to toe in *Field and Stream* fashion, with extra light and whippy rods that cost a fortune – one for sunny days, one for overcast weather.
Marino Corazza, journalist

The art of fly-tying is limited only by imagination.
Robert Kirby, satirist

Marlin fishing is a sport of a kind, and quite a rip socially, but most of all the clearest indication that mankind has yet to come up with a better alternative to evolution.
Patrick Lee, writer

There is nothing as exhilarating as meeting the Evening Rise in the high country.
Tom Sutcliffe, businessman

Trout remain the nicest fish not to be actually catching.
Tom Sutcliffe

Animals

What is there to say about kudu – except that, when they become a nuisance, you shoot them?
Stephen Gray, writer

A good horse is like a good wife – very hard to find.
Germain Marquis, restaurateur

Man is the most important animal.
Ina Perlman, charity worker

The animals are going, and once we lose them, what will we have for our children?
Oom Piet Seleteng, conservationist

You only know animals if you talk to them.
Oom Piet Seleteng

Apartheid

The struggle against apartheid was a bond that hooped together a multitude of people who would otherwise have quarrelled.
Anonymous

If we'd called it ethnic cleansing we might have got away with it.
Evita Bezuidenhout, ambassador

Because you could not translate the word apartheid into the more universal language of English, the wrong connotation was given to it.
PW Botha, Prime Minister/State President, 1978-89

The acceptance of vertical differentiation with the built-in principle of self-determination must apply on as many levels as possible.
PW Botha (1981)

Apartheid has only been one of the myriad manifestations of the real enemy, which is power.
André Brink, writer, academic

Apartheid failed because of the IFP's opposition to the balkanisation of South Africa into so-called independent states, and its refusal to open negotiations with the government until and unless all political parties had been unbanned and political prisoners released.
Mangosuthu Buthelezi, IFP leader, politician

Apartheid is like slavery.
Joaquim Chissano, President (Mozambique)

Apartheid is mental violence.
Danie Craven, SA Rugby Board President

Separate development was morally justifiable if you look at it as a constitutional option.
FW de Klerk, State President, 1989-94; Deputy President, 1994-

I killed apartheid, not Mr Mandela.
FW de Klerk

Apartheid is the most logical and the most ludicrous and the most loathsome theory for solving the problems of ethnic diversity.
Nicholas Fairbairn, politician (UK)

Now the National Party has disowned it, but the little bastard won't leave home.
Arthur Goldstuck, journalist

The end of apartheid isn't the end of life, it's the beginning of everything else.
Nadine Gordimer, writer, Nobel Prize for Literature

I belonged to a world, in terms of my background, which I think suffered the worst extremes of apartheid, a world where our mothers and sisters would walk 3 km, sometimes 6 km, whenever there was a drought to fetch water.
Chris Hani, Umkhonto we Sizwe chief of staff, SACP general secretary

The process of segregation was aided and abetted by English-speakers.
Anthony Heard, editor

I do not accept that a policy of differentiation on a basis of race and ethnicity represents legalised racial discrimination.
Chris Heunis, politician

I carried a pass book that defined me as a gardener because I couldn't be recognised as an artist by law in this country; blacks must be labourers.
John Kani, actor

The disgraceful spectre of over 30 black men of all ages, all sizes, handcuffed together in twos, snaking through the dusty streets, under the incredible escort of two unarmed policemen was part of the essence of apartheid.
Aggrey Klaaste, editor

Apartheid was structurally programmed to fail.
Piet Koornhof, politician

The policy had no safety valve; it was immutable.
Graham Leach, correspondent, BBC Radio

Many shops had to have two doors; one for us blacks and one for whites.
Patrick 'Terror' Lekota, politician

We were herded into squalid townships to rot away, or into Bantustans to starve to death; we were shot and maimed, or killed at random, housed in overcrowded single-sex hostels to lead abnormal lives, or locked up in prisons to be tortured or hanged for dubious crimes.
Patrick 'Terror' Lekota

Apartheid was not only a caste system but a statement about reality amounting to a denial, which then sought to be self-enforcing.
Joseph Lelyveld, editor (USA)

Apartheid – in theory and in practice – is an effort to make Africans march back to tribalism.
Albert Luthuli, ANC President General, Nobel Peace Prize

Apartheid seems utterly indifferent to the suffering of individual persons, who lose their land, their homes, their jobs, in the pursuit of what is surely the most terrible dream in the world.
Albert Luthuli

Coming to the Post Office now, and having to wait and do all that jazz because there were three whites; we had to wait hours on end, we being a hundred or so.
Solly Madlala, Soweto resident

I wanted to cut off the hand of apartheid.
Gabriel Mahokoe, murderer (explaining why he shot a white family)

The principle of apartheid is that we have two separate spheres, not necessarily with an absolute dividing line, not separate territorial spheres.
DF Malan, Prime Minister, 1948-54

If there were no apartheid, if blacks had the vote, if we were able to live where we like, there would have been no need for liberation movements in this country.
Nelson Mandela, President, May 1994-

Apartheid itself was a war against the people.
Nelson Mandela

Segregation serves not simply as the institutional and ideological buttress of the white monopoly of power at a time of rapid social change; it is the central mechanism for the reproduction of cheap and coercible migrant labour.
Shula Marks, historian

Apartheid has contaminated a very beautiful jurisprudence.
Mandla Mchunu, street lawyer

To shut other people out, as successive governments have programmed white society to do to the black communities, is to shut oneself in.
Es'kia Mphahlele, academic, writer

As regards all the various nations we have here, the White nation, the Coloured nation, the Indian nation, the various Bantu nations, something to which we have given too little regard is the fact that numerically the White nation is superior to all other nations in South Africa.
Daan de Wet Nel, politician (1966)

Black people may find it hard to believe, but the main purpose of apartheid was not racial separation, nor even racial domination; it was to enrich the ruling class.
Ken Owen, editor

It (apartheid) ranks as one of this century's most disastrous feats of social engineering.
Edward J Perkins, ambassador (USA)

It would appear that the policy of the Union Government was to have two nations in South Africa.
Councillor Qamata of Xalanga

South Africans are sick of waiting for apartheid to be expelled from the bowels of our country.
Gavin Relly, businessman (1988)

Apartheid is the policy that has been applied in South Africa ever since Jan van Riebeeck landed three hundred years ago; it is the policy that brought civilisation to this country, that changed this country from a state of barbarism into one of the most sought-after countries of the world.
PJ Roos, politician (1948)

It is a myth that apartheid is a safeguard for the Afrikaner's survival.
Anton Rupert, businessman

The demon of racialism must be buried and forgotten; it has shed among us sufficient blood. We are one people.
Pixley Ka Isaka Seme, lawyer

I remember the humiliation to which my parents were subjected by whites in shops and in other places where we encountered them, and the poverty.
Mosima Gabriel Sexwale, class of '76, convicted of high treason

Apartheid: A system of institutionalised discrimination applied to South African citizens wishing to visit Australia.
Gus Silber, journalist

We woke up one morning to hear that Malan had won the election and that meant he shut the door on our faces.
Walter Sisulu, politician

The long struggle against apartheid has bred a culture of revolution.
Allister Sparks, journalist

If we reject the Herrenvolk idea and the principle that the white man cannot remain master, if the franchise is to be extended to the non-Europeans, and if the non-Europeans are developed on the same basis as the Europeans, how can the Europeans remain master?
JG Strijdom, Prime Minister, 1954-58

It's important that we show that white people are also victims of apartheid.
Dali Tambo, TV chat show host

Not only has South Africa segregated areas, it also has the technology to create segregated airwaves.
Derrick Thema, journalist

I myself was an aspirant Springbok with a desire for national colours but that was denied me because of my skin.
Steve Tshwete, politician

It is no longer a pigment of the imagination.
Pieter-Dirk Uys, satirist

Apartheid has been such a horrendous experience in black lives that only if it is exorcised in a single, all-encompassing, all-cleansing ritual will the psyche be satisfied.
Stanley Uys, journalist

Grand apartheid was really one of history's all-time scams.
Phillip van Niekerk, journalist

On the matter of apartheid the English pot can certainly not call the Afrikaner kettle black.
At van Wyk, academic

It will take a very long time to complete the separation between races, but we have set our foot on that road, and we will do it eventually.
HF Verwoerd, Prime Minister, 1958-66

We did what God wanted us to do.
HF Verwoerd

Differentiation is not discrimination.
HF Verwoerd

Just as the damage and humiliation of the past provokes sadness, it also induces anger.
Lloyd Vogelman, academic

It Italy it's called Fascism, in Germany, national socialism, and in South Africa, Christian nationalism.
John Vorster, Prime Minister, 1966-78 (1942)

If separate development is not maintained, South Africa will not be worth it for me any longer.
John Vorster (1963)

We felt very strongly that we had to preserve our identity, because that is a God-given right that every man has, the black man, the coloured and the white.
Koot Vorster, dominee

Apartheid's greatest failing may yet prove to have been economic and not political: for poor people are not naturally inclined to democratic tolerance.
Patti Waldmeir, correspondent, Financial Times (UK)

Non-discriminatory norms can be given the force of law, but the emotional and cognitive step into 'non-racialism' as a quality that penetrates the warp and weft of society is a long, long way off.
David Welsh, academic

Architecture

In the geology of South African structures are to be read the accretions of our history and the choices we have made.
David Goldblatt, photographer

When buildings cease to exist as coherent structures, their remains or footprints may yet be eloquent not only of what ruined them but of what may follow.
David Goldblatt

Armed Struggle

Attack is part of defence.
Benny Alexander, politician

We need to kindle and rekindle the struggle and bypass the fears and collective prejudices, unless we are all to go down in that barbaric insanity of one person, one bullet.
Breyten Breytenbach, poet, writer

The reason why I was never attracted to the armed struggle is that there will be no spoils of war. There will be no beautiful women to bring home.
Mangosuthu Buthelezi, IFP leader, politician

Whoever touches my security forces touches me.
FW de Klerk, State President, 1989-94; Deputy President, 1994-

We will go to war with a 100 per cent effort.
Dougie, skinhead, apprentice vehicle designer (1993)

When men rebel against their own government, a cause is usually to be found in some form of injustice, grievous oppression, unendurable evil.
George and Knysna Herald (1914)

The place was like a war zone – bullets, road blocks, rocks through the car windscreen. I blasted my way out of there.
Juhan Kuus, photographer

Our struggle was ever alive – now low tide, then high tide.
Patrick 'Terror' Lekota, politician

In the face of the uncompromising white refusal to abandon a policy which denies the African and other oppressed South Africans their rightful heritage – freedom – no one can

blame brave, just men for seeking justice by the use of violent methods; nor could they be blamed if they tried to create an organised force in order to establish ultimately peace and racial harmony.
Albert Luthuli, ANC President General, Nobel Peace Prize (1964 – after the Rivonia Treason Trial)

Every means of a state and community or society becomes a weapon; every capability in whatever field of endeavour at the disposal of an enemy becomes a target.
Magnus Malan, soldier, politician

Armed struggle must be a movement intended to hit at the symbols of oppression and not to slaughter human beings.
Nelson Mandela, President, May 1994-

Together, hand-in-hand with our sticks and matches, with our necklaces, we shall liberate this country.
Winnie Mandela, politician

Suffering is not enough. We must struggle.
Winnie Mandela

There is only one way out of the troubles in South Africa, reform or war.
Alfred Milner, British High Commissioner

It has been suggested that our aim was to annihilate the white people of this country; nothing could be further from the truth.
Mosima Gabriel Sexwale, class of '76, convicted of high treason

The difference between now and the time government will negotiate is the body count, how many people will have to die.
Frederik Van Zyl Slabbert, academic

The distinction between 'soft' and 'hard' is going to disappear in an intensified confrontation, in an escalating conflict.
Oliver Tambo, ANC President (1986)

We cannot and should not allow a situation of relative peace and tranquillity to obtain in the white areas of the country while black townships are in flames. We must take the struggle into the white areas of South Africa and there attack the apartheid regime and its forces of repression.
Oliver Tambo (Radio Freedom, Addis Ababa, 1985)

In the end, the government together with the ANC will have to suppress our people.
Andries Treurnicht, CP leader

Over my dead body will we have guns in the manse.
Paul Verryn, cleric

There is no end to the arms smuggling, by road from the Transkei to the southern ANC cadres – and by sea to an unprotected coast for Inkatha.
David Willers, editor

Army

There's a lot of fellatio going on in the army.
Ian Fraser, playwright

The majority of South Africans regard the SADF as an enemy, an army of occupation.
Mzukisi Gaba, activist

There is no army in Africa which could last more than an afternoon against the South Africans if they put their backs into it.
RW Johnson, political scientist

A defence force is like an insurance policy, and it's up to the future government to decide what sort of insurance policy it needs and what sort of premiums it is prepared to pay.
Kat Liebenberg, soldier

The immense military machine, built up at the cost of so many billions, stands useless, its nuclear weapons dismantled, its ageing aircraft grounded, its rockets and wondrous artillery pieces pointing uselessly into an empty sky.
Ken Owen, editor

The defence force provides the means to a political end.
Pierre Steyn, soldier

The army is the killing machine of the state.
Buti Thagale, cleric

A voluntary army made up only of gays – male and female – could quite well serve our defence needs for the foreseeable future.
Peter Wilhelm, editor, poet

Art/Artists

Art cannot be channelled; art is a question of grasping the ungraspable.
Beezy Bailey, artist

The eruption of creativity with which many South Africans of all races and cultures have responded over the last decade or so to the crushing convulsions of apartheid, holds the real promise of amplifying its scope as it moves from 'protest' and 'resistance' art towards affirmation, celebration, interrogation and enquiry on a wide front.
André Brink, writer, academic

Great artists in all genres are great because they are givers of joy.
Guy Butler, writer, academic

One of the biggest problems in this country is that our playwrights are consumed by their own importance.
Walter Chakela, playwright

Creating a character takes place by a process of alchemy rather than mimicry.
Jeremy Crutchley, actor

There is this funny thing about allowing ourselves to like a picture only if we can recognise what's in it.
Mark Dixon, artist

Whether Azapo likes it or not, there is an increasing number of artists living in Paul Simon's global village.
Alex Dodd, journalist

Can it be true that the Soweto String Quartet provided musical accompaniment to Sol Kerzner's most bizarre wet dream?
Alex Dodd

The debate that used to get people in a froth was whether poems could serve as AK-47s.
Alex Dodd

We should be wary of artistic calls to the blood; and sceptical of Art by Edict.
Neville Dubow, academic, artist

In the lonely act of creativity, the artist is left with his greatest responsibility: a commitment to truth as he sees it.
Neville Dubow

Photography as a medium is a polished mirror of violence.
Neville Dubow

To photograph is always an act of seizure.
Neville Dubow

A study of history indicates that in periods of crisis, art does not stop being made; that long winters of discontent often act as a stimulus to art-making in a way that piping dreams of peace do not; that a sense of urgency brings with it a release of energy.
Neville Dubow

We use art in order to justify our moral values, and morality to justify art.
Hazel Friedman, art historian

Selecting actors is like the flirtation that happens before you get someone into the sack.
Athol Fugard, playwright

Art is just another language, and if you don't know the symbols, a roll of barbed wire is a roll of barbed wire.
Kendell Geers, artist

To say that the arts are spiritually enriching and therefore should be subsidised is twaddle.
Chris Gibbons, broadcaster

Theatre audiences love strong women and weak men.
Robert Greig, journalist

If theatre in South Africa is to grow, it has to find new enemies.
Robert Greig

Our arts are no more than a sullen backwater.
Robert Kirby, satirist

No other country in the world offers you such exquisitely crafted art for so little.
Reg Lascaris, businessman

So, are we saying it's protest theatre that has changed the face of politics in South Africa?
Felicia Mabuza-Suttle, businesswoman, TV show presenter

We need drama that will give us steel in our bones for the battle that we will still have to fight.
Nico Malan Theatre on the banning of Die Plaasvervangers

The arts have got the words and power to heal and to change people's attitudes towards one another.
Gcina Mhlope, director, actress, storyteller

South Africa is such an abnormal society that one has become accustomed to silence among people on works of art generally.
Es'kia Mphahlele, academic, writer

In this country, if you're not poor and suffering and wearing the same clothes every day, you aren't considered a real artist.
Nataniel, performer

If I had the money, I would simply do opening nights all my life.
Nataniel

When I am on stage it's as if I'm in direct communication with God.
Mbongeni Ngema, playwright

The theatre is not an optimistic weather centre, where an approaching hailstorm can be ignored by looking hopefully at a warm front shaping up on the other side.
John Peter, journalist

A playwright's political conscience is a delicate plant: he puts it on the stage at his peril.
John Peter

Auctioneers of art and *objets d'art* have a stately, elitist private language that could give rise to mirth or even to offence in these resolutely democratic days.
Ivor Powell, journalist

If being unhappy under apartheid was all it took to make an artist, we would all have our names in lights at the Lincoln Centre.
Barry Ronge, journalist

I hope that local artists, black and white, will come to realise that having suffered at the hands of an unkind oppressor does not immediately confer talent on you.
Barry Ronge

Governments can only facilitate the flowering of the arts; individuals, who can, do the creating.
John W Siemon, director, Baxter Theatre

Too much of today's art pursues the myth of trying to be PC first and entertaining second.
Clem Sunter, businessman, scenario strategist

The creative and artistic impulse in a fragmented society often comes from the ghetto rather than from the affluent strata of society.
Can Themba, journalist, writer

There is no democracy in Art.
Pieter-Dirk Uys, satirist

Some of the monumental names from the past decades of the Thousand By-Law Reich – the playwrights, the novelists, the poets, the painters, the singers, the pundits, the Afrikaner foundation rocks of the Kultuur that was to remain for ever, have pathetically faded as fast as their grip has loosened on the bloody hems of the Boer helmsman.
Pieter-Dirk Uys

Performers present part of themselves every time they open their magic closet and allow the ordinary eye to peep within.
Pieter-Dirk Uys

Satire is a mixture of tragedy and time.
Pieter-Dirk Uys

I have always thought that being an actress is not a flash in the pan thing; it's keeping it up for 10, 20 years, and still being queen of it all.
Brumilda van Rensburg, actress

Good artists survive even an art school training.
Andrew Verster, artist

Art is about shifting consciousness, not shifting goal posts.
Andrea Vinassa, journalist

It was so much more fun – and easier – to overthrow governments than actually make art.
Andrea Vinassa

If the theatre business is essentially about bums on seats, the art circuit must surely be about eyes on the art, however briefly and insincerely.
Michele Witthaus, journalist

Assassination

There is nothing unhealthier than an assassin.
Garry Brennan, journalist

Assassination is nearly as bad as killing non-political people for the sake of promoting violence.
Alan C Brown

The blood drained away like water from a bath when the plug is pulled.
Stewart Carlyle, political correspondent (on the assassination of HF Verwoerd)

Assassination is the weapon of political weakness.
Ken Owen, editor

Those who have no hope of political victory reach for the gun.
Ken Owen

Assassination is the new currency of our politics, used systematically against black municipal councillors and frequently against black policemen.
Ken Owen

Assassination of Chris Hani

Your king is dead.
Anonymous right-winger

How do you kill a communist?
You hit him with a Pole.
Anonymous, AWB

The people are shattered into a thousand pieces, everyone is just running with his own little piece of hatred.
Anonymous

You can't kill a leader of the people and expect nothing to happen.
Anonymous

It is time we told the leadership that enough is enough and now is the time to hit back so that Chris Hani will not have died in vain.
Anonymous Umkhonto we Sizwe cadre

I cried when Dr Verwoerd died and I'm gonna celebrate tonight.
Anonymous

It's difficult to see a man lying with his brains blown out, but he's one of the enemy and we wiped him out.
Anonymous

What's actually happening in this country?
Anonymous

It is as if all the anger and frustration of the past two years have created a huge boil in society, and it was lanced by his killing.
Anonymous peace worker

I never thought in my life I would see a flag at half-mast at the SA embassy (Washington) in tribute to the death of a black leader in my country.
Anonymous

He was almost the Laughing Cavalier; that familiar grin, his infectious enthusiasm leading the huge crowds in the toyi-toyi, the 'soldiers' dance' of his beloved Umkhonto we Sizwe.
David Beresford, correspondent, The Guardian

There was no hiding the fact: South Africa was bleeding.
David Beresford

Mandela's contemplation of the grave into which Hani's coffin was lowered could not but evoke in spectators the speculation that he was watching the premonition of his own death.
André Brink, writer, academic

In Hani, the soldier who carried The Collected Works of Shakespeare to the battlefield, was symbolised the man of action inspired by the conviction that we shall not live by the sword alone but by the word.
André Brink

The imminence of death was a strong reality for him.
Jeremy Cronin, politician

Let us not be fooled: he was, first and last, a revolutionary.
Richard Ellis, correspondent, The Sunday Times (UK)

If there had been a Clinton-style dictum on the peeling walls of his shabby office, it would have given a simple message: Power, stupid!
Richard Ellis

You had seen him on television: when you saw his face lying in a pool of blood it was a face you recognised.
Mark Gevisser, journalist

Hani was the darling of the left, a communist forged in Stalinism, one-time Chief of Staff of the Spear of the Nation, the kalashnikov-carrying fist of the ANC, a man who quoted Shakespeare and Donne, yet had endorsed necklacing.
Nick Gordon, journalist

They've shot my daddy, I saw it was a white man...
Nomakhwezi Hani, daughter of Chris Hani

Even in death, he is a harbinger of the South Africa that is possible.
Ronnie Kasrils, politician

He was taken to our hearts, as a people, as a nation, because he lived so that we may be free.
Nelson Mandela, President, May 1994-

We have been brought up to know that the grave of the soldier, the revolutionary, lies by the roadside on the way to freedom.
Govan Mbeki, politician

When faced with the question of whether Chris Hani was an atheist or not, a Catholic in faith or not, believed in eternal life or not, wanted a Catholic burial or not, and so on and so on – I had to be very careful not to presume that there were answers merely from the fact that he was secretary-general of the Communist Party in South Africa.
Reginald Orsmond, Catholic Bishop of Johannesburg

Power slipped visibly from the limp hands at Groote Schuur to the stronger hands at Shell House.
Ken Owen, editor

As much as it was the hand of a white man that slaughtered Comrade Chris, it was the eyes of a white woman that helped us catch the bastard.
Tokyo Sexwale, politician

Our underbelly has been ripped open.
Tokyo Sexwale

We who are left have to realise that in the history of a people there comes a time when the music stays the same but the tempo changes.
Tokyo Sexwale

Who would have imagined that such a widespread wave of shock, pain and genuine grief, transcending colour, would have been evoked by the murder of a black man, and the chief of the SA Communist Party at that?
The Star

The people who marched on Wednesday (the Day of Remembrance) were poor people, homeless people, dispossessed people, jobless people, young people with no stake or faith in the system, mourning the loss of their champion.
Phillip van Niekerk, journalist

Attitudes

Your attitude determines your altitude.
Felicia Mabuza-Suttle, businesswoman, TV show presenter

Group attitudes are unpredictably savage.
Es'kia Mphahlele, academic, writer

How far back should you go to trace a current of life now congealed into an attitude?
Lin Sampson, journalist

Azanian People's Liberation Army (Apla)

Apla is not only the youth – it is all the people of Azania.
Anonymous Azanyu leader

An Apla a day keeps democracy at bay.
Pieter-Dirk Uys, satirist

The one thing Apla did succeed in doing was breathing life back into the khaki right.
Phillip van Niekerk, journalist

Azanian People's Organisation (Azapo)

Azapo had nothing but the memory of Biko, a tradition of brave resistance, and a political line that played rather well in the townships.
Rian Malan, writer

Battles

We went along sticking our lances through them – it was a terrible thing, but you have to do it.
Anonymous lancer, Battle of Elandslaagte

As the snake runs down the hill in an attack, the first person breaks the windows and doors, the second throws in petrol bombs, then as people start running out the rest of the snake kills them with spears, knives or guns.
Anonymous policeman (Natal, 1993)

No firing, but only one volley, boys, and then give them the cold steel.
Major Black (2-24th) on the night of Isandhlwana

If you come near to the white man and find that he has made trenches and built forts that are full of holes, do not attack him, for it will be of no use.
Cetshwayo, King of the Zulus (1879)

Let the experts fight it out with the terrorists in the shadows.
Johan Coetzee, policeman

Inspan the gun, gallop it three thousand paces back; then blaze away again as fiercely as you can!
Christiaan de Wet, soldier, Second Anglo-Boer War

We were especially careful, as it was rumoured that the English had armed the Zulus of Natal. Had this been true, it would have been necessary to exercise the utmost vigilance to guard against these barbarians.
Christiaan de Wet (Second Anglo-Boer War)

All round the laager were the guns of the English, belching forth death and destruction, while from within it at every moment, as each successive shell tore up the ground, there rose a cloud – a dark red cloud of dust.
Christiaan de Wet (Battle of Paardeberg, Second Anglo-Boer War)

First one position and then another was abandoned by our burghers, who followed one another's example like sheep; few made any attempt to defend their posts, and in spite of my efforts and those of the officers under me, they retreated to the north.
Christiaan de Wet (Fall of Bloemfontein to the British, Second Anglo-Boer War)

Tell my mother and the ladies that they have no cause to be alarmed at the idea of my going to fight the blacks. There will be much running and riding, but no danger.
John Graham, founder of the Cape Regiment

Now quietly, lads. Remember Majuba, God and our country.
Bobby Gunning, 60th Rifles (Battle of Talana Hill)

I came beside him and stuck my assegai under his right arm, pushing it through his body until it came out between his ribs on the left side. As soon as he fell I pulled the assegai out and

slit his stomach so I knew he should not shoot any more of my people.
Kumbeka Gwabe, soldier uMcijo regiment, Isandhlwana

Taking a Spitfire into the sky in September was rather like entering a dark room with a madman waving a knife behind your back.
Adolph Gysbert (Sailor) Malan, pilot, farmer

An army from another century, abristle with spears and shields, squaring off against a line of nervous policemen while traffic roared by and smoke belched from the steelworks in the background.
Rian Malan, writer (on Boipatong)

The ground in front of me was literally rising in dust from the bullets, and the din echoing between the hill and the wood below and among the rocks from the incessant fire of the Mausers seemed to blend with every other sound into a long drawn-out hideous roar.
Captain Nugent, 60th Rifles (Battle of Talana Hill)

Here they come, black as hell and thick as grass.
George Smith, cleric (Rorke's Drift)

A single battle cannot exterminate a nation.
HJ van Aswegen, academic

Don't swear, boys: fire low.
Father Walsh, Rorke's Drift

Beauty

If you're blonde you don't have to be beautiful.
Michele Bestbier, actress

While beauty may be skin deep, ugliness goes all the way to the bone.
Andrew Donaldson, journalist

Could anyone really successfully shield off beauty?
Albert Luthuli, ANC President General, Nobel Peace Prize

Bill of Rights

A bill of rights will only endure if the rights so enshrined are instinctively and intuitively felt to be binding at a deep ethical level by a substantial majority of the governed.
Laurie Ackermann, judge, academic

It is an NP solution to a problem of its own making: how to depart from an overtly race-based and illiberal society without making concessions to the fundamental assumptions of an open pluralist and non-racial tolerant society.
Kader Asmal, academic, politician

We are being sold a pup with the danger that it may become a rottweiler.
Kader Asmal (on the NP draft Bill of Rights)

The history of struggle in our country, the rights claimed and gained in struggle and the international context provided the inspiration for our drafting.
Kader Asmal (on the ANC draft Bill of Rights)

The Freedom Charter, adopted in Kliptown in 1955, is the greatest source of any Bill of Rights in our country.
Kader Asmal

Kader Asmal is wrong on one point – the bill is not a rottweiler – it is a poorly drafted combination of a jurisprudential dinosaur and a political shark.
Firoz Cachalia & Dennis Davis, lawyers

To expect from a bill of rights goods which it cannot deliver will not merely be futile but will subject it to strains damaging perhaps to its capacity to perform the work it can do well.
Kobie Coetsee, politician

Its purpose is to prevent the authorities from infringing certain fundamental rights of the citizen, not to grant rights to or to impose duties on people *vis-à-vis* one another.
Kobie Coetsee

A Bill of Rights which is not ideologically neutral may turn judges into politicians.
Peter Leon, lawyer

With no hint of irony, the same government which trampled upon rights as a matter of routine has hitched its somewhat overburdened wagon to the star of civil liberties.
Tony Leon, lawyer, politician

No Bill of Rights can be introduced into a society which has descended into a Bosnian polar night of icy darkness.
Tony Leon

The Bill of Rights of the Democratic Party is designed as both a shield and a sword.
Tony Leon

Behind the campaign for a Bill of Rights lies one of the saddest features of the apartheid era, the craven betrayal of South African common law by South African lawyers, not excluding eminent judges and judges of appeal.
Ken Owen, editor

This is a document written by people who have only a passing acquaintance with the rights that lie beneath the 'Western civilisation' which they profess to share – the rights that were enshrined in our common law, and violated by our legislators and our lawyers.
Ken Owen

The purpose of a bill of rights is to ensure that never again in this country will a policeman be able to say to a citizen *'Waar's jou pas, kaffer?'* and claim for such brutality the blessing of the law and the approval of all three branches of government.
Ken Owen

It is a charter not for the common man but for the strong, the privileged, the clever; it is tailored for elites.
Ken Owen

Birthrate/Birth Control

Because of the danger of hidden Coloured blood in their donor-fathers, the propagation of test-tube babies may be banned in South Africa.
Anonymous (1950)

To people like ourselves, part of the bulwark of Western civilisation, the use of the pill is tantamount to racial suicide. If persisted with, it could mean the end of the white man in Africa.
JJF du Toit, businessman

The relationship between a nation's GNP and its rate of population growth tends towards a straight line.
Aidan Edwards, businessman

Those who can best afford to encourage a high birth rate do not do so, and those who can least afford to encourage it have growing populations, accelerating their desperate dependence on those who have been more prudent.
Aidan Edwards

Family planning as a strategy to reduce South Africa's black teeming millions is seen by most Blacks as crude, and Blacks perceive it as a subtle genocide plan in the Black-White conflict which exists in South Africa.
John Hanks, academic, conservationist

In any state we visualise there will have to be soil conservation measures which will mean control over the human and cattle population in any area to ensure that it does not exceed the carrying population of the land.
Albert Luthuli, ANC President General, Nobel Peace Prize (1959)

If the population growth is much faster than the economic growth or job creation, any country can only head for disaster and the expectations for a better life and a prosperous future could be a mere pipe dream.
Nthato Motlana, doctor, businessman

Soon after the turn of the century there won't even be enough whites to fill the demand for wealthy mugging victims.
Ken Owen, editor

No one, not even our husbands, has the right to tell us how many children we should have, or when.
Jane Raphaely, editor, publisher

Each black person threatens the continued existence of whites, even an 88-year-old woman. They are known to breed very fast.
Barend Strydom, murderer

The Bantu have wonderful characteristics, but their genetic composition and cultural evolution is so different from that of the Coloured people that a mixing of the two cannot in this respect be advantageous for the Coloured man or woman.
FD du T Van Zyl, academic (1968)

Our enemies naturally want that we should mix on the social, economic and other levels because if White and Coloured first accept each other socially, then blood-mixing follows unavoidably and if we Whites here in South Africa have been bred out of existence, there will be no more opposition to the communists and the various 'Black Power movements'.
JD Versfeld, businessman (1984)

Black Sash

They are faded icons, these women, of liberal times past.
Mark Gevisser, journalist

They are middle class and mainly middle-aged housewives from the northern suburbs, moved by common humanity for their fellow South Africans.
David Harrison, documentary film maker, author

Mainly English-speaking, it endured jibes from cabinet ministers, physical abuse, and attack from white right-wingers and the reserve of some husbands prominent in business.
Anthony Heard, editor

Blacks

We are equally under one yoke.
Anonymous

They have been made to feel inferior for so long that for them it is comforting to drink tea, wine or beer with whites who seem to treat them as equals.
Steve Biko, Black Consciousness leader

Sometimes you come across a good kaffir who is faithful and upright and a true Christian and doesn't let the wild dogs catch the sheep. I always think it isn't right to kill that kind of kaffir.
Herman Charles Bosman, writer (Oom Schalk Lourens)

Most blacks are happy, except those who have other ideas pushed into their ears.
PW Botha, Prime Minister/State President, 1978-89 (1978)

If a black man gives you his word, you can trust him.
Dirk Coetzee, policeman, assassin

Their estimate of the value of human life is very low; plunder and bloodshed are engagements with which their circumstances have rendered them familiar since their childhood; they are crafty and cunning; at once indolent and excitable; averse to labour; but bloodthirsty and cruel when their passions are inflamed.
Report of Commission on Native Policy (1854)

The black South African has simply been required to sacrifice too much of himself in order to get through each day: he has suffered too many humiliations, great and small, too much government mendacity, too much unnecessary anxiety and, above all, he has seen too great a distance develop between himself and his African roots.
Wessel Ebersohn, journalist

It's odd to feel so connected with blacks and yet so cut off.
Nadine Gordimer, writer, Nobel Prize for Literature

After being suppressed for so long, blacks are suffering too.
Katryn Hattingh, housewife

They served, they cleaned, they dug, they rinsed, they mopped, they polished, they carried, they delivered, they cared for white children.
Anthony Heard, editor

We greatly outnumber the other groups because this country is our home, we are not settlers.
Albert Luthuli, ANC President General, Nobel Peace Prize (1959)

The African people do not want crumbs. They demand what is their rightful heritage in the land of their birth – Africa.
Albert Luthuli

No race has shown greater self patriotism than the native.
DF Malan, Prime Minister, 1948-54 (1933)

We suffered a particular kind of genocide which previous generations hadn't suffered.
John Matshikiza, writer, actor, director

You have only to sacrifice 'the nigger' absolutely and the game is easy.
Alfred Milner, British High Commissioner

When black people interact with white people, they lose everything.
Eric Miyeni, comedian

I don't have to wear an African outfit to be black.
Jacqui Mofokeng, beauty queen

They are by nature a cheerful race; if you make their souls happy they are a dancing, singing, happy race.
MC de Wet Nel, politician (1950)

Suppose an uprising by the blacks were to take place, would every native go on the rampage, raping every white woman and child in sight?
Lewis Nkosi, writer, academic

Above all things, mistrust a Kafir who speaks English and wears trousers.
A Paynton, diamond digger

If you are really one who loves the natives, you must make them worthy of the country they live in, or else they are certain, by an inexorable law, to lose their country.
Cecil John Rhodes, Imperialist

In South Africa the black is still reared on a diet of Zulu savagery, Hottentot sloth and Bushman indolence.
Richard Rive, writer

The negro and the negroid Bantu form a distinct human type. It has largely remained a child type, with a child psychology and outlook.
Jan Christian Smuts, Prime Minister, 1919-24 & 1939-48

I sympathise entirely with the native races of South Africa, but I don't believe in politics for them.
Jan Christiaan Smuts

We represent the fresh fragrance of flowers in bloom.
Robert Mangaliso Sobukwe, PAC founding president

I grant blacks the right to live, but not in our country.
Barend Strydom, murderer

The entire black history throughout the centuries is an experience of the wilderness.
Buti Thagale, cleric

We were these sensitive might-have-beens who had knocked at the door of white civilisation (at the highest levels that South Africa could offer) and had heard a gruff 'No' or a 'Yes' so shaky and insincere that we withdrew our snail horns at once.
Can Themba, journalist, writer

Our very oppression is the flower of opportunity.
Can Themba

Black man, you are on your own.
Abraham Ongopotse Tiro, activist

There is no place for him in the European community above the level of certain forms of labour.
HF Verwoerd, Prime Minister, 1958-66

It is nonsense to suppose that the interior of Southern Africa belonged to the Bantu and that the white man took it away from him.
Voortrekker Monument Guide Book (1970)

We have no feelings of guilt towards the non-white because we have not robbed him of anything.
John Vorster, Prime Minister, 1966-78

The Body

Muscles are just great in their right place but what about dangerous curves?
Glenn Cowley, journalist

Your body is a battleground and, if you don't demand the right to control it, someone else will.
Andrea Vinassa, journalist

Boers

The Boers' biggest problem is a lack of good men – all they have got is a bunch of punks who drink too much and fall off their horses.
Anonymous SADF soldier

A Boer can never live without freedom – never.
Anonymous AWB farmer

He will not have a gun in the open; he is not proud, but he is safe.
John Black Atkins, war correspondent, Second Anglo-Boer War

Boers are much easier to mislead than to lead.
Andries Botha, soldier, Second Anglo-Boer War

Beards are the only crop the Boers have ever grown without a government subsidy.
Roy Campbell, poet

His simple ignorance is unfathomable, and this in stolid composure he shares with his wife, his sons, his daughters, being proud that his children should grow up as ignorant, as uncultivated, as hopelessly unprogressive as himself.
Randolph Churchill, politician (UK)

The Boer is only half a man without his horse.
Christiaan de Wet, soldier, Second Anglo-Boer War

With the Bible as his only instrument of culture, with his gun to shoot game and protect him against those he regarded as savages the Boer was perfectly adjusted to his environment.
David Harrison, documentary film maker, author

A verifiable Dutch boer is the very skunkiest white man in existence.
HA Hornsby, author

The average Boer extremist will readily testify to how blacks are mentally subnormal, how their wish is to drink and copulate all day, how they smell like sheep and steal whenever the boss's back is turned.
Fergal Keane, correspondent, BBC Radio

I have fought against many barbarous kaffir tribes, but they are not so barbarous as the English, who burnt our farms and drove our women and children into destitution.
Paul Kruger, President, Transvaal Republic

They had their own language, their own customs and traditions, and a myth to light their way, a mystic Christian mission on the Dark Continent.
Rian Malan, writer

First beaten, then fairly treated, and not too much worried on his own 'plaats', I think he will be peaceful enough.
Alfred Milner, British High Commissioner

The Boers were as nimble as centaurs.
Thomas Pakenham (Lord Longford), writer

The real fighting Boer is ever a tolerant, good-natured fellow.
Deneys Reitz, soldier, politician

The Boer has to the full the defects of his qualities; that scintillating intellectual brilliance and versatility, so common

and so charming in the Frenchman and the Irishman, the Boer, even when highly cultured, seldom has: he is deep and strong rather than broad and brilliant: indomitable when he does act, it takes much to rouse him into action; he is slow and often heavy.
Olive Schreiner, writer

I learnt that in the African Boer we have one of the most intellectually virile and dominant races the world has seen; a people who beneath a calm and almost stolid surface hide the intensest passions and the most indomitable resolutions.
Olive Schreiner

A Boer without a weapon is a dead Boer.
Eugene Terre'Blanche, AWB leader

Young men greatly daring in fanciful suits, but lacking originality in cravats.
Edgar Wallace, war correspondent, Second Anglo-Boer War; writer

The only white race that has been steadily going backwards to barbarism.
Viscount Wolseley, soldier, Second Anglo-Boer War

We may admire their sturdy love of independence and in their rugged characters see much that is manly.
Francis Younghusband, journalist, explorer

Broederbond

The Broederbond has sponsored a sort of spiritual Great Trek of the Afrikaners in the twentieth century, by which they have removed themselves from 'dangerous' contact with other

elements of the population and withdrawn into cultural isolation.
Brian Bunting, lawyer

The ability of the old broeders to survive, whether in the security establishment, the SABC or the Department of Finance, would make any dinosaur green with envy.
Dennis Davis, lawyer

If you're turned on by secret societies that don't allow women and plot absurd ideologies until the early hours of the morning, look no further.
Arthur Goldstuck, journalist

There can be no doubt that we have today in the Broederbond to deal with a secret political association, leading political spirits of whom are determined to rule South Africa over the heads of the English-speaking among us.
Barry Hertzog, Prime Minister, 1924-39

Since 1948, every National Party policy decision has been first approved by the Broederbond before being tabled in parliament.
Patrick 'Terror' Lekota, politician

The Broederbond is a malignant cancer in our body politic and only the knife can remove it.
Ernie Malherbe, educationist

When the blacks take over, what are they going to do with the Broederbond?
Jaap Serfontein, civil servant

It is untrue to say that the Afrikaner Broederbond is a secret, racially exclusive power bloc masquerading as a cultural organisation, since everyone knows that the Afrikaner

Broederbond is a racially exclusive power bloc masquerading as a cultural organisation.
Gus Silber, journalist

After the cultural and economic needs, the Afrikaner Broederbond will have to devote its attention to the political needs of our people.
JC van Rooy, academic

Our solution for South Africa's troubles is not that this or that party shall obtain the upper hand, but that the Afrikaner Broederbond shall rule South Africa.
JC van Rooy

The Bush/Bushveld

The bushveld, when it comes to man's survival, is neutral.
James Clarke, journalist

The great silent bush is so lonely; the strain of being on the look-out all the time is so great; the uncertainty as to what may start up – anything from a partridge to a lion – is so trying that the beginner is wound up like an alarm call and goes off at the first touch.
Percy Fitzpatrick, politician, writer

The savannah, the trees and wooded grasslands of Africa are all peopled by ghosts.
David Lambkin, writer

The bushveld is a place where the human element indeed shrinks into utter insignificance, and grips you and subdues you and makes you one with yourself.
Jan Christian Smuts, Prime Minister, 1919-24 & 1939-48

Business

The only point at which the malcontents join issue is niggers being allowed to hold claims.
Anonymous

In the first year of Dingiswayo's chieftainship he opened a trade with Delagoa Bay, by sending 100 oxen and a quantity of elephants' tusks to exchange for beads and blankets.
L Alberti, explorer

If you do what must be done because of your responsibility to your shareholders and your group, does this make you a moral avenger?
Piet Badenhorst, businessman

To those who have placed their money in well-managed companies, I say they do not need to fear.
Barney Barnato, mining magnate

It was plain that if one had a little money there was a fortune to be made.
Alfred Beit, mining magnate

Business people are notoriously naive.
Willy Breytenbach, academic

No one has yet quantified the part played by guns and drugs in earning the rand to pay for hidden exports.
Rob Davies, academic

There are no ladies in business.
Susie Jordan, editor

Businessmen like to invest just like a farmer likes to farm.
Derek Keys, businessman, politician

I believe that the trend of all effective businesses in this country will be their willingness to get involved no matter how excruciating their day-to-day pressures are.
Reg Lascaris, businessman

You can't play the stock exchange from a good stretch of trout river.
Patrick Lee, writer

Where he must stand in the breach for his people, the Afrikaner of the new Great Trek meets the non-white at his Blood River, half-armed or even completely unarmed, without a barricade, without a river between them, defenceless in the open plains of economic competition.
DF Malan, Prime Minister, 1948-54

The only thing we are looking at is greenbacks.
Lawrence Mavundla, businessman

The battleground might have shifted from the streets to boardrooms, but the war for the black person's self-determination and the black person's voice to be taken seriously is far from over.
Vusi Mzilikazi, journalist

Once people participate in free enterprise they become financially literate overnight.
Tony Norton, businessman

Business can influence things, not so much by doing anything directly, but by running business in such a way that produces a state of affairs which any government in power has to take into account.
Harry Oppenheimer, businessman

The free market is only an instrument, not a god.
Ken Owen, editor

There is no doubt that world class businesses exist in South Africa and that ultimately they will attract a global following.
Tim Read, financier (UK)

I don't want to see a system that is so feeble in its regard for realities that it allows the vital economic engine to deteriorate into a Marxist fungus.
Gavin Relly, businessman

If we are selling overseas we have to be better than our competitors, and they include every country in the southern hemisphere.
Anton Rupert, businessman

Our market is characterised by a handful of companies which produce through a chain from the cradle to the grave.
Pat Sidley, journalist

Tax-free and on the nail, the colour of money is luring more and more South Africans off the streets and on to the pavements.
Gus Silber, journalist

A fascination for entrepreneurs, the more flamboyant the better, is an abiding characteristic of our small community.
Linda Stafford, journalist

The nature of the market economy is to promote liberty.
Conrad Strauss, businessman

Big business has a responsibility to support the Government, provided the Government brings about positive change.
Bill Venter, businessman

If we allow ourselves to be bamboozled into buying into the consumerist ethos of advanced capitalism, we probably deserve everything we get.
Andrea Vinassa, journalist

After 20 years with a private secretary, you miss them very, very much indeed.
John Vorster, Prime Minister, 1966-78

You must never have a board that doesn't represent the shareholders.
Gordon Waddell, businessman

Caution

Oppose whatever your enemy supports and support whatever your enemy opposes.
Benny Alexander, politician

Everywhere the crustacean mentality is on display: tuck into your hard shell, make yourself small and inconspicuous, scuttle rather than swagger, protect what you have and take no chances.
Shaun Johnson, journalist

Censorship

We do make the occasional cut in a film, but that's just to shorten a particular scene.
Braam Coetzee, censor

Things fall apart, the censor cannot hold.
Mark Gevisser, journalist

Censorship is always ideological, whether this is explicit or implicit.
Marjorie Heins, lawyer

For these men who saw themselves as the scissors of God, censorship was not merely a job, it was a vocation, a divine mandate.
Christopher Hope, writer

The Publications Appeal Board, consisting usually of heavily powdered middle-aged women, dominees and retired security police officers, would sit solemnly debating the relative offensiveness of, say, the audible fart versus the visible scrotum.
Robert Kirby, satirist

Where else in the world today could you hope to encounter sombre debate on the 'desirability' of the breasts of dead women?
Robert Kirby

Political censorship has always been cherished by totalitarian establishments for its subversive properties; it not only controls what may not be seen, it defines what may.
Robert Kirby

Essentially an art of the hypocrite, censorship offers unlimited scope for the politician.
Robert Kirby

Censorship is a dastardly, cowardly deed.
Don Mattera, poet

We do not have censorship in South Africa. What we have is a limit on what newspapers can report.
Louis Nel, politician

The consequences of censorship are always perverse.
Ken Owen, editor

The girly mags should be marketed in black plastic – rubbish bags would be highly appropriate.
Dene Smuts, politician

Thanks to a Monty Pythonesque publications law, plays were banned only by their title, not content.
Pieter-Dirk Uys, satirist

Self-censorship probably destroyed more inspiration and motivation than the blue pencils did in Pretoria, and this mainly because the ideas that surged vividly to the forefront were not acceptable to the Kultuur of the day.
Pieter-Dirk Uys

We cannot divulge too much and you have to accept our bona fides for a while.
Stoffel van der Merwe, politician (1987)

We give all the basic information, but, of course, we don't give the story behind the story.
Adriaan Vlok, politician (1988)

Change

Change in this country, good and bad, involves a sense of loss.
Andrew Donaldson, journalist

Change is the one characteristic common to all periods of time, and those who best adapt to change are the most successful.
Aidan Edwards, businessman

The trick, in a conflict situation, is to manage change.
Jannie Geldenhuys, soldier

For years everyone had said white minority rule could not last because it was repressive, corrupt, inefficient and power-hungry; now these became the reasons we could not get rid of it.
Anton Harber, editor

To change a constitution through peaceful and evolutionary means involves persuading those who hold power to change.
Chris Heunis, politician

Change cannot mean staying the same.
Shaun Johnson, journalist

We can't leave the future to holocaust without doing everything possible to get change without South Africa becoming a charnel house.
Neil Kinnock, politician (UK) (1988)

Nobody controls change, but some benefit from riding the wave.
Patrick Lee, writer

A difficult and painful process of evolution is going on, evolution for the better.
Alan Paton, writer

Anyway, *plus ça change,* etc, and socially it's going to be much of the same old charred-to-bits muchness, only more of the wors and less of the boere.
Hilary Prendini Toffoli & Carolyn Sacks, journalists

Change – what you don't get left over from a Krugerrand these days, unless you're buying a Krugerrand.
Gus Silber, journalist

The winds of change carry many exotic fragrances.
Jessica Smith, journalist

If you really want to change society, it's bottom up, not top down.
Clem Sunter, businessman, scenario strategist

Change? Who said anything about change?
Andries Treurnicht, CP leader (1981)

Charity

We should have taught our people to fish instead of giving them fish long ago.
Jan Boland Coetzee, rugby player, wine farmer

I agree with everything I have just said.
Piet Koornhof, politician

It would be fatal for industry to barge in with a big purse and try to fix society's ills.
James McLuskie, businessman

Probably the most dangerous of philanthropic breeds is the white liberal do-gooder whose main project is the social upliftment of those beneath him or her.
Andrea Vinassa, journalist

Children

A good child can only be said to be a good child by example of the parents.
Anonymous Azanyu leader

All children are children until they grow up, then they become black or white.
Evita Bezuidenhout, ambassador

Nine days is too long for any child's wonder to last.
Guy Butler, writer, academic

Those keenest and kindest of critics, best of friends, and most delightful of comrades, the likkle people.
Percy Fitzpatrick, politician, writer

They have become so acclimatised to Western culture that they wouldn't recognise their ancestors if they saw them walking in the road.
Karl Hechter-Schulz, health worker, museum curator

Who wants nursery rhymes when kids can play with AK-47s and burning necklaces?
Johnny Johnson, editor

With the first-born child it is like moving into a moonless night, on an unfamiliar terrain with only a pen-light for illumination.
Patrick 'Terror' Lekota, politician

Our children must at last play in the open veld no longer tortured by the pangs of hunger or ravaged by disease or threatened with the scourge of ignorance, molestation and abuse and no longer required to engage in deeds whose gravity exceeds the demands of their tender years.
Nelson Mandela, President, May 1994-

A child's eyes are always glowing even when it sees danger and chaos.
John Matshikiza, writer, actor, director

When they are young they are still not indoctrinated.
Gcina Mhlope, director, actress, storyteller

Black children are developing political consciousness – complete with revolutionary romanticism – at the age of 10.
Ken Owen, editor

Children should have a sense of belonging and that education comes before liberation.
Donald Pupuma, paediatrician

If it is true that a people's wealth is in its children, then South Africa is bitterly, tragically poor.
Percy Qoboza, editor

Only when all the children of South Africa learn together from the earliest possible moment, will the process of equality really begin.
Jane Raphaely, editor, publisher

If a child lives within his own universe and has no knowledge of other universes, there's no way he will ever develop empathy for people who inhabit those other universes.
Clem Sunter, businessman, scenario strategist

The scary thing about these children of apartheid is their bravado, their brutality and their unwavering commitment to the struggle for liberation.
Derrick Thema, journalist

Small children have become so accustomed to corpses that instead of running away in fear, they do hair-raising things to the corpses.
UmAfrika

Children very early on in life learn to mistrust the addiction of their elders to masterful pronouncements on the obvious.
Laurens van der Post, soldier, writer, philosopher

Christianity

I fear the Almighty and I respect His works, but I could never understand why He made the kaffir and the rinderpest.
Herman Charles Bosman, writer (Oom Schalk Lourens)

Let us do our duty and leave the rest to God.
PW Botha, Prime Minister/State President, 1978-89

There is no doubt that Christ is and will be the way for Africa.
Michael Cassidy, evangelist

Having become committed to Christ, one becomes committed to people.
Michael Cassidy

God came to me and said, hey chick, woman, come here, let me show you what you are supposed to be.
Brenda Fassie, singer

My son asked me, mom, why has Jesus got white hair? and I said ja, and took down all the pictures of Jesus in the house.
Brenda Fassie

The NG Kerk supported the system of apartheid but made it clear that in order to justify it biblically it should be applied as a total policy with total justice.
FE O'Brien Geldenhuys, cleric

God has ordained a diversity of races, peoples and cultures and therefore there is nothing wrong with an indigenous church adapted to the language and culture of the people concerned.
FE O'Brien Geldenhuys

The church is only responsible for propagating certain theological, ethical and moral principles which should form the basis for a political system.
Johan Heyns, theologian

Religious organisations are selling a product, just like anybody else.
Bafana Khumalo, journalist

Christianity does not exclude, but unites.
Marie Koopmans-de Wet, housewife, charity worker

Those who deny the humanity of African people in this country do so while falsely proclaiming that they follow God's word.
Patrick 'Terror' Lekota, politician

No one who has freely and for years mingled with this people (the Boers) can doubt that they have persuaded themselves by some wonderful mental process that they are God's chosen people, and that the blacks are the wicked and condemned Canaanites over whose heads the divine anger lowers continually.
John Mackenzie, missionary

We believe that the only road is that which fulfils the demands of our Calvinist creed.
WA Maree, politician

In the Free State it was customary to have the domestic servants (not the labourers) in for family prayers. They sat on low stools which they brought into the dining room with them, and slightly apart from the family.
L Marquard, traveller

God wants to meet your needs.
Ray McCauley, born-again cleric

Under certain circumstances a Christian is morally justified to ask for disinvestment in the same way as he is morally justified to call, for instance, for strike, boycott or a radical peaceful measure in order to avert a greater danger.
Beyers Naudé, cleric

Where a basic Christian truth is threatened by any political action or any political policy, that priest must stand up and speak out – not to criticise and condemn a specific political party but to state clearly what Christian truth, justice and love demands of everyone.
Beyers Naudé

How do the poor know God loves them unless someone comes and makes them feel precious?
Ethel Normoyle, nun

We may be able to bluff ourselves about God, but we cannot bluff God about ourselves.
Jack Penn, surgeon, philosopher, artist

Fortunately, not a single white South African will ever have a say on who sits where or next to whom in Heaven; my own feeling is that racist 'Christian' South Africa is bitter against the Creator for not letting them have a say on the residential arrangements in Heaven.
John Qwelane, editor

Bombs and bullets may blow our lives away, but the word of God will live for ever.
Frank J Retief, cleric

The wonderful thing about Calvinism is that it's kept sex a mystery.
Lin Sampson, journalist

God is my gun and ammunition.
Lorenzo Smith, businessman

A real faith cannot mean filing God at the back of my head while I get on with my own business.
Franklin Sonn, educationist, ambassador

God is a white man because the Bible says God blushes and everyone knows a black man can't blush.
Barend Strydom, murderer

That the gospel or the life-history of Christ makes no room for the use of violence to right the wrongs of society remains a massive scandal among the oppressed.
Buti Thagale, cleric

Maybe we (in the church) need to say we have a dream, a vision, and you the politicians have a duty to meet it.
Desmond Tutu, cleric, Archbishop of Cape Town

Any religion which does not engage all the concerns of human beings is an abomination.
Desmond Tutu

I've always been religious and I always wanted a man who would be able to take me to church.
Brumilda van Rensburg, actress

How is it possible that some Christian Afrikaners, knowing about the terrible things that have been done to fellow human beings, still find it impossible to confess the sins committed under apartheid?
At van Wyk, academic

God is more dead in South Africa than he is in other places.
Francois Venter, playwright

Although we have Catholics and Protestants, Zionists and Muslims, atheists and totemists, our political battles have remained free of the most irresolvable of all animosities – religious conflict.
Lester Venter, journalist

God save us from priests who make of their work a career rather than a calling.
Peter Younghusband, foreign correspondent

We do not know what Jesus looked like, whether he ever got married or what he did for fun on Saturday after Shul.
Jeff Zerbst, academic, journalist

The resurrection almost seems an anticlimax after the crucifixion, but, as Gore Vidal or Robert Altman might say, a happy ending was definitely required.
Jeff Zerbst

Chutzpah

Chutzpah is when a mugger mugs someone famous and then asks for his autograph.
James Clarke, journalist

Civilisation

There is indeed confrontation between civilisation and barbarism.
Magnus Malan, soldier, politician

After two thousand years of civilisation how can you make a road without trees on either side?
Robert Mazibuko, conservationist

The hunting packs are not yet loose amongst us, but they snarl and snap at the fringes of civilised order, and sometimes they break through to kill, to maim, to burn or simply to set a dog on fire.
Ken Owen, editor

Civilisation, as waves and waves of barbarians have discovered, is essentially a matter of acquiring new and expensive tastes.
Ken Owen

As good orchestration requires a multitude of different instruments, so an interesting world requires a multitude of differing genes.
Jack Penn, surgeon, philosopher, artist

Everywhere in our civilised world there tends to be a terrible cleavage between thinking and doing.
Laurens van der Post, soldier, writer, philosopher

Civil War

It's an easy way to lose everything.
Anonymous CP farmer

We shall reach the bottom, at last, probably amid the upheaval of a war with our Native races (then not the poor, savage, but generous races whom we might have bound to ourselves by a little generosity and sympathy, but a fierce and half-educated, much brutalised race who will have come into their own).
Olive Schreiner, writer

The idea of a civil war is horrendous.
Clem Sunter, businessman, scenario strategist

In a civil war mobilised masses are as effective as tanks and aeroplanes.
Mordechai Tamarkin, academic (Israeli)

Codesa/Multi-Party Talks

In the rush for a 'settlement in our time', I detect a strong whiff of Munich.
Jack Bloom, politician

In the end, the great unstated truth of the South African negotiations has been that the new deal has emerged from a historic bargain between those who have the numbers and those who have the guns.
John Carlin, correspondent, The Independent (UK)

Two years of tortuous negotiations characterised by walk-outs and postponements as well as political violence in the black townships on a scale not seen since the Boer War.
John Carlin

The ANC and the NP at negotiations are like two mating dogs. The dog in front is blind and the dog at the back is pushing it home.
Robin Carlisle, politician

I bind myself and my party to the letter and the spirit of the new constitution.
FW de Klerk, State President, 1989-1994; Deputy President, 1994-

Women are strange animals. They're petty and jealous and I don't see why they should be represented at the negotiating council when very few of them have any contribution to make.
Patricia de Lille, politician

For the centralisers at the World Trade Centre it would be good to remember that a well-functioning federal system is the best antidote to secession.
Hermann Giliomee, academic

For all their inelegance, discursiveness, irritation and cant, the Kempton Park days have been very special.
Shaun Johnson, journalist

The voice of the radical is louder than the shuffling of papers at the negotiations table.
Bill Krige, journalist

From now on no force can stop us from our emancipation from our painful past.
Ishmael Mahomed, judge

From the outside, the process resembled nothing so much as sumo-wrestling, the resolute giants of the ANC and NP locked arm-in-arm and eyeball-to-eyeball, neither giving an inch.
Rian Malan, writer

Attending negotiations was like having all one's teeth extracted and then being taken to an equal opportunity braaivleis and told to eat all the meat you want.
Gomolemo Mokae, activist

During the Kempton Park circus, songs were sung and music was played, yet there never was victory for us black people.
Kgosimang Monnakgotla, activist

Codesa is a new way of handling politics in this country.
Murphy Morobe, politician (1992)

Even for those who get a good night's sleep, the agreements flash past in a blur, like telephone poles past the window of a train.
Ken Owen, editor

Mr Roelf Meyer flung out concessions like a Siberian sleigh-rider throwing passengers to the wolves.
Ken Owen

It's a good package. We got a good deal.
Cyril Ramaphosa, politician

No hymns or anthems marked its passing.
Claire Robertson, journalist

Those gripped by this irritating country from birth or out of a horrible fascination kept watch as South Africa's future was sealed in the dead of night.
Claire Robertson

There we all sit, our belts tightened to the point of dismemberment, watching with horror as children in cars and bakkies become the *victims du jour,* and they are arguing about what to call the talks, as if they were suburban newly-

weds squabbling about whose granny the new baby should be named after.
Barry Ronge, journalist

Even in the distant, rosy-tinted days of Codesa I and II, war had always been somewhere on the constitutional agenda, politely preceded by 'civil' and evoked as the ultimate South African nightmare by any delegate who believed his or her submissions were not being taken seriously.
Gus Silber, journalist

The negotiating moves from multilateral to bilateral forums and back again as it flows like some glutinous substance around the obstacles in its path.
Allister Sparks, journalist

A revolution has been negotiated at the conference table.
Peter Storey, cleric

There have never been so many monsters in a room together all dressed up as good fairies.
Pieter-Dirk Uys, satirist

The way the transition has been set in stone, the gang at the multi-party talks needed the NP to remain the government, even if they have to carry them over the line.
Phillip van Niekerk, journalist

A bygone era where everyone tried to front-load the new political dispensation.
Phillip van Niekerk

The delegates to the Convention for a Democratic South Africa – or whatever body actually draws up the new South African constitution – will have no excuse for not being supremely well informed on constitutional issues.
David Welsh, academic

The multi-party process is probably the ultimate boys' game.
Elsabe Wessels, journalist

Colonialism

You have a fancy for building an Empire in the north, and I suppose you must have your way.
Barney Barnato, mining magnate, to Cecil John Rhodes, Imperialist

The evils of the old traditional policy of maintaining and subsidising the chiefs within the colonial territory having at last culminated in the miserable war now raging, the whole Cape Colony seems to be inspired with one over-mastering wish and determination to have no more of this mischievous mixture of authorities – this *imperium in imperias* – but to have the whole population of the country placed, as speedily and as thoroughly as possible, under one law and one administration.
John Buchanan, cleric

As colonies we were only sources of materials to feed the factories that the exploiters built in South Africa, as well as those in metropolitan countries.
Kenneth Kaunda, President (Zambia)

Whites in colonial areas were generally regarded as lowly by those who remained in their mother countries.
Patrick 'Terror' Lekota, politician

Colonialism is a total process which deprives the colonised of political, cultural, economic, religious and other freedoms.
Patrick 'Terror' Lekota

The so-called 'half-dressed barbarians' who engaged the colonists in defence of this country were the youth of our people; they so valued freedom that they were prepared to pay the supreme price for it – they paid with their lives.
Patrick 'Terror' Lekota

Our continent has been carved up by the great powers; alien governments have been forced upon the African people by military conquest and by economic domination; strivings for nationhood and national dignity have been beaten down by force; traditional economics and ancient customs have been disrupted and human skills and energy have been harnessed for the advantage of our conquerors.
Albert Luthuli, ANC President General, Nobel Peace Prize

There must be one flag, the Union Jack, but under it equality of races and languages.
Alfred Milner, British High Commissioner

Wherever the missionary places his standard among a savage tribe, their prejudices against the colonial government give way; their dependence upon the colony is increased.
John Philip, missionary

Africa is still lying ready for us, it is our duty to take it.
Cecil John Rhodes, Imperialist

If there be a God, I think He would like me to paint Africa British-Red as possible.
Cecil John Rhodes

All-Red: my dream.
Cecil John Rhodes

These white men did not just bring things of wonder: the floating house, the booming stick, the gaudy beads. They also brought ideas – evil, good, indifferent – ideas such as could subvert and demolish our tribal system.
Can Themba, journalist, writer

As so many untoward events have happened in our intercourse with these people, and so many clashing interests now exist; and as the Kaffir tribes have now become so thoroughly imbued with hatred to the 'white man', and appear so resolutely determined on his destruction, or to lose their political existence in the struggle, and above all as they have so resolutely and so perseveringly refused to give to the Gospel even an attentive hearing, it seems to me that the sword must first break them up as tribes, and destroy their political existence; after which, when thus set free from the shackles by which they are bound, civilisation and Christianity will no doubt make rapid progress among them.
JC Warner, government agent (1856)

I have never regarded Responsible Government as applied to a colony, more properly speaking a Dependency, as anything less than an absolute contradiction.
Philip Wodehouse, Governor of the Cape & High Commissioner

Coloureds

'Brown Afrikaners' are fast becoming an integral part of Afrikanerdom.
David Beresford, correspondent, The Guardian

Their desire to be white was linked up with their desire to be human.
Allan Boesak, cleric, politician

All coloureds are not skollies.
PW Botha, Prime Minister/State President, 1978-89

I still want to understand why we coloureds get the short end of the stick.
Cheryl Carolus, politician

The definition of a coloured in the population register is someone that is not black, and is not white and is also not an Indian, in other words a no-person. They are the left-overs.
Marike de Klerk, housewife; First Lady, 1989-94

Coloured people see the ANC, DP and PAC as devils, but the NP is the devil they know.
Patricia de Lille, politician

It was not just passing sailors who produced so many pale skins among those now called Cape Coloureds.
David Harrison, documentary film maker, author

They were rejected with a special vehemence by the Afrikaner Nationalist establishment because they were a living denial of the racial tidiness it sought to impose on all things.
Anthony Heard, editor

Once so close to whites, they were elbowed aside by apartheid.
Anthony Heard

Coloured people wryly noted how olive-skinned immigrants from places like Mozambique and Madeira could move, technically as whites, into their homes after they, the coloured families, had been displaced by the Group Areas Act.
Anthony Heard

Occasionally genes with long memories would throw up a dark child in an otherwise 'white' family – testimony to racial mixing in years past.
Anthony Heard

Many children were born of an intermingling by the Dutch with both slaves and Khoikhoi.
Patrick 'Terror' Lekota, politician

It is no disgrace to be a coloured person. One is not responsible for one's own birth.
JH Loock, politician (1950)

Our Dutch masters taught our people to respect the white man.
Joe Marx, fish and vegetable hawker, politician

It is one of the meanest traits of white South Africans that they are able to feel such a contempt for the people they themselves have fathered.
Alan Paton, writer

They are a rejected people.
Alan Paton

As a distinct ethnic group with over three million members, we deserve a capital letter.
Paul Stober, journalist

Coloureds are our 12-year-old children and must remain under our guardianship.
Andries Treurnicht, CP leader

Few if any of the unworthy steps taken by the National Party over the past 40 years of its administration had at so early a stage soiled its name as the disenfranchisement of the Cape coloured voters.
At van Wyk, academic

Commentators

Viewers of sport on TV1 can't seem to escape the mediocrity of the ubiquitous Quirk and Locke (tennis at Wimbledon, golf at Sun City, cricket in New Zealand, Australia and the Caribbean).
Roy Goldberg

They should learn from the overseas commentators who only give background information and whose voices do not interfere with one's viewing pleasure.
VO Kent

The snivelling commentary is a sign of our times.
Douglas Livingstone, scientist, poet

Our commentators exude a Currie Cup-centred parochialism.
Jon Swift, journalist

Too many commentators subconsciously overlook the dodgy decisions which go the way of the country they come from.
David Williams, journalist

Communication(s)

If the pen is mightier than the sword then the voice has to be the scud missile of human communications.
Vanessa Bloom, journalist

A discussion between two adult, civilised human beings is hardly a big deal; people do it all the time, the ability to communicate verbally being one of the defining characteristics of a human being.
Cosmas Desmond, cleric

It is our great ability to communicate that makes us human.
Wessel Ebersohn, journalist

The only way to communicate is to have a vehicle and to have a cause to communicate.
Michael Edwardes, businessman

The demolition of any form of human communication can only be negative in its ultimate consequences.
Robert Kirby, satirist

Like the missionaries of the past and the free market advertisers of today, if you wish to communicate with the people, you must speak their language.
Kole Omotoso, academic

Of the three great hypocritical myths of our time (personal liberation and the guiltless orgasm are the other two) the easiest one to swallow but the most difficult to digest is the one about the value of honest communication.
Barry Ronge, journalist

The key to our survival might be communication and co-operation, rather than violence.
Phillip Tobias, academic

Human beings communicate in a way far more profoundly with one another through the nature of what they are, than through their words.
Laurens van der Post, soldier, writer, philosopher

Although walkouts express a form of communication, it is one that South Africa can do without.
Goodwill Zwelithini, King of the Zulus

Communism

The free world wants to feed South Africa to the Red Crocodile, to appease its hunger.
PW Botha, Prime Minister/State President, 1978-89

It might no longer be a threat to the essential interests of the United States of America, but communism is of terrifying relevance to the people of this country.
Mangosuthu Buthelezi, IFP leader, politician

Scratch a local communist and you'll probably find a capitalist being reborn.
Pieter-Dirk Uys, satirist

After decades of blue-murder yellin' and screaming, with a Red under your Bed being worse than the black in it, communism is alive and powdering its peeling nose.
Pieter-Dirk Uys

Conservation

It's terribly difficult to focus on what needs to be done first, because everything needs to be done now, immediately, before another species disappears, before another donga snakes along the eroded earth, before someone throws another stompie into dry grass.
Julienne du Toit, journalist

Conservation concepts, as understood in the Western world, have little relevance for the homeless and the hungry.
Anthony Hall-Martin, conservationist

Lounge conservationists are dangerous.
Hazel Muller, hunter

Conservation is a dirty word to the hard core of the development lobby, groomed in the traditional South African ethic that resources exist solely for exploitation.
Wilf Nussey, journalist

We need to recognise the mutual dependency of eco-tourism and nature conservation, and then rationalise responsibly these aspects.
Anton Rupert, businessman

Conservation of the big and the hairy is a lost cause if people don't understand the habitat.
Clive Walker, conservationist

It's important for all of us to realise that, in a sense, we are custodians and we can't allow what is around us to disappear.
Clive Walker

Conservative Party (CP)

Its road is one which curves away from the Low Road, runs over a precipice and plunges down into an abyss.
Willem de Klerk, businessman, academic

What they are trying to do in the last desperate days of the old order is to bring into being what more than four decades of relentless social engineering utterly failed to do.
Hugh Roberton, journalist

As the Official Opposition in the House of Assembly, the Conservative Party stands at the forefront of the struggle to trade the New South Africa in for a second-hand model.
Gus Silber, journalist

They may not have known it, but as they stood solemnly in the doomed legislature, singing *Die Stem* from the bottom of their hearts, they were, in fact, performing the funeral rites of a system they so desperately want to keep alive.
Mike Siluma, journalist

They (the Conservative Party) offer a crystal-clear vision of what they stand for.
Clem Sunter, businessman, scenario strategist

I have said that the Conservative Party has no obsession with apartheid signs, but we have no allergy against measures necessary to protect a particular community.
Andries Treurnicht, CP leader

Conspiracy

The conspiracy began to buckle under the weight of its own grandeur.
Rian Malan, writer

The Constitution

In a virile nation, surely no constitution can be final.
PW Botha, Prime Minister/State President, 1978-89

Violent challenges will not strengthen the sinews of the new constitutionalism nor the protection of human rights.
Princeton Lyman, ambassador (USA)

It is a mission boy constitution, a hodge-podge of sorry borrowings from old colonial powers.
Rian Malan, writer

Liberty, democracy and human rights can only be protected superficially by a constitution and a constitutional court.
Pierre Olivier, judge

A constitution must enjoy the faith of the people if it is to work at all.
Ken Owen, editor

If constitutions were written by angels, they wouldn't be necessary.
Peter Soal, politician

We must know who's who, who's real and who's a pretender, before we begin the serious business of drafting a new constitution on behalf of 'the people'.
Allister Sparks, journalist

No constitution is perfect, and our constitution needs still to be infused with the spirit of democracy.
Sunday Times

A piece of paper like a new constitution – even if it is carefully crafted by the slickest lawyers in town – is not going to hold clans together.
Clem Sunter, businessman, scenario strategist

Political parties are singularly unfit to write a lasting constitution.
Herbert Vilakazi, academic

The fitting first line of a constitution is, indeed, 'We, the people ...'
Herbert Vilakazi

We have always had a basically wrong constitution in South Africa because it never really gave space to the accommodation of all people.
Constand Viljoen, soldier, politician

Constitutional niceties are a red herring in Africa.
Geoffrey Wheatcroft, journalist

Conversation

It's not enough to fill a room with gold if the conversation is not equally great.
Anonymous

A housewife would have to say something more than 'I'm a housewife' to knock up a conversation.
James Clarke, journalist

There are times when you get more out of a conversation by asking intellectually testing questions.
David Frost, TV interviewer (UK)

Dialogue is our important weapon.
Nelson Mandela, President, May 1994-

Conversation's like a dress pattern: once you have a basic design, you can adapt it to any situation.
Lin Sampson, journalist

No true conversationalist is entirely without French.
Lin Sampson

It was a South African who came up with the stunning riposte: 'Is it?'
Lin Sampson

Corruption

Corrupt ideologies breed corruption.
Anonymous

Rampant greed – exemplified by insider trading, unauthorised dealings in financial rands, bank robberies, the incidence of bribery and corruption, tax evasion, sharp business deals – has become the accepted norm.
Bob Aldworth, banker

The bribery market in this country has been spoiled by the millionaires.
Winston Churchill (on his efforts to bribe guards at the State Model School, Pretoria)

Successful campaigns against corruption don't stop with denunciations.
Robert Klitgaard, academic (USA)

Corruption in South Africa and the homelands is more than a disease, it is an instrument of State power.
Victor Nell, community psychologist

What brought the Nats to their knees, and President de Klerk to the negotiating table, was simply the bankruptcy of a nation which had been looted until it could no longer honour its debts.
Ken Owen, editor

I'm not saying I wouldn't put these people in jail, but I can understand how it happens.
Anton Rupert, businessman

The outrage over tales of corruption among the whiter sections of the community is somewhat curious, after all that has been done to people in this country during the past 40 years.
Phillip van Niekerk, journalist

The corruption in the returned exiles committee provides an ominous inkling of the capacity for incompetence and corruption in the ranks of the new bureaucrats.
Phillip van Niekerk

Cosmetic Surgery

I want a Barbra Streisand kink in my nose, and I have enough chins to cover the width of the N1 so they must take some away – I want a neck.
Nataniel, performer

One thing about a face-lift: the word always gets around.
Hilary Prendini Toffoli, journalist

Credibility

Credibility is what you lack if you don't think what the majority for the moment thinks you ought to think.
Denis Beckett, journalist

Cricket

We just bowl well at the death.
Wasim Akram, captain, Pakistani touring team (February 1993)

Fans want the stuff that gives them the excuse to rip out their seats for lack of something better to wave about in delight as their team goes in search of a target which they must reach... or die trying.
David Anthony, cricket fan

Shout it in English. Shout it in Afrikaans. Shout it in Xhosa. Shout it in Sotho. Shout it in Tswana. This was a phenomenal victory. A priceless moment in history.
The Australian (on SA's winning the test match against Australia by five runs, 1994)

I believe we could approach the Oxford Dictionary who are one of the custodians of the English language and ask them to use the word 'KEPLER' as a synonym for 'SLOW'.
B Barker

So, they reckon one Clive Rice was worth five Transvaal players, Clive Rice the batsman, Clive Rice the bowler, Clive Rice the fielder, Clive Rice the captain and Clive Rice, the ****** Holy Ghost.
Eddie Barlow, wine farmer, sportsman

As the one-day game consolidates more and more in the cricketing landscape the gap between the great and the merely very good becomes more pronounced.
Mark Beare, journalist

Cricketers, by and large, are honest men except in the case of catches to the wicketkeeper.
Colin Bryden, journalist

Cricket has become the sport of national unity, putting paid to the soccer/rugby, black/white thing.
Andrew Donaldson & Adam Levin, journalists

Cricket can rightly claim to have added something to the terms of our continued climb towards true nationhood.
Drew Forrest, journalist

A test match is played out at two levels: consciously as athletic performance and subliminally as myth.
Drew Forrest

Rhodes leaping forward, horizontally, to dismiss Lara; Rhodes hurling himself to mid-on to get Simmons, one-handed; Rhodes cradling the chance offered by Adams into his chest; Rhodes defying belief to move from backward point almost to gully to clutch, left-handed, a thick edge from Cummins; and, finally, Rhodes caressing the steepling hoik of Haynes from the stratosphere to safety.
Ian Hawkey, journalist (on Jonty Rhodes's five catches against the West Indies, Bombay, India, 1994)

I felt like an executioner pressing the button.
Karl Liebenberg, umpire (after the first dismissal in Test history based on a TV replay)

We just fought and fought and fought.
Mike Procter, cricket coach (on SA's victory over Australia, Sydney, 1994)

The quickest route was through the air.
Jonty Rhodes, cricketer (after 'diving out' Inzamam-ul-Haq, Brisbane, 1992)

If there is one great truth about cricket, it is that it is a game of opinions.
Peter Robinson, journalist

To be 'Waqared' generally refers to the receipt of a fast, inswinging yorker on the big toe.
Peter Robinson

No one who watched this game will forget it because it was a game, and a last day, of a hundred gasps and a hundred roars, a game of noise and silence, of comments and cries. It was one of the greatest of Test matches.
Peter Roebuck, cricketer (UK) (on SA's victory over Australia, Sydney, 1994)

The image of (Jonty) Rhodes, full length and horizontal above the ground, knocking over all three stumps, has etched itself into the lore of SA cricket.
Sunday Times

Perhaps the greatest thing about the game of cricket is that even the players, officials and spectators have been unable to kill it.
Jon Swift, journalist

One-day cricket is generally relegated to the second division by the aficionados, though it has acquired international status.
Donna Symmonds, cricket commentator (West Indies)

Crime

It's not the muggers that kill you, it's the wankers.
Anonymous

Criminal elements would descend on Durban in the July season like flying ants after rain.
Anthony Heard, editor

When crime, especially of an economic nature, becomes as common amongst civilised people as it is now in South Africa, we must conclude there has been a breakdown of moral conscience.
David Lapin, rabbi, academic

All the burning rage and intense hatred I felt when I stared intently at the bowed head of Kobus Petrus Geldenhuys as the judge sentenced him five times to death vanished when I looked into his eyes: dark brown and fringed with thick lashes, they were so gentle when he asked me for forgiveness. He began to cry and, despite myself, I wept with him.
Janine Lazarus, journalist (on the Norwood rapist)

Electric fencing on outside walls sends 24 000 volts through uninvited visitors who prefer to clamber over walls rather than ring the doorbell.
Katy Macdonald, journalist

Northern suburbia has come to the puzzling conclusion that whites cannot be criminals.
Katy Macdonald

The criminals who rob, rape and murder seem to grow in number every day, and seem to get more desperate and brutal with each passing moment.
Nelson Mandela, President, May 1994-

As long as there are people on this earth, there will be counterfeiters.
Mossie Myburg, policeman

To be able to commit many forms of economic crime it is a prerequisite that there is access to a facility or opportunity which may be suitably exploited.
Barry Rider, criminologist

The way things are going, the Mafia would be advised to hurry up while there is still something in this country to steal.
Phillip van Niekerk, journalist

There is a class sympathy for a man such as (Bob) Aldworth from people who never venture down into the magistrate's courts to see people routinely sentenced to jail for stealing bicycles.
Phillip van Niekerk

Crime is an issue made for the National Party: an acceptable synonym for swart gevaar in the white suburbs, and a seemingly non-political phenomenon that includes among its victims most law-abiding people in the townships.
Phillip van Niekerk

The dividing line between what is sharp but acceptable business practice and what amounts to fraud is deliberately being blurred as imaginative criminals increasingly breach and overstep the permissible, by degrees.
Klaus von Lieres, lawyer

It could be argued that the terrifying growth in crime represents a malign extension of the informal economy.
Peter Wilhelm, editor, poet

Criticism

As far as criticism is concerned, we don't resent that unless it is absolutely biased, as it is in most cases.
John Vorster, Prime Minister, 1966-78

Culture

If the Johannesburg City Council has culture at heart, I would like to see Ron Finkelstein and Christopher Till dance Swan Lake.
Anonymous

You cannot separate politics from culture.
Anieta Armand, broadcaster

In situations of complete powerlessness, people recognise that they have only one thing left – their culture.
Emile Boonzaier, anthropologist

The only shared culture in this country is the culture of killing.
Breyten Breytenbach, poet, writer

The same relationship exists between creative work and culture as between revolution and politics.
Breyten Breytenbach

A culture of resistance can become a habit like any other.
André Brink, writer, academic

There is more culture in an Aussie billabong than we have in our biggest city.
James Clarke, journalist

In African tradition the bonds between the people and the earth are indissoluble, but for generations, African tradition has been in disarray and these bonds have been in disarray.
Wessel Ebersohn, journalist

You can't use culture to perpetuate something that is wrong.
Mojanku Gumbi, activist

Local is not only lekker but also intelligent, witty and sophisticated.
Marilyn Hattingh, editor

Every day there is an overlapping and overlaying of cultures; the focus shifts, the meanings change.
David Kramer, entertainer

Somehow casinos have become the central metaphor for South African culture, and appropriately.
Patrick Lee, writer

When you accept that your children are going to grow up to a different narrative strain than you did, then you cut a certain connective cord for ever.
Patrick Lee

By promoting different ethnic groups as exclusive entities bound to an unchanging culture, the South African government effectively undermined the dynamics of traditional culture while at the same time co-opting the efforts of anyone who took pride in dance and music.
Fiona Lloyd, journalist

The violence we are having is a part of African culture: the signing of a paper doesn't mean anything to Africans.
Albert Mncwango, commander, Inala regiment, IFP

If we lock up culture, regiment it, so that anybody is suspect who doesn't have the stamp of approval, we are in deep trouble.
Es'kia Mphahlele, academic, writer

We black people cannot allow our culture to die in darkness.
Vusamazulu Credo Mutwa, storyteller, sangoma

Like the political stew, the cultural arena has its fair share of limelight-hungry protagonists.
Heather Robertson, journalist

The beaded, bare-breasted African choir singing along to tribal drums has become the most overworked cliché of the decade, and it really is quite insulting to the rest of us.
Barry Ronge, journalist

There can be little doubt that the Toyi-Toyi has overtaken the Sakkie-Sakkie and the Phatha-Phatha as South Africa's favourite cultural dance.
Gus Silber, journalist

Our culture encourages men to exaggerate their prowess and women to understate theirs.
Dene Smuts, politician

Our aim must be to have a cultural mosaic, not a melting pot.
Allister Sparks, journalist

There is inter-cultural influence but a culture has, of necessity, to exercise the right of exclusivity.
Andries Treurnicht, CP leader

'iCulture' threatens to place its well-rounded behind in the still-warm seat of departed 'Kultuur' and allow itself to be used by the new fundis of fundamentalism to steer the ship of state along another barren and narrow channel of expression.
Pieter-Dirk Uys, satirist

Most societies use their culture to control their citizens.
Pieter-Dirk Uys

The spice of taste that is sprinkled on the blandness of a community.
Pieter-Dirk Uys

Customs

Conscious of the warrior ethic, which is based on mutual respect, but also on an awareness that one can kill the other at any moment, I said to them: 'I come to you like a goat (in the knowledge that you can kill me), not a cock flapping his wings.'
Johnny Clegg, anthropologist, musician

Every person present takes up a stone and, just before the vow, lays it on an evergrowing pile, the symbol of united Afrikanerdom.
David Harrison, documentary film maker, author

Lobola is about buying a woman.
Jacqui Mofokeng, beauty queen

In the special area at the back of the main hut, *emsamo,* surrounded by broad-shaft spears, sacrificial strips of meat, and sacred herbs, he prayed to the ancestral spirits, *amathonga,* sprinkling the floor with *intelezi,* burning incense and licking medicine from his fingers after dipping them rapidly in a burning clay container.
Lewis Nkosi, writer, academic

Ever and anon may be seen a *paterfamilias* emerging from the shop with a pair of brand new shod boots in his hand, the good wife with a piece of voerchitz under her arm, the ruddy-cheeked buxom lass with a rainbow coloured shawl, the ogling amorous swain with a brass-knobbed horsewhip, and a little brass-edged looking glass, and even the antiquated *'au motjie',* the maid of all work of the family, the bloom of the red stone adorning her shrivelled skin, with a prodigious wooden pipe between her jaws – all returning to their wagons carefully to stow away the purchased articles.
Olive Schreiner, writer

Behind the ribs and just over the belly the Kafirs had peeled off a large slab of skin, about three feet square, and through the trap-door thus formed dragged out the stomach and intestines; they had also cut out the heart, liver, and lungs, so that what was left was merely a hollow shell, in the lower half of which the blood had formed a pool a foot deep. Into this cavity they and the Bushmen now kept entering by twos, disappearing entirely from sight, searching eagerly for small pieces of fat along the backbone and about the kidneys, and bathing in and smearing themselves all over with the blood. They do not wash it off again, but let it dry on them, and remain there till it gradually wears or gets rubbed off.
Henry Courteney Selous, hunter (with reference to an elephant carcass)

Under African norms and value systems when a warrior has fallen you return the remains or spear or rags, no matter the circumstances surrounding the death.
Wetsho-otsile Seremane

Male relatives of bride and bridegroom wear skirts made from strips of leopard-skin or other fur; the groom wears a crown of black plumes and cow-tail bracelets on his shins and upper arms.
Patti Waldmeir, correspondent, Financial Times (UK)

Dance/Dancing

The history of dance in South Africa shows that dance politics and dance power have to do with moral issues as well as political, economic, organisational and cultural issues.
Peter Brinson, dance educationist, writer

Choreography is a form of research.
Peter Brinson

Alongside music, painting and sculpture, dance can convey its knowledge of those areas of human experience that cannot be expressed in words or numbers.
Peter Brinson

Just to hear 30 000 guerrillas toyi-toying, knees beating their chests, arms high up in the air holding AK-47s, sweat streaming from their uniformed bodies, was a moving experience.
Mkhululi Dliwayo, Umkhonto we Sizwe

In the courteous world of ballroom dancing, men are gentlemen, women are ladies and the tango is a secret danced by two.
Pnina Fenster, journalist

There are few social levellers as effective as standing in line with 80 other people for a formation version of the Achy Breaky dance.
Pnina Fenster

There's nothing more uplifting than looking around you and seeing a thousand people dancing and smiling together.
G-Force Graeme, disc jockey

The toyi-toyi ranges from a friendly frolic to a combative capriole.
Justinus Maluleke, journalist

Ballet, like drama, fiction, lyrical poetry, the opera, cinema and pop music, idealises romantic love and along with this, the woman.
Stanley Peskin, critic

All the dancing I've done has been alone in the veld, when I've jumped in the air and thrown up my arms and shouted with the mere joy of living.
Olive Schreiner, writer

It takes two to tango but more to toyi-toyi.
Tokyo Sexwale, politician

To see South African contemporary theatre dance from an international perspective is to see a cross between mausoleum and crucible.
Adrienne Sichel, critic

Death

Death seems to come like a crossbow bolt, its flight disclosed only by the sight of a relative, a friend or acquaintance falling.
David Beresford, correspondent, The Guardian

You are either alive and proud or you are dead, and when you are dead, you can't care anyway.
Steve Biko, Black Consciousness leader

Dying in a just cause is not a vain death.
Frank Chikane, cleric, politician

Necklacing is the most singular and spectacular form of murder in living memory.
Wessel Ebersohn, journalist

The fire of the necklace is the fire of Africa's own purgatory.
Wessel Ebersohn

When children are being treated in this way and dying, we are simply ranging the deepest passions of the human heart against British rule in Africa.
Lloyd George, Prime Minister (UK) (on the Second Anglo-Boer War concentration camps)

The full realisation of the position dawned on me – it was a death rate such as had never been known except in the times of the Great Plagues.
Emily Hobhouse, humanitarian (on the Second Anglo-Boer War concentration camps)

They may have graves, or their graves may be the stomachs of hyenas, but they will always be honoured.
Patrick 'Terror' Lekota, politician (on fallen MK cadres)

I know tonight, as I sit here with a crown on my head, there are people dying in the townships. I have not forgotten them.
Jacqui Mofokeng, beauty queen

My biggest fear is that I'll die alone – I want to die with a family of 70 sitting round my bed, knowing that until I die no one will inherit anything.
Nataniel, performer

Death Penalty

On the mornings the hangings took place, long before the sun rose, sirens began to wail from behind the koppie which flanked the prison, adding to the rising chants and hymns of inmates which always accompanied the condemned on their way to the gallows.
Vusi Dlamini, convict

There exists no stronger argument against the death penalty than its irrevocable nature.
Wessel Ebersohn, journalist

A return to the rope is an admission by our rulers that they cannot break with the mechanics of apartheid.
Hugh Lewin, author

When I was sentenced to death I thought that I was one of the soldiers who fell on the field.
James Mange, Umkhonto we Sizwe

I wouldn't want to be part of a government that continues to hang people – you can't teach lessons to corpses.
Robert McBride, politician

The rope used for blacks is rarely changed, so around your neck is the blood and puke of compatriots who have been executed before you.
Phyllis Naidoo, author

Africans have been expendable under the death penalty ever since Dingaan and Chaka and the other chiefs.
Robert van Tonder, Boerestaat Party leader

Decisions

To make decisions without thought is like participating in a steeplechase with bandaged eyes.
Jack Penn, surgeon, philosopher, artist

Décor

I have fitted all up in the stile of a comfortable plain English house, Scotch carpets, English linnen & rush bottom chairs with plenty of lolling sophas.
Lady Anne Barnard, socialite

Have you noticed how no one ever looks ugly in a pink room?
Sharon Dickenson, businesswoman

What a lot of people want now from the decorator is the undecorated room.
Stephen Falcke, interior designer

Décor should be extremely flexible and tolerant.
Marianne Fassler, dress designer

A good decorator is one who is not judged so much by the quality of her work as by the quality of her clients.
Jane Fraser, journalist (Australian)

The in colour is green and the ultimate accessory is the fringe of electrified, razor-edged spikes mounted ever so discreetly on top.
Reg Lascaris, businessman

When an abundance of useless, painted wooden fruit and flowers finally left affirmative action decorators feeling a little silly, it was agreed that there's nothing politically incorrect about a real orange.
Adam Levin, journalist

Whether it's made of North American cornhusks, South American bark, Philippine cane, Madagascan raffia, French vine branches or Sowetan chicken wire, there's something essentially honest about a basket.
Hilary Prendini Toffoli, journalist

We are fast getting to the stage where there will not be a single item in a room that has not got a drape around it.
Lin Sampson, journalist

A bare wall is a dead wall.
Lin Sampson

Cottage furniture was politically correct, not only as an answer to dralon and Gomma Gomma, but part of an ethnic pride we newly-found Africans were nurturing.
Peta Thorneycroft, journalist

The very real danger of purist restoration is being left with something that is too stripped, too new, too, in the end, like a wedding cake.
Graham Viney, interior designer

To the discerning, one of the most challenging and fascinating aspects of collecting is the striving for quality and the expression of personal taste.
Stephan Welz, auctioneer

I always say you can't have too much good gilt. You shouldn't save it for the confessional.
Rodney Wright, interior designer

One should hardly have to decorate more than once in every generation.
Rodney Wright

Democracy

Democrats never surrender.
Ken Andrew, politician

Whereas you certainly cannot have democracy without universal suffrage, you do not acquire it simply by announcing that everyone can vote.
Denis Beckett, journalist

Harness the wisdom of the masses in an effective democracy and they become a bulwark against tyranny.
Denis Beckett

Democracy, the new position we've never tried before, is going to be as much fun as sex – only safer.
Evita Bezuidenhout, ambassador

We believe that a democratic system of government, which must accommodate all legitimate political aspirations of all the South African communities, must be negotiated.
Pik Botha, politician (1986)

Is democracy not about each party freely taking its own stands on principle and conviction?
Mangosuthu Buthelezi, IFP leader, politician

That democracy cannot succeed in diverse societies is a myth.
Zach de Beer, politician

Pretending that one's identity is created by oneself only is undemocratic.
Johan Degenaar, philosopher

The conflict between poverty and democracy is South Africa's greatest dilemma.
Philip Gawith, journalist

Despite our fondest hopes, democracy does not really rest on the rational foundation of individual rights and a constitution, but on the notion of national self-determination.
Hermann Giliomee, academic

A relatively smooth transition from minority rule to a democracy is difficult at the best of times, and even more so under conditions of growing poverty, rising unemployment, and a battle for scarce resources.
Rudolph Gouws, economist

Can an infant democracy heal the searing wounds of past injustices and bind up all the diverse people of South Africa?
Paul Gray, correspondent, Time International (USA)

The process of democracy was initiated by the peoples of this country in their struggle against overseas colonialism and was originally and primarily led by the white population group.
Chris Heunis, politician (1985)

Democracy has a price tag: political change also depends on the financial ability of a country to satisfy reasonable demands.
Chris Heunis

People should not believe that democracy solves all problems.
Samuel P Huntington, academic

The transition from autocracy to democracy entails a simultaneous shift from discipline to self-discipline.
David Lapin, rabbi, academic

Democracy is such a lovely thing that one can hardly hope to keep it from other people.
Albert Luthuli, ANC President General, Nobel Peace Prize

There are certain rules around democracy – you must accept that you might lose.
Gerhard Maré, sociologist

I don't know anything about democracy except that I was once told to become a member of the Inkatha Freedom Party.
Fungu Mbangokawupheli, local leader, Natal

I am not sure it is the poor people who will vote radical.
Harry Oppenheimer, businessman

The danger to a viable democracy is a lack of expertise from within and its destruction from without.
Jack Penn, surgeon, philosopher, artist

Radical pedagogy is going to be the foundation upon which the democratic culture of this nation is founded.
Zwelakhe Sisulu, editor, businessman

I have always said that the easiest way to make a democrat out of a tyrant is to confront them with the prospect of the opponent being in power.
Frederik Van Zyl Slabbert, academic

The abiding virtue of a democracy is that it is the easiest way for a society to change its mind to meet changing circumstances.
Frederik Van Zyl Slabbert

Democracy is a state of societal living, a culture, to be taken care of consciously and carefully: a thing of beauty.
Adam Small, writer

We are stumbling along the road to democracy, and the country has become a place not only to stir the soul, but also to test the pieties.
Richard Steyn, editor

Democracy, while it never eliminates corruption completely, is a way of minimising it.
Clem Sunter, businessman, scenario strategist

Democracy must actually be the rule of the people: not of a white hobo over a black MA.
Can Themba, journalist, writer

No point in democracy if everyone is demented as *mal* loonies, because we've not found a valve that can let off the steam.
Pieter-Dirk Uys, satirist

Once too good to share with just anyone, democracy is now the most used, most familiar, most misunderstood word in the land.
Pieter-Dirk Uys

Democracy means everybody gets the chance to have an ulcer.
Pieter-Dirk Uys

People become scared of laughter, and laughter is opinion and without opinions you can't have democracy because democracy is an orgy of opinions.
Pieter-Dirk Uys

In time we will get a sufficient number of prominent leaders to participate in the democratic game so that eventually those who still lust after revolution will become as irrelevant in South Africa as they are in the US or Britain.
Stoffel van der Merwe, politician (1988)

Democracy is not a state of mind which leads to the ballot box; it is not created by the ballot box.
Laurens van der Post, soldier, writer, philosopher

Democracy is an attitude of mind, not a polling booth.
Laurens van der Post

Our own passivity is the greatest threat to democracy.
Phillip van Niekerk, journalist

Democracy is an ongoing process of using rights, of taking the gap.
Phillip van Niekerk

Democracy is scarcely the obvious solution for a country where the majority is poor, black and impatient and the minority white, rich and powerful.
Patti Waldmeir, correspondent, Financial Times (UK)

Where inequality is great, and racially defined, democracy is the victim.
Patti Waldmeir

If we could establish a durable and democratic accommodation, it would not only be one of the major feats of political engineering in the modern world, it would also stand as a

beacon to numerous other societies that are wracked by racial and ethnic conflict.
David Welsh, academic

Democracy, in whatever shape or form it ultimately comes to South Africa, is unlikely to usher in a heaven on earth.
David Welsh

The democratic cast of mind is not a gift from on high; it is not created (or destroyed) by politicians and constitutions.
David Welsh

Democratic Party (DP)

More than anything else, we are the party for humanitarianism.
Hennie Bester, politician

Its philosophy begins with the proposition that the individual human being is all important.
Zach de Beer, politician, former DP leader

We are the only party with no blood on its hands.
Zach de Beer

Who else can you trust?
Zach de Beer

They lurk in doorways and never miss an opportunity to flash their itchy white liberal morality at the passing public.
Robert Kirby, satirist

We don't even have our own army!
Tony Leon, lawyer, politician

The DP can do no better than whimper, plaintively, that people are stealing its clothes.
Ken Owen, editor

They do not want to be the top act, they reckon second-best or third-rate will do them just fine.
Jon Qwelane, editor

There is a grasp, and respect, for its role as the cutting edge of change in white thinking and as a champion of civil liberties.
Hugh Roberton, journalist

We have always been a niche party.
James Selfe, politician

It's the only party that I know will continue to uphold the values I fought for for all those years.
Helen Suzman, liberal, retired politician

Where would we be without them?
Pieter-Dirk Uys, satirist

Diamonds

I aim to control the whole diamond business before long.
Alfred Beit, mining magnate
That's funny, so do I. We'd better join hands.
Cecil John Rhodes, Imperialist

The discovery of diamonds had resulted in a sudden change of policy on the part of the British government; the policy of benign indifference towards the Boer republics suddenly became one of profound concern about their future.
Graham Leach, correspondent, BBC Radio

Men don't buy flawless diamonds for funny girls. They get the chunks with the chinks in them.
Lin Sampson, journalist

Gentlemen, this is the rock upon which the future success of South Africa will be built.
Richard Southey, Cape Colonial Secretary

Diamonds and gold brought enterprise, investment and trade – the engines of imperial enlightenment – as they also brought northward expansion, subjugation and racial repression.
WT Tyler, critic

A life without looking for diamonds would be like dying before you're dead.
Flippie van der Merwe, diamond digger

Dars a mooi klippe voor en borst spelt (There's a pretty stone for a woman's brooch).
Schalk Jacobus van Niekerk (on seeing children playing with bright pebbles near Hopetown, Cape Colony)

The men who first dug at Dutoitspan did not know that there were diamonds literally embedded in the walls of the farm.
Geoffrey Wheatcroft, journalist

Diplomacy

Diplomacy is the art of getting on with those whom you cannot stand.
Pieter-Dirk Uys, satirist

Doctors

A doctor, like anyone else, wants, above all, to satisfy his ego.
Chris Barnard, surgeon

While patients expect their doctors to be technically conversant, they also require a little soul.
Hedi Lampert-Kemper, journalist

When you take antibiotics you are cutting down a veritable forest in your gut, and few doctors will do anything to try to minimise the damage or build you up afterwards.
Leslie Pleass, homoeopath, editor

With some admirable exceptions, doctors don't seem to care about quality of life. They don't have to live with the consequences.
Andrea Vinassa, journalist

Options make doctors jittery.
Andrea Vinassa

Dompass

A reference is like a rough chain on the black man's neck.
Anonymous Sharpeville survivor

I also realise that the pass system was seen as a major stumbling block.
PW Botha, Prime Minister/State President, 1978-89 (1986)

If anyone took the trouble to find out how many black people have spent some time in prison as a result of the pass laws, I think they would find about half or more of them have.
Pik Botha, politician

Our people have been so conditioned to the 'dom' pass that they have been known to buy it for 15 pounds sterling or risk death in an attempt to salvage it from a burning building.
Philip Kgosana, activist, 'The Black Messiah'

The pass or reference book was called the Dompass, or the Stinker.
Aggrey Klaaste, editor

If there is anything that made criminals out of the African people, it was the question of the passes.
Walter Sisulu, politician

My object is to provide every Native with a handy holder for his identification card in the form of a little pocket book in which the most important date concerning him will appear, as, for example, his employment contract and tax receipts.
HF Verwoerd, Prime Minister, 1958-66

Dorps

It was the focus of light and life for the stock farmer and husbandman, the breeding ground of his noblest traditions, the protector of his own language and culture, the watchman of the people's moral fibre and the centre of worship.
JR Albertyn, traveller

On Sundays in the Afrikaner dorps there is more activity around the video shops than the Dutch Reformed churches.
Andrew Kenny, journalist

Even the tiniest dorp in the Free State today has experienced a consumer boycott or some other form of organised resistance.
Phillip van Niekerk, journalist

Dress

Clothing is really touch-feel-see art.
Anonymous

Men in Safari suits are the worst. I hate the hairy Persian carpet legs.
Jani Allan, journalist

Dressing with style is akin to issuing a manifesto; dressing fashionably is like signing a petition.
Jani Allan

I always wear black underwear on Fridays to mourn all the opportunities I missed during the week.
Tracy Brown, PR

It's more or less a given that Winnie Mandela will personally save South African couture.
Andrew Donaldson & Adam Levin, journalists

What you wear determines how people respond to you, and there is a place for the feminine, the frivolous.
Marianne Fassler, dress designer

There may not be a soul in a particular town but the shoes in the store will sell like hot cakes.
Pamela Mabizela, businesswoman

I look like a *doos* and dress like one, I catch people off guard.
Nataniel, performer

If I took my clothes off on stage I'd wear fishnet stockings and stiletto heels – people may think that's camp, but I just think they go nicely with the G-string.
Nataniel

Many formerly fashionable fundis are agonising about how to make a splash when they go out on the gown.
Jenni Newman, PR

Hardly a Marxist among us does not have his suits tailor-made.
Ken Owen, editor

All I've got in the whole whole world is my wardrobe.
Susie Park, socialite

Why do South African women wear shoes that look as if they have been cut out of the chump end of a piece of sirloin?
Susie Park

I am nervous
of men
who wear
grey shoes
thinking
that this
is the solution
to the problem
of colour.
Andrew Putter

It is very difficult for a woman to be successful without the confidence of being well dressed.
Elzbieta Rosenwerth, couturier

Her shirt is made of that extraordinary new fabric that's slapped and shrunk and sucked at to produce something so unrecognisably delicious that you could go to bed with it without ever touching the person inside.
Lin Sampson, journalist

The dress seemed more responsive than the person in it.
Lin Sampson

Sometimes, if you wear suits for too long, it changes your ideology.
Joe Slovo, politician

It's hard persuading women, especially South Africans, that they should treat their wardrobes in the same way gourmets treat their stomachs.
Linda Stafford, journalist

We have a corporate climate where pin-stripes – even on the brain – are the norm.
Janet Wilhelm, journalist

Drink/Drunkenness

I drank to forget, then I forgot what I was trying to forget.
John Berks, talk show host

We have cane for the pain and voddy for the body, rum to light the fire in your soul and gin to put it out.
Garry Brennan, journalist

A couple of Ohlssons is like having sex beside Zoo Lake.
Paul Dean, restaurateur

When compared with other nations, the Afrikanders are remarkable for their sobriety, and it is considered by them a disgrace for a man to be drunk.
Christiaan de Wet, soldier, Second Anglo-Boer War

During the day I switch from gin and tonic to iced vodka accompanied by a little zakuski such as a bit of caviar or a gherkin or a piece of anchovy on a biscuit.
Peter Noel-Barham, gourmet

If a drunk physically mishandles one's wife, he must be knocked out as a matter of urgent necessity.
Jack Penn, surgeon, philosopher, artist

Yet nightly we repaired to the House of Truth, swinging bottles of brandy filched from the dark cellars where the white man hid his courage from us, and drank ourselves cold.
Can Themba, journalist, writer

Ecology

The reason why the black people did not significantly affect the ecological status quo was not so much their sympathy with nature, but more because they lacked the technology to make major change.
Anonymous

Economy

South Africa's economy is in poor shape to meet the expectations of blacks, who may suppose that greater power over their own affairs will be accompanied by a higher standard of life for all.
William Deedes (Lord Deedes of Aldington), politician, editor (UK)

There is agreement that economic policy in the new South Africa should simultaneously address the problems of no growth on the one hand, and large income and wealth disparities on the other.
Rudolph Gouws, economist

The economy is as strong as a horse, but it's got too many jockeys at the moment.
Derek Keys, businessman, politician

We might not have the skills of a Harvard graduate but what we have is our access to the market, and our labour, and if nothing else, our sweat equity.
Jabulani Mabuza, businessman

I couldn't see myself battling to get a job against a white guy who had less education than me, and still having to call him 'boss' – so I went into business for myself.
Lawrence Mavundla, businessman

Every day, more and more middle-class South Africans watch the guts being torn out of the economy and their own businesses, and long for a strong hand to restore order.
Victor Nell, community psychologist

Education

It is customary among us, the Afrikaners, to send our children to school for three months and then to expect them to be fully educated.
Anonymous

Education presents a tortured dilemma: the millions whom politics has rendered incapable of meeting the basic intellectual and disciplinary standards for secondary and tertiary education are precisely those on whose behalf affirmative action is clamoured for.
Lionel Abrahams, poet, novelist

We must not say that the native caste is there primarily to be a hewer of wood and a drawer of water.
ER Browne, politician (during a Senate debate and incorrectly attributed to HF Verwoerd) (1953)

Female students are undertaking manned rocketry with vigour, while simultaneously practising for the international jet-ski championships – and they wonder why impotence is on the increase.
Alastair Campbell, student

Whatever happens, we must not lose sight of the most significant person in the education process – the child.
Margaret de Paravicini, journalist

There are still not human rights in the classroom.
Colin Douglas, politician

We no longer have the time, even if we had the resources, to teach several million people just to read.
Chris Gibbons, broadcaster

Despite snipers to the right and to the left, I believe that these (private) schools will serve South Africa's needs in the years that lie ahead by pursuing excellence long after the extremist dialogues have extinguished themselves in clouds of bluster and fulmination.
Neil Jardine, teacher

It was an agonising task for us to search for our past while studying at educational institutions designed along Bantu education policies and, therefore, devoid of anything that might inspire resistance to our servitude status.
Patrick 'Terror' Lekota, politician

An illiterate person is like a blind person, you have to do what somebody tells you to do.
Mina Macu, domestic worker

They'll hate your bush colleges so much that I bet you they burn the bloody places down.
Ernie Malherbe, educationist, to John Vorster, then Acting Minister of Education (1957)

The aim of the Education Department was to give the Natives the same education as the Europeans were getting.
J McLaren, civil servant (1908)

There is a crying need for imagination and creativity to be infused into the educational process.
Merlyn Mehl, educationist

South African education represents perhaps the greatest challenge for lateral thinking in the world at the present time.
Merlyn Mehl

What use could anyone make of the learning acquired there in a land where life is still primitive and Company rule is law?
OF Mentzel, geographer

A good world history would be worth anything. Everything that makes South African children look outside South Africa and realise the world makes for peace.
Alfred Milner, British High Commissioner

The only way to avoid working on the mines is to go to school and get educated.
Mpumelelo Miya, miner

Who was it who said education is the whole difference between civilisation and barbarism?
Harry Oppenheimer, businessman

For the student, copulating over the telephone might be absolutely wonderful because there are a lot of advantages.
Nina Romm, artist

Teaching is liberation.
Nina Romm

No country has ever been run by illiterates.
Albertina Sisulu, politician

The terrain of education needs more radicalism – not less.
Zwelakhe Sisulu, editor, businessman

When the history of this time is written, education could stand out as the factor which led our country to unity or it may signify the Achilles' heel through which a troubled yet promising and beautiful country bled itself to a sad end.
Franklin Sonn, educationist, ambassador

Is there one South African school that is running classes in how to be an entrepreneur and open up a business as part of its core curriculum?
Clem Sunter, businessman, scenario strategist

The foremost characteristic of a 'winning nation' has to be the quality of its education system.
Clem Sunter

The old Nationalists used it to lobotomise a nation and churn out a generation of Ja-Oom and Ja-Baas clones, while the old Liberation Czars used the slogan 'Liberation before Education' as a sly way of mobilising the passion of youth to storm the barricades of oppression, while the educated comrades sat in Swedish hotels sipping whisky paid for by various anti-apartheid movements.
Pieter-Dirk Uys, satirist

What is the use of teaching a Bantu child mathematics when it cannot use it in practice? Education must train and teach people in accordance with their opportunities in life.
HF Verwoerd, Prime Minister, 1958-66

When I have control of Native education, I will reform it so that Natives will be taught from childhood to realise that equality with Europeans is not for them.
HF Verwoerd

Election 1994

Before . . .

Fighting a losing election campaign, the NP has abandoned its Saatchi and Saatchi gloss and has gone back to its old propaganda mentor – Goebbels.
Anonymous Cosatu House circular

Indians will remain the filling in the sandwich.
Anonymous Indian

FW de Klerk is 'n kaalkop, maar hy's 'n groot kop. Hy's my man.
Anonymous Natal voter

I have no question in my mind that we'll win three provinces, except Natal.
Benny Alexander, politician

I have a huge constituency, so how could I not have confidence?
Mangosuthu Buthelezi, IFP leader, politician

I'm not worried. I will get my pension.
Mangosuthu Buthelezi

We are entering a period of resistance politics.
Mangosuthu Buthelezi

The climate in this country is so serious that our participation is the best thing I can do for this country.
Mangosuthu Buthelezi (on the IFP's entering the election)

If you think of Trevor Manuel as the future minister of finance you can understand why the Egyptians worshipped cockroaches.
Robin Carlisle, politician

A lot of money, a lot of investment and a lot of opportunity is going to be needed to sort of jump-start South Africa.
Bill Clinton, President (USA)

It's an uhuru election.
Zach de Beer, politician

If all goes as planned, there will be some brief cheering.
William Deedes (Lord Deedes of Aldington), politician, editor (UK)

We are going to storm South Africa.
FW de Klerk, State President, 1989-94; Deputy President, 1994-

Mr Mandela and his party are searching for a new species of flora to finance its promises. It's called the money tree and banknotes grow on it to pay for the ANC's promises.
FW de Klerk

We are not a mouse: you will hear the roar of the NP lion when the results come out.
FW de Klerk

Nelson Mandela has so much egg on his face he needs two bars of soap to get it off.
FW de Klerk

Every tarmac he (Nelson Mandela) lands on when he flies about the country in this election has been built under National Party government.
FW de Klerk

We say: use the Boer's bakkie, but vote for the PAC.
Barney Desai, politician

We never killed people, only apartheid.
DP advertisement

Each black voter becomes apartheid's personal executioner.
Chris Gibbons, broadcaster

South Africans are not just voting to affirm history, they're voting for a direction and a set of policies.
Stanley Greenberg, election adviser (USA)

An election is not a duchess's tea party.
Independent Electoral Commission (IEC)

We are ready. You are ready. Let's do it.
IEC advertisement

The last shall be first.
IFP advertisement

Was it necessary to fix on a specific day, and to make it a hill to die for?
Shaun Johnson, journalist

Unless the position of the king is addressed and he is very clearly accommodated, I don't for the life of me see how you can have an election.
Kobus Jordaan, politician

Without exception, every black party in the election aspires to the things of white Western civilisation and not to the things of black African civilisation.
Andrew Kenny, journalist

I wish the parties all the best.
Henry Kissinger, mediator (on the failure of mediation between IFP, ANC and government)

(This election) is not about sandbags and machine guns. It is a festival.
Johann Kriegler, judge, IEC chairman

Madam, have you been present at these proceedings?
Johann Kriegler (to an SABC reporter)

We will remain cool, calm and elected.
Tony Leon, lawyer, politician

You haven't lived until you've tried it with the woman on top.
Des Lindberg, entertainer (on Frances Kendall's Federal Party)

On April 27, we'll bury the NP together with its black surrogates.
Nelson Mandela, President, May 1994-

Do not expect to be driving a Mercedes the day after the elections.
Nelson Mandela

We are not going to live as fat cats.
Nelson Mandela

If there is anything I am conscious about, it is not to frighten the minorities, especially the white minority.
Nelson Mandela

We are not going to war, we are going into an election.
Dikgang Moseneke, advocate, IEC deputy chairman

How are you going to get to the polling stations when you can't even get to the shops?
Gertrude Mzizi, politician

They're brandy and coke terrorists.
Jay Naidoo, politician (on the arrest of 32 right-wingers following two car bombs)

When you have a situation where people have lost trust, you need an outside person who understands them and whom both sides can trust. It happened that both of them trusted me.
Washington Okumu, ambassador-at-large (Kenya) (on his mediation between the IFP and the government/ANC)

If we vote, we can hope to complete the transition from minority oppression to democracy, not bloodlessly but in reasonable order; if we do not vote, we shall continue to be trapped in the spiral of violence and disorder from which we may never escape.
Ken Owen, editor

One family, one piece of land.
PAC Natal election campaign slogan

Don't think if you don't vote you'll be protected – some sucker will still be elected.
Prophets of the City, rap group

Choose your party carefully. The last one went on for more than 40 years.
Radio 702 advertisement

The chocolate layer covering the hard niggerball.
Fanus Schoeman, politician (explaining the ANC's government policy)

This whitey belief that if you are illiterate, you can't vote – it doesn't hold water.
Tony Seeber, IEC

This election is the ritual by which South Africans liberate themselves from a bitter, blood-soaked past, and accept the fate that history has fashioned for them: one people, many races, many languages, many clashing beliefs.
Sunday Times

If you touch a right-winger before or after the election then we will donder you harder than we have ever dondered you.
Eugene Terre'Blanche, AWB leader

There are 29 parties – it's a supermarket of choices.
Pieter-Dirk Uys, satirist

At last, after 340 years of waiting in the shadows, we can throw the dice for the first time and move up the democracy board.
Pieter-Dirk Uys

Any Afrikaner, whether my own son or anyone else, who actively promotes the ANC's election campaign is a traitor to his own people.
Wilhelm Verwoerd, academic

If you are in now you can always get out, but if you are out now you can never get in.
Constand Viljoen, soldier, politician (on why he chose to register his Freedom Front party for the election)

The NP's is the Alzheimer's campaign: you have to have a failing memory to go along with it.
Weekly Mail & Guardian

During . . .

There is no doubt that if there were a bloodbath here, blood would lead.
Anonymous journalist (USA)

And we call these white suburbs!
Anonymous northern suburbs white voter (looking at the polling station queues)

When you've got polling stations without electricity and phones, and electoral officers without much education or experience, then you mustn't expect things to work like they do in Seapoint.
Anonymous electoral officer

Peaceful isn't the word – it's been wonderful.
Anonymous ANC worker

This story doesn't end with bombing Saddam Hussein to bits; it ends with the people of this country receiving what they've been fighting for for so long.
Peter Arnett, correspondent, CNN

This means freedom to me. Now I can die with happiness in my heart. Now I can walk like a real man.
Samuel Bhene (80), on 27 April 1994

Our approach is to look at this as a moment in history, not a week in the news.
Dennis Dunlavey, correspondent, ABC

This is one of the great stories of the 20th century.
Charlayne Hunter-Gault, correspondent, McNeill/Lehrer News-hour (USA)

You'd be a fool not to be here, blood or no blood.
Charlayne Hunter-Gault

A political miracle is taking place.
The Independent (UK)

People laid down their lives for the election; if I can't lay down my time I don't deserve to be a South African.
Stan Jabour, businessman

We can't be too pink-lensed about this, but it was a wonderful day.
Dale Lautenbach, journalist

I cry not only because of joy, but for the human resources that went to waste for us to vote.
Sipho 'Hotstix' Mabuse, musician

They walked like a people freed: free even before they had put pen to ballot paper.
Justice Malala, journalist

This election is the realisation of our hopes and dreams that we have cherished over decades.
Nelson Mandela, President, May 1994-

We hope by the mere casting of a vote the results will give hope to all South Africans and make all South Africans realise this is our country.
Nelson Mandela

I have waited for this day for all my life, and I will wait for the whole day if needs be.
David Mashigo, voter (on 27 April 1994)

Not like Sunday – it was like Christmas morning in Soweto.
Beauty Mokhele, housewife

I was grateful it happened in my lifetime.
Kaizer Motaung, businessman

The only station Eugene Terre'Blanche visited on voting day was a petrol station.
Morgan Naidu, journalist

For South Africa, the election marks the end of 342 years of white hegemony; for Africa, it completes the liberation of a continent; for the world, it is the final repudiation of institutionalised European racism.
Ken Owen, editor

That slow shuffle towards the polling booths became a journey of rediscovery, of ourselves and of our nation.
Claire Robertson, journalist

It is good to get a vote while you are still alive.
Klaas Sethakge, voter (64)

I never thought I would be proud to be a South African again.
Anthony Sher, actor

This time has been long and difficult in coming.
Adam Small, writer

Freedom in our lifetime
Sowetan (headline)

Vote, the beloved country
The Star (headline)

We will always remember this day as the day of the vow.
Eugene Terre'Blanche, AWB leader (of 27 April 1994)

I am walking on clouds. It is an incredible feeling, like falling in love. We South Africans are going to be the rainbow people of the world.
Desmond Tutu, cleric, Archbishop of Cape Town

And after . . .

Q: How many IEC commissioners does it take to change a light bulb?

A: Nobody knows, the light bulbs haven't arrived yet.
Anonymous (one of a series of IEC jokes)

Young men carried their elderly fathers on their backs to the polling booths; black voters came on crutches and in wheelchairs, travelling for miles and waiting for hours in this great march to freedom.
Bill Clinton, President (USA)

South Africans, all of them together, showed a respect, a tolerance and a spirit of unity which transcended everything else.
Zach de Beer, politician

Mr Mandela has walked a long road and now stands at the top of the hill. A traveller would sit down and admire the view, but a man of destiny knows that beyond this view there is another and another and another.
FW de Klerk, State President, 1989-94; Deputy President, 1994- (conceding defeat, 2 May 1994)

The election had a kind of wholesome, healing character to it.
Colin Eglin, politician

Uhuru wears off, like war paint.
Rex Gibson, editor

For whites at least, democracy means having to queue.
Anton Harber, editor

The abiding image of the day that South Africa began to become one nation, all together, was in the orange, autumn sun rising over a new country teeming with extraordinary, renewed people.
Shaun Johnson, journalist

Material desire was not the deepest emotion on April 27: white South Africa has always underestimated the depth of the psychological slur of disenfranchisement, apart from the social poison it unleashed.
Shaun Johnson

And the oppressed masses: they did not attack, loot and wreak revenge on the day of the wrong's righting. They grasped their precious votes, the repository of dignity, to their hearts and celebrated.
Shaun Johnson

A free-for-all but not necessarily fair.
Frances Kendall, Federal Party leader

Free at last. Thank God we are free at last.
Nelson Mandela, President, May 1994- (on 2 May 1994)

Now we should come together with our political opponents, pick up the pieces and build our country.
Nelson Mandela

I stand before you humbled by your courage with a heart full of love for all of you.
Nelson Mandela

I hold out the hand of friendship to the leaders of all parties and their members and ask all of them to join us in working together to tackle the problems we face as a nation.
Nelson Mandela

I pledge to use all my strength and ability to live up to your expectations.
Nelson Mandela

The people of South Africa have spoken in these elections. They want change! And change is what they will get.
Nelson Mandela

You have mandated us to change South Africa from a country in which the majority lived with little hope, to one in which they can live and work with dignity, with a sense of self-esteem and confidence in the future.
Nelson Mandela

We place our vision of a new constitutional order for South Africa on the table not as conquerors, prescribing to the conquered. We speak as fellow citizens to heal the wounds of the past with the intent of constructing a new order based on justice for all.
Nelson Mandela

A kind of toilet town of an election, a fitting epitaph to Nationalist rule.
Ken Owen, editor

To have lived to see, in one lifetime, the defeat of Nazism, the collapse of communism, and the end of apartheid is almost too much good fortune, but even so, I cannot forbear to look back once more on the past, even if it carries the taste of salt.
Ken Owen

Remember that on May 10 1994, the people of this blood-soaked nation were united in prayer, and hope, and an unselfconscious, unqualified patriotism.
Ken Owen

We have accomplished what few people anywhere in the world thought we could do: we have freed ourselves, and made a democracy, and we have done so without war or revolution.
Sunday Times

They came, they saw, they reported and they are leaving.
Christina Stucky, journalist (on the hack pack)

On the ballot list of the ANC, democracy starts to disappear after his (Mandela's) name.
Sueddeutsche Zeitung (Germany)

There is need, now, more than ever before, for a realism tinged with iron.
The Times (London)

We are free today. We are free today. All of us, black and white together, free today.
Desmond Tutu, cleric, Archbishop of Cape Town

It was hard to believe that such a thing could have happened in South Africa.
Constand Viljoen, soldier, politician

Only the unflagging human spirit made it a day to be proud of.
Weekly Mail & Guardian

Dawn of freedom, my foot. Black majority rule in South Africa should send a shudder around the world.
Peregrine Worsthorne, journalist (UK)

Emigration

When someone calls to say they can't make drinks on Sunday because they're 'on the run', you know they don't mean from the security police – they've got a date with Lufthansa.
Anonymous

I just want one last boom so I can sell my house at a profit and head for New York.
Anonymous (1982)

There's nothing more thrilling than walking into a stylish social gathering and being greeted by a chorus line of gaping, gold-draped gullets and the syncopated refrain: 'So you're off as well?'
Kathy Berman, TV producer

Leaving your country is in some way a desertion.
Hilda Bernstein, writer, artist

The young oaks are going to America, Canada and Oz.
Garry Brennan, journalist

Keep Boipatong. I'm Boeing.
Patrick Bulger, journalist

Paying a reconstruction levy is cheaper than emigrating. And you can pay in rands.
Dennis Davis, lawyer

In matters of emigration, rather as in love affairs, or tales about money, people tell wild, inventive and unreliable stories.
Christopher Hope, writer

I look forward – with no malice intended towards those who are still to go – to the morning when we finally stop this incessant talk of 'leavers' and 'stayers', and get on with throwing our talents and energies into building a better new country out of the old.
Shaun Johnson, journalist

We are going to be saved the expense of emigrating: a brand new country is coming to us.
Patrick Lee, writer

The number one reason why single South African women between 28 and 38 are emigrating is not the current socio-political turbulence, it's the prospect of finding a suitable mate.
Mike Lipkin, marketer

There came a time when you could go into the nicer parts of LA, the whitest of white middle-class suburbs, and find the air thick with Johannesburg accents – the nasal whine of Highlands North on this side, the plummy ripeness of Saxonwold on that.
Rian Malan, writer

When you flee SA, make sure you flee SAA, the people's airline.
Joel Mervis, editor

If one stays in South Africa, it is an act of faith.
Stephen Mulholland, publisher (now living in Australia)

Sage advice to those thinking of fleeing the beloved country and fearing how they will support a comfortable lifestyle in pastures new: remember that one's standard of living is very different from one's quality of life.
Jenni Newman, PR

First it was called the Chicken Run, then the Brain Drain, then Asset Relocation; now those who are getting out of the country are simply known as Nick-of-Times.
Jenni Newman

Moving is a luxury of capitalism.
Jo Noero, architect

If the ship sinks, I shall drown, but I'm not going to jump overboard.
Harry Oppenheimer, businessman

Some who have gone resent the fact that there are some who have stayed.
Alan Paton, writer

It is a mistake to think South African emigrants arrive at Heathrow with only the price of a currant bun.
David Rees, academic

Despite everything, there are still enough whites left in the country to fill an Emigration Seminar to the seams.
Gus Silber, journalist

There is always a brain drain after political incidents.
Helen Suzman, liberal, retired politician

They say that when the Jews start packing, it's time to go; when the Portuguese start packing, it's too late already!
Pieter-Dirk Uys, satirist (a joke told to him by Helen Suzman)

If you were inclined to pack for Perth, you would have a full armoury of reasons to bolster your intentions.
Lester Venter, journalist

Emotions

Without pain, there is no joy.
Pik Botha, politician

Joy is a higher category than morality, although it can comprise it.
Guy Butler, academic, writer

When you grow up as a moffie in a country ruled by Neanderthals, you soon learn there's nothing to fear but your fear.
Steven Cohen, artist

Who hasn't, at some stage, been lonely and in need of flattering pink lighting?
Pnina Fenster, journalist

Emotional insecurity more than anything precludes generosity of spirit.
David Lapin, rabbi, academic

Passion burns itself out remarkably rapidly, leaving nothing but the ashes of two burnt-out relationships.
Mike Lipkin, marketer

The fellow who was not afraid didn't live very long.
Adolph Gysbert (Sailor) Malan, pilot, farmer

I have never had a single moment of depression, because I know that my cause will triumph.
Nelson Mandela, President, May 1994-

Bitterness is not a productive emotion.
Kogila Moodley, academic

Hope is really much more fundamental than either pessimism or optimism.
Beyers Naudé, cleric

Loneliness is listening to a Radio Oranje request programme.
Obie Oberholzer, photographer

Fear is a journey, a terrible journey, but sorrow is at least an arriving.
Alan Paton, writer

Anger and lust, these are volcanic sins.
Alan Paton

Covetousness, like hatred, is a destroyer of personality.
Alan Paton

One cannot argue with passion.
Alan Paton

Gratitude is a highly civilised emotion if it is spontaneous.
Jack Penn, surgeon, philosopher, artist

Emotion is a noble thing, sentimentality is suppressed brutality.
Ian Player, conservationist

Euphoria subsides, it always does.
Adam Small, writer

Bitterness is to the tongue what darkness is to the eye; darkness and bitterness are forms of one another.
Laurens van der Post, soldier, writer, philosopher

Vengeance, revenge, and bitterness are all reactions of the retarded Corsican in ourselves: they play no role in the abiding assertion of life.
Laurens van der Post

There are times when fear is a rational response to events.
Peter Wilhelm, editor, poet

Once hope is destroyed, value of existence is diminished.
Musa Zondi, politician

England/The English

Anglo-African Whites by and large squat flabbily behind the ramparts of Afrikanerdom – carping, but profiting hugely.
Breyten Breytenbach, poet, writer (1985)

An Englishman cannot keep up with a Boer on the march.
Christiaan de Wet, soldier, Second Anglo-Boer War

The weather is absolutely vile and how any person who has ever enjoyed South African sunshine can settle down to this sort of thing I cannot understand.
Percy Fitzpatrick, politician, writer

God may hear my prayer; England does not.
Piet Joubert, soldier (after the Battle of Majuba)

England does not want the truth from us, they want their own truth – that truth which will suit the scheme of their own Ministers; that is the truth for them, and whatever we say that is not the truth.
Piet Joubert

They have asked for my trousers and I have given them; for my coat, I have given that also; now they want my life and that I cannot give.
Paul Kruger, President, Transvaal Republic

Gold is their goal and expediency their watchword.
DF Malan, Prime Minister, 1948-54

For many English-speakers, it has simply become impossible to envisage a South Africa in which their most treasured values – indeed, their view of themselves – can remain viable.
Ken Owen, editor

I contend that we are the finest race in the world, and that the more of the world we inhabit, the better it is for the human race.
Cecil John Rhodes, Imperialist

If the British Empire had needed a universal symbol beyond the Union Jack, a cricket bat and a set of falling bails would have done.
Barry Ronge, journalist

Most leading businessmen are English-speaking, but then so are most of the socially visible white tramps in the cities.
Lawrence Schlemmer, academic

I remember it as often a subject of thought within myself at this time, why God had made us, the English, so superior to all other races, and, while feeling it was very nice to belong to the best people on earth, having yet a vague feeling that it was not quite just of God to have made us so much better than all the other nations.

Olive Schreiner, writer

There are many, particularly English-speaking whites, who have been as guilty of oppression as everyone else and who have gotten away with political murder.

Adam Small, writer

What are the British good at any more?

Janet Suzman, actress

When the British arrow enters the shoulder blades, it is always on an oblique trajectory.

Stanley Uys, journalist

Although British power has vanished, there is still a British Empire of the Mind.

Laurens van der Post, soldier, writer, philosopher

We English speakers have a softness, a fastidiousness and a lack of cunning that makes us second-best to Afrikaners in matters such as rugby or politics.

Peter Younghusband, foreign correspondent

Environment

It's sad that when you mention the ozone layer, the image that springs to mind is a rallying call of unwashed hippies and hardcore vegetarians, who all use fridges when they're at home with their tofu burgers.
Ian Fraser, playwright

In the environment, job satisfaction is more guaranteed than in occupations like advertising.
Sam Mhlungu, environmentalist

The 1980s will be remembered as the decade the environment hit back.
Clem Sunter, businessman, scenario strategist

Equality

In the lending of corkscrews, the splitting of six-packs, the sharing of salt, all are equal.
Denis Beckett, journalist

Trusting to the liberality and elasticity of the British Constitution, the native considered he had equal rights with the white man, and by paying the usual fee for a claim licence he saw no reason why he should be debarred from becoming a full-blown digger.
G Beet, diamond digger

The basis of equality is choice.
Cheryl Carolus, politician

We cannot possibly hope for equality until we begin to undo inequality.
Tony Leon, lawyer, politician & Etienne Mureinik, academic

There are serious problems if the law says that all citizens, including chiefs, kings and ordinary people, are equal in status.
Mwelo Nonkonyana, Chief of the Amabhala, Transkei

It is our responsibility to break down barriers of division and create a country where there will be neither whites nor blacks, just South Africans, free and united in diversity.
Oliver Tambo, ANC president

Failure

Failure in South Africa – which is still on the cards – will move remorselessly from the negotiating tables of Cape Town and Pretoria on to the conscience of the world itself.
William Deedes (Lord Deedes of Aldington), politician, editor (UK)

Thirty years of my life have been spent knocking in vain, patiently, moderately and modestly at a closed and barred door.
Albert Luthuli, ANC President General, Nobel Peace Prize

Failure is devastating only if it affects other people, or if it leads to disillusionment to the point of despair.
Jack Penn, surgeon, philosopher, artist

There is no point in our conquering the world and failing in southern Africa.
Neil van Heerden, diplomat

Farming/Farmers

The purchase of imported stock for the improvement of his flock, the disposal of his clip of wool, and last though not least, the indulgence of the good wife's craving to invest some

of the superfluous cash brought in by it in the various tempting articles of personal adornment and domestic refinement, which the well-filled winkels of the dorp exhibit, brought the farmer more frequently into contact with the inhabitants of the towns – an intercourse which not only tended to enlighten his previous crude notions of the usages of civilised life, but greatly to benefit the trading portion of the community.
Anonymous

When you go out to plough, never leave your guns at home.
Jacob Cuyler, landdrost of Uitenhage

As the men were away on commando, the Kaffirs reaped the corn under the supervision of the Boer women; and where Kaffirs were not obtainable the women did the work with their own hands, and were assisted by their little sons and daughters.
Christiaan de Wet, soldier, Second Anglo-Boer War

It is clear that the 'farm Native' has lost economically by contact with Europeans. Working very much harder than he did under tribal conditions, he has no more nourishing or varied a diet than the rawest Pondo of the reserves; a servant or 'labour tenant' dismissed by his employer has no hut site or land to cultivate.
Monica Hunter

In direct contradiction to the custom and example of the original inhabitants, the Hottentots, the colonists turn their cattle out continually into the same fields, and that too in a much greater quantity than used to graze there at the time of the Hottentots.
Andrew Sparrmann, botanist

Burn our cities and leave our farms and tomorrow the cities will bloom, but burn our farms and tomorrow grass will grow in the cities.
Eddie von Maltitz, farmer, activist

Feminism

While women have been going through the process of change, men have been standing outside it all.
Tersia King, businesswoman

The idea of women's oppression is just a convenient excuse women use to blame others for their own limitations.
Mamphela Ramphele, academic

Manifestations of feminist thinking in South Africa have been as fragmented and confused as the country itself.
Dene Smuts, politician

Food

A skilful man would so arrange the meat on his spit as to have alternate pieces of fat and of lean, and thus get what we used to call a *bont span* (team of oxen not all of the same colour).
Christiaan de Wet, soldier, Second Anglo-Boer War

Lettuce should not be cut to fit bread; it should billow out loosely and asymmetrically.
Susan Edelstein, cook

We had our breakfast there – the liver roasted on the coals, and a couple of 'dough-boys', with the unexpected addition of a bottle of cold tea, weak and unsweetened.
Percy Fitzpatrick, politician, writer

Business lunches are the only liquid centre in this hard city of gold.
Jane Fraser, journalist (Australia)

People don't want to be seen feasting when everyone else is starving.
Paddy Gibb, floral artist

The outstanding characteristics of Malay cookery are the free, almost heroic, use of spices and aromatic flavourings, the prolonged steady, but slow, application of moist heat to all meat dishes, and the skilful blending of many diverse constituents into a combination that still holds the essential goodness of each.
C Louis Leipoldt, doctor, writer, cook

Zebra flesh I should without hesitation deem the tenderest, most savoury, and best flavoured of all game meat, especially when the animal is young.
C Louis Leipoldt

Boerwors is now a thing of the past, although it often appears on the table – a travesty of what it should be and a disgrace to the modern cook.
C Louis Leipoldt

The pumpkins, as big as oxwagon wheels, looked as if they dabbled with the same syringe as athlete Ben Johnson.
Charles Leonard, journalist

The cakes I make require an act of faith; they may be to die for, doll, but they don't look like it.
Barbara Ludman, journalist, author

For a brief moment I savoured that exquisite delectableness that comes when oyster, tongue and palate meet in a first gentle caress that leads to a frenetic erotic embrace and the lingering gustatory climax that gently subsides in the afterglow of ingestion.
Peter Noel-Barham, gourmet

A meal in Cape Town is distinguished by its substantial dishes and, what is most welcome to voyagers, plenty of vegetables which are as sweet as they can possibly be, for the situation of this climate is so happy that all European and most tropical fruits and vegetables grow as well as in their native soils.
Mary Ann Parker, wife of a ship's captain (1791)

When we talk braais, we're talking about the cuisine of the Trekkers, with its roots in the ver verlate vlaktes and the kreun van ossewa, when improvisation was the order of the day and if you didn't use some kind of spice, your freshly killed kudu would have crawled off long before you'd creaked your way up the next koppie.
Hilary Prendini Toffoli, journalist

The South African braai is not so much a tradition as a compromise, designed to enable women to make salads while the men stand around the fire lying to each other about their sex lives.
Peter Robinson, journalist

Giraffes are splendid eating and usually in good condition, and fat is a luxury that no one can properly appreciate till he has lived for a time on nothing but the dry meat of the smaller antelopes.
Frederick Courteney Selous, hunter

I tasted elephant's heart, roasted on a forked stick over the ashes, which I thought then, and still consider, to be one of the greatest delicacies that an African hunter is likely to enjoy.
Frederick Courteney Selous

The most famous of all South African delicacies is 'biltong', strips of petrified beef or game hung out in the veld to dry and traditionally eaten with liberal sprinklings of salt, herbs, aromatic spices, and a hacksaw.
Gus Silber, journalist

If men are moderate in their habits what can be more delightful in the early morning to breathe the fresh air of the South African climate and to be fully awakened from sleep by a cup of well-made coffee?
Transvaal Times

A restaurant is like a theatre: it's a stage and you have a set.
Johan van den Berg, TV producer

200 pounds salted beef, 150 pounds salted speck, 150 pounds dripping, 80 pounds of butter, 13 muids wheat, 2 muids flour, $1^{1}/_{2}$ muids green peas, $1^{1}/_{2}$ muids yellow peas, $1^{1}/_{2}$ muids white beans, $^{2}/_{3}$ muid broad beans, 250 pounds of barley, 100 pounds rice, brown beans, black beans, Madagascar beans, princess beans, sago and groats, 274 pounds coffee beans, 34 pounds castor sugar, 150 pounds lump sugar, 38 pounds black pepper, 7 pounds white pepper, 31 pounds tamarind, coriander, mustard and cumin seeds, 1 pound white bird's nests, one sack Japanese rice, 7 bottles English olives in brine,

18 pounds currants, 6,000 almonds, preserved plums, a half-aum coconut oil, a bierpijp white vinegar, 100 tallow candles, 220 pounds hard soap, six loads kindling, 400 bottles imported and Cape wine. (Contents of a pantry, 1754)
Joachim von Dessin, secretary to the Orphan Chamber

Forced Removals

We had no choice, the guns were behind us.
Anonymous

We do not force people in South Africa to move to new homes, we coerce them.
PW Botha, Prime Minister/State President, 1978-89

Before we had even opened the front door, I just heard the hammer on the pillar of the veranda . . . a big sound that made me wonder if I was dying.
Jane Dakile, teacher

I don't think it was a good idea to tell people where to live and to kick people out of particular townships. It became forced removals.
FW de Klerk, State President, 1989-94; Deputy President, 1994-

The 'black spots' in white areas were ruthlessly eliminated, and the land turned over to whites, sometimes with names dripping in insensitivity.
Anthony Heard, editor

They lost their land. They lost their cattle. They lost their dignity. They lost themselves.
Tshepo Khumbane, social worker

The resettlement of Black people is resorted to in order to ensure their national unity, to protect their ethnic and political interests and to improve their living conditions and standard of life.
Piet Koornhof, politician

The compensation that was given to landowners can never be compared to the suffering endured by them.
Horatius Mabaso, activist

Since we were tossed out we have little land to farm, our cattle died because there was not enough water for them, some were living from fishing in the lake and we are no longer allowed to do so.
Phillip Mfeka, former householder

If the government says go, then you go.
Petrus Ndlovu, former householder

I have studied the photograph from all angles, I consulted the experts about this, but I am still looking for the 'Bulldozer'. There is no bulldozer. What is shown in the photograph is an excavator.
SMJ Steyn, politician (re an Argus report saying a bulldozer demolished shacks, 1977)

They came in buses and trucks with guns and clubs; the women and children were crying.
Temba Xayimpi of the Mfengu

Forgiveness

Reconciliation is not a human possibility but a divine gift.
David J Bosch, theologian

There can't be healing in this country without the past being put on the table and dealt with.
Dirk Coetzee, policeman, assassin

When I eventually spoke out it was such a relief. For the first time in nine years my soul was at peace. Not that I'm redeemed now and going to heaven.
Dirk Coetzee (1994)

You cannot forgive people without knowing what they have done.
Bantu Holomisa, politician

Nothing is forgiven, nothing forgotten, nothing settled.
Rian Malan, writer

True reconciliation can only be based on justice.
Beyers Naudé, cleric

We seek to create a process which will make it possible for all South Africans to come to terms with our painful past – with dignity and in a spirit of forgiveness but with due consideration for acknowledgement and the need to provide reparation or compensation for victims.
Dullah Omar, politician

Not only the white NGK should go on its knees and ask for forgiveness, we should be there too.
Elia Tema, cleric (NGK)

Amnesty says nothing if those who gave the orders and the politicians do not themselves apply for it.
Joe Verster, policeman (CCB)

Freedom

The arse-side of freedom does not exactly smell of roses.
Breyten Breytenbach, poet, writer

Perhaps the long walk to freedom knows no final destination.
Breyten Breytenbach

Because freedom is a new, exotic sound on our tongues, we are in danger of resorting to counting nipples as a barometer of our liberation from a Calvinist past.
Joanne Fedler, academic

How real a concept is freedom? You start to function when coming to terms with a set of limitations.
Athol Fugard, playwright

Those who fight the freedom struggle will always be free.
Ferdi Hartzenberg, CP leader

To conquer and to want power is not noble, but to fight for freedom is.
Ferdi Hartzenberg

Freedom of association also implies freedom of disassociation.
Johan Heyns, theologian

What is the use of liberty if there is starvation?
Peter Leon, lawyer

The urge and yearning for freedom springs from a sense of divine discontent and so, having a divine origin, can never be permanently gagged.
Albert Luthuli, ANC President General, Nobel Peace Prize

The road to freedom is always full of difficulties.
Albert Luthuli

Only free men can negotiate.
Nelson Mandela, President, 1994-

There is no easy walk to freedom.
Nelson Mandela

The greatest honour a people can pay to a man behind bars is to keep the freedom flame burning to continue the fight.
Winnie Mandela, politician

White freedom is threatened if blacks are free.
Kole Omotoso, academic

Deprivation of freedom nurtures irresponsibility.
Ken Owen, editor

To give up the task of reforming society is to give up one's responsibility as a free man.
Alan Paton, writer

In my day and in my country I have seen freedom go under, and I have seen freedom rise again, indestructible, deathless, immortal.
Jan Christian Smuts, Prime Minister, 1919-24 & 1939-48

Freedom is the most ineradicable craving of human nature.
Jan Christian Smuts

What motivates blacks in their struggle for liberation, beyond mere rage, hatred and frustration, is the belief, whether stated or implied, that black rule will bring freedom and dignity.
Mordechai Tamarkin, academic (Israeli) (1986)

In the long run one must decide when a people's real freedom is at stake, and what is not negotiable.
Andries Treurnicht, CP leader

Freedom is not cheap, but it is inevitable.
Desmond Tutu, cleric, Archbishop of Cape Town

Like a priceless diamond necklace on a table, freedom carelessly allowed to be taken for granted gets taken by politicians who replace it with a paste copy.
Pieter-Dirk Uys, satirist

Friends/Friendship

I just want to say that where I welcome this legislation 100 per cent, I should have gone still further and I should have provided legislation that even social intercourse between Europeans and non-Europeans should be limited properly, so that if one found a sailor or a soldier here in the street who embraced or linked arms with a Coloured person, we should be able to take steps at once.
JN le Roux, politician (re the Immorality Amendment Bill, 1950)

Our allies must have the right to make their own mistakes, but they should not have the right to repeat ours.
Vladimir Shubrin, politician (USSR) (at ANC Congress, 1991)

It does not matter what your enemies say about you. What really matters is what your friends think about you.
John Vorster, Prime Minister, 1966-78

The Future

We cannot ignore the past when moving into the future, as aspirations feed off past injustices.
Anonymous

In future I'll put my faith in something more solid – like corn circles.
Jani Allan, journalist

We stand on the brink and gaze into the abyss, wondering whether it's going to be sink or swim, now or never, do or die, truth or consequences, none of the above or some combination of them all.
Arnold Benjamin, columnist

Blind-folded, we stagger into the future.
David Beresford, correspondent, The Guardian

From my heart I ask you to share in the future. To share in the new South Africa.
PW Botha, Prime Minister/State President, 1978-89 (1986)

All will be well if everyone does his duty.
JH Brand, OFS President

We need not insult the future.
André Brink, writer, academic

Fears that a future ANC government will be corrupt are unfounded. There'll be nothing left to steal.
Robin Carlisle, politician

The task ahead outstrips the means to meet it; and if, a settlement reached, South Africa is then to avoid social unrest, this is something which the world must urgently apprehend.
William Deedes (Lord Deedes of Aldington), politician, editor (UK)

The new era which is dawning in our country will lift us out of the silent grief of our past and into a future of lasting peace.
FW de Klerk, State President, 1989-94; Deputy President, 1994-

Foreign investment is sought as the imprimatur that the outside world believes South Africa has a reasonable future.
Philip Gawith, journalist

In truth, no one really cares much about our future.
Chris Gibbons, broadcaster

Whether the future turns out to be triumph or tragedy, or something in between, will be determined by mortal men and women, not signed documents.
Shaun Johnson, journalist

At some point it is a mistake to focus on the past if it obscures a vision of the future.
Robert Klitgaard, academic (USA)

We have seen the future, and it wears skirts.
Bill Krige, journalist

Search in your past for what is good and beautiful. Build your future from there.
Paul Kruger, President, Transvaal Republic

We have a tryst with history, and whenever the right hour strikes I would like to be with the people of South Africa when they shall redeem their pledge.
Patrick 'Terror' Lekota, politician

Only the joint sacrifices, successes and setbacks of black and white democrats in the prisons, during the pitched battles on the streets of the nation's cities, and in exile, will solder the people of South Africa into one harmonious and indivisible nation that will march tirelessly into the dim and distant future with a confidence never before known to us.
Patrick 'Terror' Lekota

Strange terrors and ecstasies await us in Africa, but that is the choice we face: either we take up arms and fight, or we open the door to Africa and set forth into the unknown.
Rian Malan, writer

When I try to see the future, all I get is static.
Rian Malan

We live with the hope that as she battles to remake herself, South Africa will be like a microcosm of the new world that is striving to be born.
Nelson Mandela, President, May 1994-

It is a reality that if one does not plan one's own future that someone else may do it for you and you may not like what you eventually get.
Georg Meiring, soldier

I do think there are very great risks.
Harry Oppenheimer, businessman

Does the present justify sufficient faith in the future in so far as moral rectitude is concerned on the part of both our public and private-sector leaders?
Jon Qwelane, editor

Geography is destiny.
Sheila Roberts, writer

We have all the problems of tomorrow without the sympathy of the world of today.
Anton Rupert, businessman

I want to see a great, equitable society of which every citizen will be proud.
Anton Rupert

Let us abandon fear of the future and free ourselves from the damming-up of creative energy.
Anton Rupert

I may not be here to enjoy it, but I certainly don't despair for the future of my children.
Frederik Van Zyl Slabbert, academic

Prediction of the future is a difficult thing on the level of throbbing flesh and blood: on the level of persons rather than things.
Adam Small, writer

When I consider the future of the Natives in South Africa, I must say I look into shadows and darkness, and then I feel inclined to shift the intolerable burden of solving that sphinx problem to the ampler shoulders and stronger brains of the future.
Jan Christian Smuts, Prime Minister, 1919-24 & 1939-48

Whatever comes, South Africa's gonna make it.
Jimmy Swaggart, evangelist (USA)

Hell! and here we are, feuding in God's dressing-room even before the curtain rises!
Can Themba, journalist, writer

Once we have got it right, South Africa will be the paradigm for the rest of the world.
Desmond Tutu, cleric, Archbishop of Cape Town

To someone who had democracy and abused it, the future just means the loss of past gains and a new life in Australia.
Pieter-Dirk Uys, satirist

A massive task of reconstruction awaits us if we are to skirt the apocalypse.
Phillip van Niekerk, journalist

How on earth are we supposed to build our future together when we are so polarised that we can't even pray together?
Basil van Rensburg, cleric

It's a future hovering between a wistful vision of a women-power wonderland and a more pragmatic acceptance that women won't automatically make a difference.
Janet Wilhelm, journalist

Gardening

Old gardeners never die, they only spade away.
Anonymous

Small children differ from old ladies and are not capable of respecting flowers.
Guy Butler, writer, academic

If everything were to bloom at once the bees would have heart failure trying to get round them all.
Sylvia Clark, housewife

Peace is in and so is gardening – it's calming, grows on you and you can eat off it.
Margaret de Paravicini, journalist

I do not suggest that herbs can solve every problem, but they can facilitate in the solution of most problems.
Samuel Jamile, politician, herbalist, murderer

A garden is a metaphor for death and regeneration.
Di Paice, journalist

There is a cruel edge to all elites, and gardeners are no exception.
Di Paice

There is something peremptory about an arum lily. These are flowers that are not to be trifled with.
Lin Sampson, journalist

Worship, and pass on.
Jan Christian Smuts, Prime Minister, 1919-24 & 1939-48

The best time in any garden is the honeymoon period when gardener and plants have not learned too much about each other.
Andrew Unsworth, gardener

Sooner or later, every gardener is forced into discipline and here we fit in with the national way of thinking, as we do like to have things under control.
Andrew Unsworth

Pruning contains more mythology than the whole pantheon of ancient Greece and you can safely ignore it all.
Andrew Unsworth

A garden should be a bit secretive; you shouldn't be able to see all of it at once.
Kathy Waddell, housewife

Making a garden is like composing a symphony – you have all the notes but you have to orchestrate them.
Patrick Watson, gardener

Gold

The gold rush to the Rand was from the first, dominated not by a crowd of men who wished to make their fortune, but by a few who had already made it.
Anonymous (1886)

Mining has been reduced by a number of factors to an economic paradigm of exploitative capitalism.
Guy Butler, writer, academic

Pray and implore Him Who has stood by us that He will continue to do so, for I tell you today that every ounce of gold taken from the bowels of our soil will yet have to be weighed up with rivers of tears.
Paul Kruger, President, Transvaal Republic

The wealth of our gold mining industry is not so much due to the richness of the gold as it is to the poorness of black wages.
Alan Paton, writer

Gold hastens the development of a country more than anything.
Cecil John Rhodes, Imperialist

Now we have a bogus gold mining industry, its reputation is kept going for the purpose of still further swindling the investing public of Europe.
Jan Christian Smuts, Prime Minister, 1919-24 & 1939-48

I prophesy that the gold mines are going to rule South Africa.
Richard Solomon, lawyer, politician

The gold mining industry has been the flywheel of the South African economy for a long time.
Clem Sunter, businessman, scenario strategist

Golf

There's a big difference between people who play golf and golfers.
Fulton Allem, golfer

Golf is a selfish game and out there you take all the decisions on your own.
David Frost, golfer

When you're in love, you know you've got it – just like rhythm in a golf swing.
Tony Johnstone, golfer

If the pin at the 18th had been placed behind the stand, Price would have found it.
Theo Manyama, businessman, golf tournament director (on Nick Price's Million Dollar Challenge win, 1993)

The harder I practise, the luckier I get.
Gary Player, golfer

Fear, pride and stupidity mark the world's millions of weekend golf hacks.
Howard Preece, journalist

One year doesn't make a great player.
Nick Price, golfer

The golfing gods were shining down on me.
Nick Price (on his Million Dollar Challenge win, 1993)

I have never put four rounds like that together.
Nick Price (on his Million Dollar Challenge win, 1993)

Golf imitates life.
Deon Viljoen, journalist

Government

The Government must stop believing that they can continue to rule through the barrel of a gun.
Elijah Barayi, trade unionist

You cannot govern the Xhosa with the Zulu and you cannot govern the Zulu with the Tswana but you can bring them together in conferences and talks that have a common interest.
PW Botha, Prime Minister/State President, 1978-89

What's the use of a state built on blood?
Breyten Breytenbach, poet, writer

The longer the white state, acting more in its own interests than in white South Africa's, refuses to cede control and relinquish its retentive habits of mind, the greater the chances are that the goodwill and seemingly boundless tolerance of black South Africans will start to erode.
John Carlin, correspondent, The Independent (UK)

Some members of the Pretoria gang, when free of the scrutiny that normally accompanies high office, behaved as if South Africa and everything in it were their personal possessions.
Chester Crocker, politician, businessman (USA)

The ANC complained that blacks did not have the vote, 'as if it was the Government's fault'.
FW de Klerk, State President, 1989-94; Deputy President, 1994-

Devolution of powers has given the government more tiers than a Lower Houghton wedding cake.
Pnina Fenster, journalist

The government held all South Africans in an iron grip.
Anthony Heard, editor

The government certainly does not have a monopoly of wisdom, it doesn't have a monopoly of rectitude and it certainly does not have a monopoly of ability.
Hugh Murray, publisher

To stay in power for decades, you don't need apartheid laws, all you need is an army loyal to you and the secret police.
Victor Nell, community psychologist

I am against governments which govern as the Afrikaners did here.
Harry Oppenheimer, businessman

It's not a bad idea to start a process of reform with local government.
Ken Owen, editor

I have been blessed with a government with no sense of humour whatsoever during the last 15 years of guerrilla comedy.
Pieter-Dirk Uys, satirist

A government which, by its embodiment of our own personal Head of State, bone of our bone and flesh of our flesh, will inspire and bind us in irresistible unity and strength.
JC van Rooy, academic

Government in this country has always been about the exclusive possession of power.
David Welsh, academic

Graffiti

A city without graffiti is like a hot dog without mustard.
Anonymous

No anthem, no flag, no choice, just bullshit.
Anonymous

I used to be an Anglican until I put Tu and Tu together.
Anonymous

Two and two spells 3dom.
Anonymous

Plutonium sux.
Anonymous

Jou ma se plutonium.
Anonymous

Don't womanise, condomise.
Anonymous

One man, one condom.
Anonymous

If you see a policeman, contact Apla.
Anonymous

The past is tense and the future is perfect.
Anonymous

Hang XXII
Hang 22
Hang Tutu
Anonymous

This Nelson ain't a seagull. He's a jailbird.
He's still an albatross around PW's neck, though.
Anonymous (1988)

Rong Ruler Ruined Rand.
Rather Rand than Rouble.
Anonymous (1988)

I've a bad case of the Buthelezi blues or is it just pre-Natal depression?
Anonymous (1994)

I've half a mind to vote PAC (that's all I need).
Anonymous (1994 election)

Help your local branch of the ANC/IFP on April 27. Beat yourself up.
Anonymous (1994 election)

AWB voetsek! We cannot survive on pap en boereforce.
Anonymous (1994 election)

Graffiti that is usurped by businesses ceases to be graffiti.
Susan Batty, graffiti artist

Graffiti is a violation.
Kendell Geers, artist

It's always attuned to the pulse of time; it's part of culture.
James Mabandla, artist

The graffiti street writer tells it like it is.
Lize Odenal, journalist

The writing is definitely on the wall in Soweto.
Desmond Pitoyi, journalist

When even the standard of wall defacement and vandalism has declined to boredom you know how tough times have become.
Barry Ronge, journalist

We don't talk politics with our graffiti, only weapons, burglaries, violence, smuggling, business, robberies, money.
Hein Smit, policeman

Graffiti may have an aura of non-conformity, but it is not the property of any group.
Graham Warsop, businessman

The best graffiti is lively and impertinent – and should be at odds with society.
Sue Williamson, artist

Guilt

South African whites feel they have almost cornered the market on guilt and it can make them wondrously self-righteous.
RW Johnson, political scientist

I don't want to feel that I am responsible any more for the wrongs in this country.
Rian Malan, writer

I'm so tired of carrying the white man's burden. Indeed, I wish we'd never picked it up in the first place, back in 1652.
Rian Malan

If one day we are going to evaluate the relative guilt of institutions in the tragedy of our society, the major guilt will have to be borne not by any political party but by the church – especially the NGK.
Beyers Naudé, cleric

Political guilt has turned us whites into political wimps.
Christo Nel, copywriter

The time has come to stop apologising, to stop philosophising, to stop bending over blackwards to blend in with the crowd.
Gus Silber, journalist

When you see how the blacks in the north have exploited their own people, you don't have any guilt about being white in South Africa.
Peter Wales, businessman

Handicaps

Deafness is not a sentence meant to be lived out in silent exclusion from the world.
Kerry-Ann Holloway, journalist

The general public tends to assume that the deaf won't talk – it's like assuming that blind people can only do basketwork.
Cara Loening, businesswoman

Heroes

Heroes can be dangerous, because of how they are often misused for narrow ethnic and nationalistic purposes.
Anonymous SADF soldier

Our enduring heroes are not dominees, but panners, pioneers, explorers, windgats and remittance men on the make.
Patrick Lee, writer

South Africa's heroes are legend across the generations.
Nelson Mandela, President, May 1994-

If you give me a choice between a little grey man and a hero, I will pick the hero every time.
Wilbur Smith, writer

History

History is made by people who respond sincerely to the moment – for better or for worse.
Anonymous

The lesson of history is clear: those who deny the past must never be trusted with the future.
ANC election advertisement (1994)

All of us are prisoners of history and are, as such, challenged to become prisoners of hope.
David J Bosch, theologian

Our history is responsible for differences in the South African way of life.
PW Botha, Prime Minister/State President, 1978-89

History is not made or experienced by Man, but by men, women and children.
Guy Butler, writer, academic

To stay and serve in Africa generally and South Africa specifically is to stay centre stage in one of the most breathtaking scenarios of human drama and challenge in all history.
Michael Cassidy, evangelist

I would hope that history would recognise that I, together with all those who supported me, have shown courage, integrity, honesty at the moment of truth in our history.
FW de Klerk, State President, 1989-94; Deputy President, 1994-

History tells us that political favours are not worth the paper they are never written on.
John Farquhar, editor

In South Africa there is a pervasive sense among both whites and blacks that history has finally ended.
Hermann Giliomee, academic

Those who insist on a dull repetition of the mantras of the past invite extinction.
Bobby Godsell, businessman

There is a compelling temptation to forget the past.
Richard Goldstone, judge

Generations of history, written for racist political ends, has left a space into which has moved the instant commentator, the foreign expert, the deadline-chasing journalist, the market-driven consultant, the ambitious politician, who try to turn history to their own short term advantage.
Jeff Guy, historian

We've got to take the past into the present.
Jenny Hobbs, writer

The past has had its padlocks removed.
Christopher Hope, writer

There are times when the great tides of history simply take their own unstoppable course – when individuals are incidental – and times when politicians have the power to unleash or stem the tides.
Shaun Johnson, journalist

Hindsight is a frustrating thing, because invariably the illumination it provides comes too late to be very useful.
Shaun Johnson

The great irony of our history is that the horror of apartheid elevated us to a status that neither our demographics nor our economics warrant.
Shaun Johnson

I've always said that history is the worst teacher; you don't learn, you get bitten all the time.
John Kani, actor

A historical perspective has no grab handle for those consumed by their own legendary times.
Patrick Lee, writer

Our history is of white trader bwanas pressing savages into labour, and Christianity, in that order.
Patrick Lee

To us, African people in South Africa, history has bequeathed three great tasks: to free ourselves; to teach the Afrikaners in particular, and white people in general, human worth; and to provide an example to other oppressed nations as to how freedom can be won against almost all odds.
Patrick 'Terror' Lekota, politician

It is our historic task to teach white people that we, too, are human beings.
Patrick 'Terror' Lekota

The history of mankind is the history of man struggling and striving for freedom.
Albert Luthuli, ANC President General, Nobel Peace Prize

We were taught history at school and then at university we were told we'd been duped.
Katya Lyall-Watson, a 20-something

There is so much history of inequity here, so many frustrated desires and hopes, so many needs.
Princeton Lyman, ambassador (USA)

It is not the kings and generals that make history but the masses of the people, the workers, the peasants, the doctors, the clergy.
Nelson Mandela, President, May 1994-

The tide in the annals of all countries and peoples ebbs and flows.
Nelson Mandela

History has shown that the loosening of the chains of oppression through liberal democracy without restitution means nothing.
Mosibudi Mangena, Black Consciousness Movement, C-in-C Azanla

There are no lessons to be learned from history, only images to be relearned and repeated.
Lewis Nkosi, writer, academic

Only those who were steeped in the past would have any understanding of the greatness of the present.
Alan Paton, writer

The past is another country – forgiven, forgotten, *verby.*
John Perlman, journalist

Even attempts to capture the chimera of black social history through official papers are bedevilled by public servants' vulgar attitude to history in general.
Claire Robertson, journalist

In a certain sense we are all prisoners of a past fraught with misunderstanding.
Anton Rupert, businessman

One cannot deny what history reveals.
Clem Sunter, businessman, scenario strategist

If not for History's Grand Finale, why then does God hold us back?
Can Themba, journalist, writer

The days of 'Yes Baas' and 'Ja Oom' are over. Beware of 'OK Comrade'.
Pieter-Dirk Uys, satirist

We shall never be free of the destructive aspects of our history until we can honestly look our past in the face and truly see ourselves for what we were: ordinary in our human fallibility, with much that was dishonourable and inadequate in our behaviour as well as a good deal that was brave, upright, lovable.
Laurens van der Post, soldier, writer, philosopher

History is as strong a motivating factor for the PAC as it is for the right-wing Afrikaners.
Phillip van Niekerk, journalist

South African history consists as much of oblivion as it does of heroes and martyrs.
Stephen Watson, poet, teacher

History seldom allows its flow to be placed in convenient single-year containers.
David Welsh, academic

Homelands

I do not like authority and I suppose even a Volkstaat will have traffic cops.
Anonymous University of Pretoria student

Just as our Dutch forefathers built dykes at Zeeland to keep the North Sea away from their fatherland, we are today constructing traditional dykes round South Africa to keep out the Black hordes.
HJ Botha, politician (1963)

They will be allowed to a certain extent to control their own law and order, their own health services and have a much bigger say in these matters than ordinary municipalities have at present.
PW Botha, Prime Minister/State President, 1978-89

Children of persons classified as citizens of, say, Bophuthatswana, who are born after independence and brought up in Soweto, by parents who have lived all their lives in Soweto may have no right to remain in Soweto.
Arthur Chaskalson, lawyer & Sheena Duncan, Black Sash, SA Council of Churches

They are constitutional realities and citizens who work and live outside those states look forward to going home.
Kobie Coetsee, politician (1986)

The Ciskei has, on occasions, come close to resembling Papa Doc's Haiti.
Graham Leach, correspondent, BBC Radio

Homelands are gone but casinos will be with us until the sun turns cold.
Patrick Lee, writer

Thaba'Nchu has been undisputed Batswana territory for 160 years, and it is going to remain so until the sun sets on this world.
Lucas Mangope, former president, Bophuthatswana

Some cry for the cutting up of South Africa without delay into separate areas, where white can live without black, and black without white, where black can farm their own land and mine their own minerals and administer their own laws.
Alan Paton, writer

The declaration of a volkstaat would be a charter for vigilante thuggery.
Rowland Peart, lawyer

Holland is an ideal location for a volkstaat for the Boers.
Matthew Phosa, politician

The ridiculous reality of Dr Verwoerd's vision was nowhere better highlighted than in the shape of Bophuthatswana, whose territory was broken into seven parts – as if a cartographer had shaken an ink pen over a map.
Alec Russell, journalist

The Bop regime is profoundly, if erratically and incompletely, unjust.
John Seiler, political scientist

Although many people claim South Africa is the only country in the world that recognises Bophuthatswana's sovereignty, this is not strictly true, as each fragment of Bophuthatswana is recognised by each of the six remaining fragments.
Gus Silber, journalist

Transkei is in part a special case, but also a warning.
Jonathan Steele, journalist (UK)

The Bantustans are sumps of corruption, they have always been sumps of corruption, and the government has always known they were sumps of corruption.
Sunday Times

Bantustans: the old name for homelands in the days before Bantu became Plural, became Angry, became Black that became Beautiful.
Pieter-Dirk Uys, satirist

Now there's only one homeland left: it's the independent state of mind.
Pieter-Dirk Uys

The cry for an Afrikaner homeland is inchoate, wild, desperate, hopeless.
Stanley Uys, journalist

Don't think of a volkstaat as a form of separation by way of secession.
Constand Viljoen, soldier, politician

When you think about a volkstaat, you should think about it as an area – say a 10th area – where you have, based on the principle of asymmetry, special powers, in order to satisfy the principle of self-determination.
Constand Viljoen

It is not the white man's duty to give the bantustans more land – if they become overcrowded, the inhabitants could emigrate to other countries.
John Vorster, Prime Minister, 1966-78

Hospitality

Everywhere I have travelled in these lovely lands of South Africa and Rhodesia my parents, my sister and I have been taken to the heart of their people and made to feel that we are just as much at home here as if we had lived among them all our lives.
Elizabeth II (when Princess Elizabeth, Cape Town, 1947)

No person, black or white, leaves a frontier farm without having partaken of food.
John Mackenzie, missionary

In the countryside, women brewed traditional beer regularly in order to offer it as hospitality to those who called in for a chat or even strangers who stopped for a gourd to quench their thirst on their way to distant lands.
Lewis Nkosi, writer, academic

Hostels

We can't have on our doorstep a cage with people who live in herds, who don't live with women; who cook hit-and-run meals and have only a beer-yard for their nightly entertainment.
Anonymous township resident

These zones were well-known breeding grounds for prostitution and vice – and for political education fuelled by alienation, bitterness, despair.
Anthony Heard, editor

Whenever there's fighting at the hostel, you always hear the women going 'kikiki' – it's a way of calling up the power of the men.
Gertrude Mzizi, politician

The people who live in the bleak and forbidding buildings never wanted to go there.
Can Themba, journalist, writer

The hostels resemble Bosnian ethnic cleansing camps.
Suzanne Vos, politician

Housing

It's a townhouse complex with 10m high walls, razor wire, 24-hour a day armed guards – it's wonderful.
Anonymous (1994)

Each shack evidenced the owner's individuality and quest for dignity and respectability.
Wendy Annecke, Black Sash

One does not obliterate or demolish a house any more easily than a human being.
Guy Butler, writer, academic

A house should be in a garden, not above or below it.
Sylvia Clark, housewife

Prime ministers were known to take special helicopter trips to decide where to build more townships as the unstoppable black tide swept the cities.
Anthony Heard, editor

Every rabbit must have a warren where he can live and burrow and breed, and every native must have a warren too.
Godfrey Yeatman Lagden, Native Commissioner, Transvaal

Among forty- and fifty-something South Africans, a house was almost a God-given right.
Mike Lipkin, marketer

Home is where most wallets feel happiest.
Katy Macdonald, journalist

The locations in the towns are the incubators of unrighteousness.
ML Malan, politician

If municipal locations are destined to provide accommodation for people who serve the interests of Europeans in the towns, whose occupants are thereby destined to be sub-economic units for all time, it seems to me unreasonable and unfair that they should be called upon to pay rent or for any other service at all.
H Selby Msimang, General Secretary, All-African Convention

To most whites it will not be readily evident that the successful purchase of a house demands of a black buyer as much determination and skill as might be required, say, to organise a revolution.
Ken Owen, editor

Humanity

Measurement of our fellow men is in terms of our humanity and not in terms of how much money they have or who they are in terms of their colour.
John Bishop, journalist, TV presenter

There must be something deeply ingrained in Man to live beyond himself and his own shortcomings and failures.
Pik Botha, politician

We are a violent species, but humanity – and South Africa with it – has demonstrated that it can rise above mere mindless violence.
André Brink, writer, academic

We are created in joy, and our destiny is nothing less than to enjoy God himself.
Guy Butler, writer, academic

Human beings start off with quite a lot of dignity and often it's other human beings who take that away.
Cheryl Carolus, politician

The people here are so much more human beings than the tribal leaders in, say, the former Yugoslavia.
Chester Crocker, politician, businessman (USA)

I am a human being, I am made of dust.
Jacob Geldenhuys, rapist, murderer (on being sentenced to death five times for rape and murder, 1993)

Each human society is a narrow world trapped to death in paltry evils and jealousies.
Stephen Gray, writer

Heroism is born out of struggle against odds and I think the best of human qualities as well as the worst emerge.
Ronnie Kasrils, politician

Drinking when you're not thirsty and making love all year round is all that distinguishes us from animals.
Piet Koornhof, politician

Each person must draw his own map.
David Kramer, entertainer

The human spirit doesn't take to being boxed and shrink-wrapped.
Jacqui L'Ange, journalist

While the concerns of your fellow man must be the concerns of every individual, the concerns of the nation must become the concerns of the corporation.
Reg Lascaris, businessman

It was soul – that which, for the freedom fighters of our country, makes resistance possible far beyond the limits of human capacity.
Patrick 'Terror' Lekota, politician

The spirit is a greater human force than the flesh.
Albert Luthuli, ANC President General, Nobel Peace Prize

What I want to get across is that we all bleed the same colour. Black, white, Afrikaans, Zulu, Xhosa – we are all human beings.
Felicia Mabuza-Suttle, businesswoman, TV show presenter

Let the strivings of us all prove that humanity can no longer be tragically bound to the starless midnight of racism and war.
Nelson Mandela, President, May 1994-

The human being has only so much capability for evil and no more.
Es'kia Mphahlele, academic, writer

I would like to be thought of as having been humane.
Harry Oppenheimer, businessman

The development of a conscience – a knowledge of what is good and what is evil – is probably the most important milestone along the path of human development.
Jack Penn, surgeon, philosopher, artist

Our minds are full of memorial paths of human experience.
Jan Christian Smuts, Prime Minister, 1919-24 & 1939-48

We know more than enough about how human beings should conduct themselves, thank you very much, whether or not there's a God.
Janet Suzman, actress

The trouble is, gentlemen, for me, human nature stinks, but that is all the material we have to work with.
Can Themba, journalist, writer

I pin my faith to the concept of the sanctity of human life and of all things human, humane and humanitarian.
Phillip Tobias, academic

We became human under adversity, not under genial, equable conditions of life.
Phillip Tobias

The process of evolution is not an upward striving for perfection: it's a process of adapting to changing circumstances.
Phillip Tobias

The dangers do not lie in the physical, the external, but in the denial of the human spirit and its values.
Laurens van der Post, soldier, writer, philosopher

Problems are the raw material of our humanity.
Laurens van der Post

Our aboriginal hearts know no neutrality: we are all born either Greeks or Trojans.
Laurens van der Post

Humour

One thing is certain – Mr Vorster can laugh. This is a good omen.
Willem de Klerk, businessman, academic (1966)

A man without a sense of humour is like a painting by Turner, Monet or Van Gogh without colour.
Jack Penn, surgeon, philosopher, artist

The greatest thing is our capacity to laugh with each other while we laugh at each other.
Steven Raymond, satirist

A sense of humour is a basic democratic right.
Pieter-Dirk Uys, satirist

The weapon of humour is as mighty as the gun.
Pieter-Dirk Uys

Hunting

The hunters dreamed of their dogs at a bloodied throat.
Tatam-Kulu Afrika, poet

They (the Xhosa) generally go out to hunt in large parties; and when they find game in the open fields, they endeavour to surround the animals, or drive them to some narrow pass, which is previously occupied by long files of hunters, stationed on either side, who, as the herd rushes through between, pierce them with showers of assegais.
John Brownlee, missionary

Somehow, the romance of the great white hunter still has power.
Kate de Sellincourt, journalist

Every hunter runs the risk of having his leg chopped off in a trap he himself has laid.
Joanne Fedler, academic

When you shoot an animal and it's a good shot, you don't hear anything, you don't feel anything – you're so concentrated on what you're doing.
Gail Rattray Fisher, hunter

The splendid horns of the Koodoo and Sable, and a score of others only less beautiful, could be seen nailed up, and then unnoticed and forgotten.
Percy Fitzpatrick, politician, writer

The shooting of a lion, fair and square, and face to face, was the Blue Riband of the Bush.
Percy Fitzpatrick

The hunt came at us like a cyclone out of the stillness, and in the forefront of it there burst into the circle of light an impala ewe with open mouth and haunting hunted despairing eyes and widespread ears; and the last staggering strides brought her among us, tumbling at out feet.
Percy Fitzpatrick

Conservation is a household word, eco-tourism a catchphrase and hunting an ironic means to preserve the environment.
Rhonda Klevansky, journalist

When shooting, think of nothing else.
Adolph Gysbert (Sailor) Malan, pilot, farmer

Shooting and hunting are two different things.
Hazel Muller, hunter

In the course of four months I killed to my own gun 42 elephants, 11 of which were big bulls, whose tusks averaged 44lbs apiece; I also shot several very fine cows, whose tusks weighed from 15lbs to 16lbs.
Frederick Courteney Selous, hunter

He wheeled round immediately, but, his strength failing him, only walked a few yards, and stood under a tree, and, after receiving another bullet square in the shoulder, gave a fierce shake of the head, making his huge ears flap again, and, sinking slowly down with his hind legs doubled out, surrendered up his tough old spirit – looking, for all the world, though dead, like a tame elephant when kneeling for people to ascend to the howdah.
Frederick Courteney Selous

Ideals

We must give ourselves into the arms of the Great African Mother and trust she will not drop us.
Breyten Breytenbach, poet, writer

The new era which is dawning in our country, beneath the great south stars, will lift us out of the silent grief of our past and into a future in which there will be opportunity and space for joy and beauty, and for real and lasting peace.
FW de Klerk, State President, 1989-94; Deputy President, 1994-

I would trade every one of my Comrades medals, not even for an Olympic medal, but just for the opportunity to say I was an Olympian, that once I competed in the finest arena on earth.
Bruce Fordyce, sportsman

Violence will be ended, the recession will become part of history, there will be a settlement, it will rain and everybody will live happily ever after.
John Hall, National Peace Accord

Here in South Africa, with all our diversities of colour and race, we will show the world a new pattern for democracy.
Albert Luthuli, ANC President General, Nobel Peace Prize

I have fought against white domination, and I have fought against black domination. I have cherished the ideal of a democratic and free society in which all persons live together in harmony and with equal opportunities. It is an ideal which I hope to live for and to achieve. But if needs be, it is an ideal for which I am prepared to die.
Nelson Mandela, President, May 1994- (Rivonia Treason Trial)

I want my black countrymen to see that blacks are scientists, doctors, entrepreneurs, teachers and social workers, not only messengers, gardeners and domestic servants.
Welcome Msomi, playwright

I want my child and your children to grow up in a South Africa that is free, where there is no poverty and no crime; in which we stand with dignity and pride.
Jay Naidoo, politician

It is unattractive to think one is born, gets married, has children and finally dies, and the world has not changed even a tiny bit.
Harry Oppenheimer, businessman

You can always trust the cynics to behave predictably; just beware of idealists.
Ken Owen, editor

If our country cannot secure opportunities for those who are poor, if we cannot give faith to those who are despairing, if we cannot win back the trust of generations of our youth who are on the verge of being lost to this nation for ever, the peace process will have been in vain and our new-found freedoms will be hollow.
Jane Raphaely, editor, publisher

I desire to act for the benefit of those I think are the greatest people the world has ever seen, but whose fault is they do not know their strength and greatness, and their destiny.
Cecil John Rhodes, Imperialist

One is beginning to get a very clear picture of what needs to be done now, and it's happening in some areas, is that all those energies of resistance against apartheid must now be turned around in a concrete way and focused on building the nation.
Zwelakhe Sisulu, editor, businessman

Here is a tree rooted in African soil, nourished with waters from the rivers of Africa. Come and sit under its shade and become, with us, the leaves of the same branch and the branches of the same tree.
Robert Mangaliso Sobukwe, PAC founding president

It is our responsibility to break down barriers of division and create a country where there will be neither whites nor blacks, just South Africans, free and united in diversity.
Oliver Tambo, ANC President

As long as there are hungry children in my land I won't have sugar or milk and I don't eat pudding.
Eugene Terre'Blanche, AWB leader

My political vision is a land for the white man and the sole right to be governed by my own people.
Andries Treurnicht, CP leader

As a Christian and a prisoner of hope, I am as certain as one can be that we are going to have a glorious country.
Desmond Tutu, cleric, Archbishop of Cape Town

I would wish for a system where there was a great deal more compassion; more recognition that human beings had a greater value than objects or property; a system where all the resources of our country were available to all; and an orderly society where you took from each according to their means and gave to each according to their need.
Desmond Tutu

The secret is not to impose one's desires on life, so much as to let things happen.
Laurens van der Post, soldier, writer, philosopher

What we need is a restoration of thinking.
Andrea Vinassa, journalist

I am preparing myself to promulgate the constitution of KwaZulu and Natal which will establish a monarchy modelled after the best examples of democratic and pluralist monarchies in the world. It is within my powers as king and sovereign to issue and promulgate such a constitution to enshrine in KwaZulu/Natal a kingdom and freedom, pluralism and prosperity for all its citizens for centuries to come.
Goodwill Zwelithini, King of the Zulus

Immigration

When immigrants come here and their race is not recorded, we will not be able to distinguish between an immigrant from Central Africa, a native who has adopted an English name, and an English person from England.
AI Malan, academic, politician

Inauguration 1994

Today I am proud to sing *Die Stem* for the first time.
Anonymous black man

I am emotional, I am on the point of tears because for the first time in my life I feel a South African.
Anonymous Coloured woman

I love my country, I love the people in it and until the day I die I want to be a South African.
Anonymous

I am Jewish, I am white and I am proud to be a South African. Today is the greatest day of my life.
Anonymous

There were representatives from many nations at Nelson Mandela's inauguration, but only one culture: reconciliation.
Darryl Accone, journalist

Out of the silence grew a thunder, as over the hills came helicopter gunships, jet trainers, supersonic fighters and aerobatic squadrons trailing the colours of the new South Africa flag in dedication to their first black, and surely greatest, commander-in-chief.
David Beresford, correspondent, The Guardian

Today South Africa regained its rightful place in Africa, in the UN and the family of nations.
Boutros Boutros-Ghali, UN Secretary General

A turning point in the history of the nation.
Boutros Boutros-Ghali

I was like on the verge of tears the whole time.
Hillary Rodham Clinton, First Lady (USA)

All the journalists are standing together in a pack saying 'Who's this, who's this?' because there are so many heads of state and princes and princesses here and they don't wear crowns these days.
Judith Dubin, journalist

This is lump in the throat stuff; I am very choked up – the flypast of the Mirages streaming the colours of the South African flag... I had to pass the microphone over.
Chris Gibbons, broadcaster

If words could describe the look on my (black) colleague's face as Nelson Mandela took that oath of office... it's a sight that I, as a white South African, will treasure for the rest of my life.
Chris Gibbons

We have seen a tomorrow that can be.
Rex Gibson, editor

It is triumph of hope over fear; of generosity over greed; of liberty over conquest.
Bobby Godsell, businessman

We all live but one life, and in the lives of very few in this world is this privilege of being an integral part of an epochal event bestowed.
Shaun Johnson, journalist

I didn't feel like a journalist at all – I felt like a South African.
Dale Lautenbach, journalist

We enter into a covenant that we shall build a society in which all South Africans, both black and white, will be able to walk tall, without any fear in their hearts, assured of their

inalienable right to human dignity – a rainbow nation at peace with itself and the world.
Nelson Mandela, President, 1994- (Inauguration speech, May 1994)

Today, all of us do, by our presence here, and by our celebrations in other parts of the country and the world, confer glory and hope to newborn liberty.
Nelson Mandela (Inauguration speech)

To my compatriots, I have no hesitation in saying that each one of us is as intimately attached to the soil of this beautiful country as are the famous jacaranda trees of Pretoria and the mimosa trees of the bushveld.
Nelson Mandela (Inauguration speech)

Mr de Klerk is one of the greatest reformers, one of the great sons of the soil.
Nelson Mandela

We have just witnessed history in the making: the flags are flying high, the new South Africa has started.
Dan Moyane, journalist

I am at a loss for words, I still don't believe it's happening, maybe I am in a dream. I am going to slap my face.
Dan Moyane

In the presence of those assembled here and in full realisation of the high calling I assume as President of South Africa, I, Nelson Rolihlahla Mandela, do hereby swear to be faithful to the Republic of South Africa, and do solemnly and sincerely promise at all times to promote that which will advance and to oppose all that may harm the Republic; to obey, observe, uphold and maintain the Constitution and all other Law of the Republic; to discharge my duties with all my strength and talents to the best of my knowledge and ability and, true to

the dictates of my conscience, to do justice to all and to devote myself to the well-being of the Republic and all its people. So help me God.
Presidential Oath

Influx Control

If the principle of permanent residence for the Black man in the area of the White is accepted, then it is the beginning of the end of civilisation as we know it in this country.
PW Botha, Prime Minister/State President, 1978-89 (1964)

Towns have been seen by the white population as being their preserve and their governments have used the influx control system to maintain this position and to restrict the presence of black persons in the towns to what is needed to meet the labour requirements of the white economy.
Arthur Chaskalson, lawyer & Sheena Duncan, Black Sash, SA Council of Churches

Influx control in South Africa is discriminatory and offensive to human dignity.
Zach de Beer, politician

Our information is that since November of last year (1948) more than 8 000 Natives have been removed from the Rand. Now the honourable member must not ask me where they went. I do not know. I assume they have been removed to some place where they can still earn a livelihood if they want to.
EG Jansen, politician (1949)

The white areas should not be regarded as the dumping grounds for the surplus labour which comes from the Bantu homelands.
TNH Janson, politician

Inkatha Freedom Party (IFP)

My own organisation regards me as the father of negotiations.
Mangosuthu Buthelezi, IFP leader, politician

Its roots run deep in South African history; it is the modern expression of the aims and objectives so clearly stated by the ANC's founding fathers.
Mangosuthu Buthelezi (1985)

Inkatha's Ten Year Existence As A Movement – And Reflections On What Inkatha Has Done In Non-Violent Strategies For Liberation And The Increasing Temptation And Pressure Of Mindless Violence As A Strategy Of Desperation In The Absence Of A Viable Basis For Peaceful Negotiation.
Mangosuthu Buthelezi (title of a speech)

The Inkatha movement is to all intents and purposes a Zulu version of the Afrikaner Broederbond.
Graham Leach, correspondent, BBC Radio

The IFP can't save the Afrikaner – it finds it difficult enough saving itself.
Johan Steenkamp, politician

The IFP shows a rather immature view of democracy.
Phillip van Niekerk, journalist

Jews/Judaism

It's often the loss of its Jewish citizens that people refer to unwittingly when they talk of the 'brain drain'.
David Barritt, editor

A good Jewish education is an education in morality, and innumerable South African Jews have been deeply committed to the struggle for a just society.
Victor Nell, community psychologist

Afrikaner anti-Semitism was virulent enough, but it was guilt-ridden.
Alan Paton, writer

The Jew in South Africa often feels he is about to be caught in a pincer between right-wing reaction and radical left extremism.
Harry Schwartz, ambassador

Jews should be like the Rothschilds, spread on all the continents of the world.
Lesley van Flyman, PR

What happened in South Africa was a small part of the effervescence of Jewish genius.
Geoffrey Wheatcroft, journalist

Knowledge

If you don't know, invent.
Robert Baden-Powell, soldier, scout

Labour

Yes, women have an easy time here compared to overseas, because we all have servants.
Anonymous (from Maids & Madams)

The very essence of a worker is in itself political.
Elijah Barayi, trade unionist

The Native is reasonably good at performing farm labour which does not require a high degree of individual judgement, but when it comes to consultation and planning in order to deal with unknown and unusual circumstances, he will disappoint.
WTH Beukes, academic, businessman

White workers must be weighed, not counted.
Flip Buys, trade unionist

It is most desirable that all young Natives, say between 15 and 16 years of age, to be placed in youth camps so that they can do land service, and do it gratis. There they must be taught to work with a pick and shovel, because they will need that knowledge in their lives.
HS Erasmus, politician (1956)

No one should be ashamed to work with her hands, grow her own vegetables or grind her own meal.
Tshepo Khumbane, social worker

We don't allow Bantu typists and so on working with White women in the same office and I am going to stop it.
Piet Koornhof, politician (1982)

In many cases the native stands, as it were, between the white man and manual labour.
Ernie Malherbe, educationist

If a man is going to live well, he's got to work.
Abel Mhlongo, farmer

Everybody should take his job, and not himself, seriously.
Jack Penn, surgeon, philosopher, artist

The difference between a person who is self-employed and employed is that a self-employed person works 20 hours a day in order to make the same money as another person but in order to have their own freedoms.
Nina Romm, artist

If you get people rolling their sleeves up to work towards some fairly definite objectives, that's enough, that gives the hope.
Clem Sunter, businessman, scenario strategist

The only way to get a job is to create a job.
Clem Sunter

Keep in touch with the workers.
Bill Venter, businessman

There is no place for him in the European community above the level of certain forms of labour.
HF Verwoerd, Prime Minister, 1958-66

Land

Oneness is a pivotal instrument for recapturing our land.
Anonymous

I don't mind about democracy, we only want our land back.
Anonymous

The land that has been taken away from us, was given down from generation to generation.
Anonymous

Much of white historiography has been an attempt to justify white occupation of the land; much of its counterpart an attempt to prove that blacks were here first.
André Brink, writer, academic

My people are land-hungry.
Mangosuthu Buthelezi, IFP leader, politician

From their own account they had once a better place, but a boor having asked permission first to sow a little corn, then to erect a mill, they allowed it; after which he applied to government for a grant of the whole place, which they promised, not knowing that it was in possession of these Hottentots; of course, they were driven from it.
John Campbell, missionary

The main thing is that we are all people of the same land.
Jacob Dhlomo, induna

Die saad is myne, die skare is myne . . . die span is myne, alles is myne. Die grond is syne.
Kasisanyane Maine, itinerant farmer

Each time one of us touches the soil of this land, we feel a sense of personal renewal.
Nelson Mandela, President, May 1994- (Inauguration speech)

A people without land can have neither political nor economic power.
Mosibudi Mangena, activist

Like Moses, I have seen the promised land but shall not dwell in it.
Gerritt Maritz, Voortrekker

The wounds of oppression are still wet, and the only cure is the land.
Kgosimang Monnakgotla, activist

We have lived here long before the white man came into this country.
Chief Mpefu

This land is mine. I won it in battle and I shall keep it.
Chief Ndlambe, Xhosa chief

We are all pioneers, required to colonise the piece of ground that chance assigns to us, to somehow make it our own.
Hylton Nel, potter

We will always be after the farmers who have illegally occupied our land and it will serve them right until they pressurise De Klerk for the total liberation of Azania.
Maxwell Nemadzivhenani, activist

It is hypocritical that the masses should feel sympathy for a handful of white farmers.
Maxwell Nemadzivhenani

We will always see the farmers as our targets, until they produce land certificates and tell us who sold them our land.
Maxwell Nemadzivhenani

Keep it, guard it, care for it, for it keeps men, guards men, cares for men.
Alan Paton, writer

The 1913 Land Act was an act of dispossession.
Walter Sisulu, politician

Why should I ask for land I already own?
Eugene Terre'Blanche, AWB leader

While millions of dispossessed people seek reinstatement and compensation, the white farming constituency holds the title deeds and claims it has an immeasurable investment in the land.
Marianne Thamm, journalist

Language

Dealing with the excesses of speech with more speech is the preferable way.
Floyd Abrams, jurist (USA)

The issue of compulsory Afrikaans language lessons in schools which started the Soweto rioting was a symbol of a much more deep-seated resentment.
Nicholas Ashford, correspondent, The Times

We are moving towards a kind of bubblegum language, a mumbo-jumbo language, a kind of international Fanagalo.
Breyten Breytenbach, poet, writer

God, South Africans have a terrible weakness for clichés.
Breyten Breytenbach

Language is only a fraction of a culture.
Guy Butler, writer, academic

No one can own a language.
Rian Cloete, TV presenter

A language isn't something that falls ready-made from the heavens.
Stephanus du Toit, cleric; founder, Afrikaans language movement

The Taal is the language of a people – our people – and I have never had any doubt of its ability to survive as that.
Percy Fitzpatrick, politician, writer

The visual is the new language.
Ian Fraser, playwright

Language has become one of the focal points of the whole Nationalist creed.
David Harrison, documentary film maker, author

As the extremists become more outrageously irrational and bloodthirsty, so language becomes less capable of dealing with the enormity of their acts.
Geoff Hughes, academic

The Ngoni consist of the Zulu and Xhosa, whose language customs and life style are so similar that we black nationalists

have as a fundamental philosophy the complete integration of these two into one language group.
Nthato Motlana, doctor, businessman

Language must be inhabited, it must be enlarged by usage; South Africans abridge it and stop it from referring too closely to those emotions which they spend almost all their lives trying to obliterate or deny.
Lewis Nkosi, writer, academic

We may speak English at the free market bazaar, but our moral choices and the trials of our daily existence – birth, death, worship, celebration and so on – are locked up in our mother tongues.
Kole Omotoso, academic

Brutal language can expose meaning quite as well as delicate language can hide it.
Ken Owen, editor

In any language, BMW remain the three most prominent letters in our vocabulary.
Carolyn Sacks, journalist

We don't give a damn what blacks say in their own languages.
Anna Starcke, political consultant

Whenever I hear the South African accent it always sounds to me kind of practical, common-sensical and unfussy.
Janet Suzman, actress

Any South African accent is the right accent, as long as you are grammatically correct.
Dali Tambo, TV chat show host

In the white areas of South Africa, where the government erects the buildings, grants the subsidies and pays the teachers, it is our right to decide on language policy.
Andries Treurnicht, CP leader

Sadly the good old days of the Queen's English here is went.
Pieter-Dirk Uys, satirist

Afrikaans is a lovely language; it's earthy, it's emotional and it's alive.
Brumilda van Rensburg, actress

People speak language and politicians make it a tool of politics.
Francois Venter, playwright

Law

The latest trend in the law is that people don't abide by it.
Anonymous (Natal Law Society, 1994)

For timewaste, law is a trade without rival.
Denis Beckett, journalist

Law is never daring to say you are sorry.
Patrick Bracher, lawyer

A lawyer is essentially an accountant sans the latter's personality.
Alfred Cockrell, academic

Lawyers work in institutionalised sweat-shops, the spartan furnishing of which is characterised most noticeably by the absence of Amazonian pot plants, crocodile skin-covered Law Reports or cornucopias of designer doughnuts.
Alfred Cockrell

Few black people in this country can make themselves understood in a court of law in their mother tongue, resulting in incalculable miscarriages of justice under the interpreter system.
Achmat Davids, historian

There can never be justice in South Africa nor can a legal system be rooted in healthy soil while the South African military, police and other state bureaucrats are placed above the law.
Dennis Davis, lawyer

As long as the South African system of criminal justice operates within an illegitimate political framework, the courts are on a hiding to nothing particularly in the case of political trials.
Dennis Davis

There is no substantive observation of the rules of natural justice.
David Dison, lawyer

Let those who prescribe the law administer it.
Hugh Lewin, author

Lawyers are about as much loved as Parktown prawns.
Norman Manoim, lawyer

The trouble with South Africa's system of public law, stated shortly and sourly, is that it is an instrument of power rather than justice.
Tony Mathews, academic

If kids can learn the law now and they become magistrates in future, they'll insist on representation for all accused.
Mandla Mchunu, street lawyer

Throughout history men, seeking their own ends, have employed bad law as a means to exploit their fellow men.
Stephen Mulholland, publisher

To do justice, judges must have some grasp of the lives of those they judge.
Etienne Mureinik, academic

Life's too short to endure without your writs about you.
Jenni Newman, PR

Nothing is exactly like the gorgeous panoply of a South African court: the mock ceremony, the pretence, the play-acting.
Lewis Nkosi, writer, academic

For millions of South Africans the law has been less of a shield to protect them than a whip to cow them, and that whip has been wielded by lawmakers, by the executive branch of government and by the courts.
Ken Owen, editor

What ordinary people need is not the protection of the common law but protection against it.
Ken Owen

The purpose of the law is to create criminals in order to keep the courts busy and the jails full, but too much law creates an oversupply of criminals.
Ken Owen

Like all solicitors, I, of course, travel first class.
Pixley Ka Isaka Seme, lawyer

The business of keeping people locked up without trial is the absolute death knell to the system of justice.
Helen Suzman, liberal, retired politician

Print the lies; it'll help me cover my legal costs.
Philip Tucker, playboy

On a continent where the independent judiciary is scarcely noted for its flourishing good health, it is important to remember that the South African courts did act as occasional guardians of civil liberties.
Patti Waldmeir, correspondent, Financial Times (UK)

Leaders/Leadership

We warn the Government to stop shooting and detaining our children because they are creating a leadership vacuum for the future.
Elijah Barayi, trade unionist

It is the actions of tyrants, not their abstract prescriptions, that determine the lot of their peoples.
Pik Botha, politician

It is not for me as the leader to say it will be like this or like that.
Mangosuthu Buthelezi, IFP leader, politician

It is impossible that a great enterprise or a great movement should be directed or controlled by the soul of littleness.
Percy Fitzpatrick, politician, writer

There are two kinds of leaders: there is the man or woman who creates the self – his/her life – out of the drive of personal ambition, and there is the man or woman who creates a self out of response to people's needs.
Nadine Gordimer, writer, Nobel Prize for Literature

Power-brokers on every side give off noisome fumes, much in the way that the droppings of ruminants give off methane.
Christopher Hope, writer

We need to have the type of black leadership that will decrease the fear in the hearts of the young Afrikaners.
Aggrey Klaaste, editor

The challenge before all leaders is to rise above party personal differences, and speak and act in the interests of all South Africans.
Nelson Mandela, President, May 1994-

The NP elite is getting into bed with the ANC in order to preserve its silken sheets, and the leadership elite of the ANC is getting into bed with the NP to enjoy this newfound luxury.
Winnie Mandela, politician

There are those 'leaders' whose children study abroad while Daddy stays home 'fanning the fires of the struggle' – the same fires which keep the children of most township blacks illiterate and out of school.
Nomavenda Mathiane, journalist

The leader who survives these days is the one who endorses whatever the youth says, be it wrong or right.
Nomavenda Mathiane

We have no doubt that when crises arise – as indeed they will – leaders will emerge to lead us across our own version of the Egyptian desert.
Nthatho Motlana, doctor, businessman

To be a good leader one has to have brains, courage, be a good chooser of people – which is perhaps the most important factor, particularly as a business grows.
Harry Oppenheimer, businessman

We rally behind our leaders, and get the leaders we deserve.
Ken Owen, editor

The spectacle of the mighty being cast low, and the lowly raised up, is too delicious to bear.
Ken Owen

Who can be more cruel and dangerous than the ruler who knows God's will and is determined his people shall obey it?
Alan Paton, writer

Leadership has so often passed into the hands of psychological drop-outs.
Jack Penn, surgeon, philosopher, artist

The essential character quality of leadership rests on the presence of integrity and initiative wherein imagination and creativity may take over from humdrum exercises in scholarship.
Jack Penn

When the country's political leadership has demonstrated such courage, why has the response of the overseas investors, up until now, been so timid?
Tim Read, financier (UK)

Leadership depends more upon judgement than upon mere specialised knowledge.
Anton Rupert, businessman

Leadership shows itself by going ahead of its followers during a moment of crisis, uncertainty and confusion.
Tokyo Sexwale, politician

Each person who aspires to leadership has to ask the question – what is my faith, my philosophy, my principles, my values and my attitudes, and are these in harmony with each other?
Franklin Sonn, educationist, ambassador

Most leaders project a public image of being tolerant, peace-seeking democrats; while behind their backs their supporters assault and kill and silence followers of other parties.
Richard Steyn, editor

Greatness comes from a solid bed of humility.
Dali Tambo, TV chat show host

There is no doubt that homeland leaders take this independence balderdash seriously.
Derrick Thema, journalist

To lead is largely to foresee.
Herbert Vilakazi, academic

When we look at the faces of those who have led South Africa since the days of Jan Smuts, what do we see? We see a line-up of hard faces, the sort of faces one could chop wood on.
Peter Younghusband, foreign correspondent

Liberals/Liberalism

Liberalism is a greater danger in the long run to the struggle of the oppressed than fascism; for the very reason that it seems to speak with the tongue of the people.
Neville Alexander, intellectual

My understanding of liberalism is that you don't think anybody's all right or all wrong.
Denis Beckett, journalist

This is the doing of you and your liberal friends.
PW Botha to Helen Suzman after the assassination of HF Verwoerd

Liberals must help construct a democracy that combines the necessary inclusiveness of a multicultural society such as ours, with an absolute commitment to the force of reason, rather than the reason of force.
Bobby Godsell, businessman

I came to the conclusion that much white liberalism here is a sort of great-aunt of empire-building, lingering on long after her time, poor dear.
Nadine Gordimer, writer, Nobel Prize for Literature

A liberal is just a conservative who hasn't been mugged.
Hilton Hamman, soldier, self-defence expert

Liberals are always getting it in the neck for what others have done.
Joyce Harris, former Black Sash president

Blacks did not want liberals to do things for them.
Anthony Heard, editor

When the liberal reflex finally dies under pressure of reality, we'll realise we're already way too late in saving our own lives.
Patrick Lee, writer

The private enterprise system, with its bargaining on equal terms, is the economic part of freedom and is therefore an essential part of being a liberal.
Harry Oppenheimer, businessman

The maximum individual liberty compatible with the equal liberty of others, the rule of law, constitutionality, the right to privacy and property, freedom of speech, freedom of association and tolerance for diversity.
Ken Owen, editor

The question is whether you are going to be liberal or join the barbarians.
Ken Owen

By liberalism I don't mean the creed of any party or any century. I mean a generosity of spirit, a tolerance of others, an attempt to comprehend otherness, a commitment to the rule of law, a high ideal for the worth and dignity of man, a repugnance of authoritarianism and a love of freedom.
Alan Paton, writer

Liberal: person who allows maid to watch *Dallas* while doing the ironing.
Gus Silber, journalist

In the South African context, it is quite unique that liberals get an opportunity to put their money where their mouths are.
Frederik Van Zyl Slabbert, academic

The contempt of Afrikaner nationalism and South African Marxism for South African liberalism is well documented.
Frederik Van Zyl Slabbert

What liberals do take credit for is their consistent opposition to apartheid, and for keeping alive those democratic values without which the new South Africa would be as bad as the old.
Helen Suzman, liberal, retired politician

I would like to see the white liberal run. He is going to have to run, because he has let the lions and the tigers and the pythons out of the zoo.
Eddie von Maltitz, farmer, activist

Young people could easily fall prey to liberalism, which is the forerunner to Communism.
John Vorster, Prime Minister, 1966-78 (1962)

Grassroots members of all three parties have not yet got the message that liberal values are in vogue at the top; they continue to exhibit an intolerance exceeded by few societies on earth.
Patti Waldmeir, correspondent, Financial Times (UK)

Liberty

Liberation will not bring us milk and honey, but it will help us regain that youthful sense of hope, ambition and determination which are a prerequisite for success.
Anonymous

How unhappy is that poor man who loses his liberty!
Winston Churchill (recounting his capture by the Boers, Second Anglo-Boer War)

In any country where you have a situation of reform, where the country is in transition, then it's possible that a government may have to make inroads into the liberties of individuals in order to ensure the success of reform.
Kobie Coetsee, politician

The Afrikanders, although devoid of all military discipline, had the idea of independence deeply rooted in their hearts, and that they were worthy of existing as a Free Nation under a Republican form of Government.
Christiaan de Wet, soldier, Second Anglo-Boer War

This surrender was no less than the sacrifice of our independence.
Christiaan de Wet, soldier, Second Anglo-Boer War

Our Nation has never surrendered unconditionally – not to the British nor anyone else – and never will.
Henning Klopper, founder of the Broederbond

I would rather live with my own people on a dunghill than stay in the palaces of the British Empire.
Henning Klopper

You cannot have liberation on Monday and a house on Tuesday.
Thabo Mbeki, Deputy President, 1994-

We must be the only people on the African continent whose liberation movements took no heed of tribal affiliations.
Nthato Motlana, doctor, businessman

We would rather go barefoot back over the Drakensberg to meet our independence or our death, than bow down before a government which has treated us as the British have done.
Susanna Smit, Voortrekker

I refuse to accept the simplistic notion that for blacks the mere change in the colour of the rulers is the essence and sum of liberation.
Mordechai Tamarkin, academic (Israeli)

It must never be forgotten that an authentic struggle for liberty goes hand in hand with a struggle for an opportunity to exercise responsibility.
AH Zulu, cleric

Life/Living

To hell with living in interesting times, I want to be bored.
Denis Beckett, journalist

To live as a white in South Africa and dwell on radical change is rather akin to living in California and joking about earthquakes: it is just not done.
Nigel Bruce, editor (1985)

Life is made of little steps.
Warren Clewlow, businessman

You just have to take your chances, that's the thing about life.
Fanie de Villiers, cricketer

We are living in an era when large-scale attempts are being made to sever the ties which bind us to our traditions, our country, our people and our God.
Neville Dubow, artist, academic

Our lives are gestures inscribed upon the void.
Damon Galgut, writer

Life in the fast lane demands the constant highs cocaine and sex beyond the missionary position can offer.
Stephen Laufer, journalist

We lived under a dark, suffocating blanket for several generations.
Patrick Lee, writer

In the real-life casino it's a fact that some of the nastiest people get dealt the best hands.
Patrick Lee

Life is what happens while you're making other plans.
Mike Lipkin, marketer

Many of us go through the swamplands and deserts of life swathed in a glossy kaross of self-delusion.
Vusamazulu Credo Mutwa, storyteller, sangoma

A second-grade, B-world is where it's at.
Robert Nel, musician

Everything you get out of life is what you've settled for.
Irit Noble, cabaret artist

We are living in an age where conquest has to be undone.
Alan Paton, writer

Life, no matter where you are, is just a state of mind and yours in the new South Africa should be one of effortless Zen-like acceptance.
Hilary Prendini Toffoli & Carolyn Sacks, journalists

Life is a matter of labels, symbols and archetypes.
Lin Sampson, journalist

Do we not all secretly long for more love than reason, more pardon than justice, more impulse than calculation, more heart than head and altogether for an asymmetrical start in our favour in our lives?
Laurens van der Post, soldier, writer, philosopher

Perhaps this life of ours, which begins as a quest of the child for the man, and ends as a journey by the man to rediscover the child, needs a clear image of some child-man, like the Bushman.
Laurens van der Post

One of the most moving aspects of life is how long the deepest memories stay with us.
Laurens van der Post

If one is truly ready within oneself and prepared to commit one's readiness without question to the deed that follows naturally on it, one finds life and circumstance surprisingly armed and ready at one's side.
Laurens van der Post

What people do not recognise is that it is difficult to draw back on to a white laager because the blacks are not outside – they're with us.
Craig Williamson, spy

Lifestyles

So long as those in authority do not regard the attacks made on members of the Bantu society, attacks which are almost of daily occurrence, as being more serious than the infringement of local by-laws, then I pity those who, like me, are trying to live a decent life.
Anonymous

If you and your family live through the night and you still have furniture and the car is in the garage, you take up religion.
Anonymous

I took my property to my brother at Ndebele Street where it was burnt while my brother was away.
Anonymous Tokoza resident

All I do in the morning is tell my children to lie on the bus floor if they hear gunshots and 'may God be with you'.
Annalie Barnard, housewife

The guys at the next braai are the instant friends you did not know, regardless of language, creed, T-shirt slogan, category of vehicle or place of ethnic origin.
Denis Beckett, journalist

Concerned householders are offered electronically-operated gates and garage doors, video intercoms, armed patrols, Alsatian dogs, barbed wire fencing, panic alarms, radio car

patrols, and for those who wish to take no chances, 'European supervision at night'.
Michael Holman, journalist

At some point around 1970 white South Africans overtook Californians as the single most affluent group in the world.
Bill Johnson, writer

I don't even go to the shop to buy a newspaper without taking a pistol with me.
Jan Kleynhans, farmer

They've covered the windows with wood, called a halt to their social life, no longer allow their children to play alone in the farmyard and – like most farmers in the picturesque eastern Free State – have a self-imposed dusk-to-dawn curfew.
Peta Krost, journalist

Long-term plans have become: 'What are we doing after lunch?'
Reg Lascaris, businessman

We have been evolving for X-million years to live like this: in a small circle of like-minded, like-moneyed people, in an enclosed dome consisting of the home, the car, the office, the mall and the time-share resort.
Patrick Lee, writer

Over a crackling public address system chikka-chakka boeremusiek was interrupted by messages from Oom Juk and Tannie Spikkels wishing the Western Province *alles van die beste,* an announcement that the Klipberg Boereorkes would play that night and several birthday wishes for Piet Fourie from Brakpan.
Charles Leonard, journalist

Simultaneously, we have to cope with economic holocaust and social Armageddon.
Mike Lipkin, marketer

In South Africa it's almost a life a minute as we seek to fuse a myriad different cultures towards a common goal.
Mike Lipkin

The most important character trait has become the ability to handle ambiguity laced with uncertainty.
Mike Lipkin

Threatened by the high number of burglaries and grisly crimes committed in the comfort of their own homes, South Africans are choosing to live in opulent ghettos.
Katy Macdonald, journalist

Oh, for the halcyon days of South Africa when everyone had hot and cold running servants and nary a guilt complex in sight.
Jenni Newman, PR

The wary secretaries, who have learnt to lock their cars, and wear no jewellery, and jump the red lights if they must, now try to master new survival skills: which is the safe route home? Is it better to abandon work and go early, or try to vanish in the rush, or stay late and drive fast?
Ken Owen, editor

We shall live from day to day, and put more locks on the doors, and get a fine fierce dog when the fine fierce bitch next door has pups, and hold on to our handbags more tenaciously; and the beauty of the trees by night, and the raptures of lovers under the stars, these things we shall forgo.
Alan Paton, writer

South African beaches are littered with beautiful bodies wearing the minimum of covering and presenting a picture of vitality and a wonderful zest for life.
Molly Reinhardt, columnist

The only heritage that counts is African, so the dancers and musicians slip out of their Hilton Weiners, their Daniel Hechters and their Bruno Maglis and into tribal costumes they would never be seen dead in if people did not pay them money.
Barry Ronge, columnist

Aside from the thluckity-thluck of an automatic pool-cleaner sucking up algae, the most common sound of everyday life in the suburbs of South Africa is the guinea-pig squeal of a car alarm being ignored by everybody, particularly the person stealing the car.
Gus Silber, journalist

Whites have built a Western world at the southern tip of Africa. If all this were quietly cut off, towed away and attached to Europe, few people would notice the difference.
Nico Smith, cleric

Life for the whites derives its essential character from the idea that they are not in Africa, or, if their physical presence in the continent is too much to deny, that they are not really *of* Africa.
Allister Sparks, journalist

We've been geared towards a world that no longer exists – brought up to believe that our integration into society is as unproblematic as booting a disc... but the disc doesn't slot into the mainframe.
Anne Store, honours degree graduate

To have Mandela attend the wedding of a daughter or to celebrate a birthday in the company of high-profile ANC executives, becomes a status symbol of the true corporate insider.
Stanley Uys, journalist

We sat on stools in the driveway and drank tap water while the madam stood in the doorway drinking orange juice.
Frank Wilderson, writer

When he arrives at his official residence a lone bugler blows a fanfare, the dogs come out barking at the sound and a delighted Mrs Elize Botha tells guests: 'Pappie is home.'
Peter Younghusband, foreign correspondent (on PW Botha and Westbrooke)

Literature

Writers writing in South Africa are served, as one is served a summons, their subject matter: apartheid – its scandals; its moral and political consequences; the separation, the misunderstanding, the un-understanding it produces.
Anonymous

Appreciation of good writing, like fine wine or great sex, is a mature skill honed by years of experience and focused desire.
Anonymous

The Afrikaans writers were like a bunch of bourgeois uncles who had the privilege of access to the houses of the wise whores, pretending it was for prayer meetings.
Breyten Breytenbach, poet, writer

Writing is always rewriting the world.
Breyten Breytenbach

The experience of struggle has enriched rather than impoverished local literature.
André Brink, writer, academic

Writing is neither defined nor circumscribed by politics.
André Brink

Only by dreaming and writing the impossible can life be made possible once again.
André Brink

The country is too big and various to be evoked by one author.
Guy Butler, writer, academic

Literature is literature, a major human activity which should be studied in its own right, rather as we study music or painting.
Guy Butler

Plays should be written in poetry.
Guy Butler

If you have an enemy whose soul you would visit with a heavy vengeance and into whose heart you would place living vipers which will live and cramp and torment him through life, you have only to place one of these novels in his hands.
SA Christian Watchman

A tax on books is the next worst thing to a tax on food.
Tim Couzens, academic, writer

There is a lot of snobbery attached to writing in this country.
Achmat Dangor, poet, writer

'White Sunset' will go like 'Mein Kampf'.
Janet Fry, mother of journalist Jani Allan (on Ms Allan's proposed best-seller on South Africa)

When I began writing, I did not know what politics were.
Nadine Gordimer, author, Nobel Prize for Literature

We writers played a part in liberating the country, because we were helping to liberate thought.
Nadine Gordimer

Writers stand out from the conflict, even if they cannot stand aside.
Christopher Hope, writer

Is there literary life after apartheid?
Christopher Hope

South African writers did much to expose the fact that apartheid, together with its human cruelty and absurdity, did grievous linguistic harm.
Christopher Hope

Literature is a splendid mistress, but a bad wife.
Rudyard Kipling at the City Club, Cape Town

You have to enter the womb of Africa and be part of it, and not see. Your eyes must be closed, but you must feel all the rhythms of the body.
Mazisi Kunene, academic, poet

The political classes usually tend to produce turgid anti-intellectual prose, generally as appetising as a warmed-over piece of stale haddock.
Tony Leon, lawyer, politician

South African polit-lit critics are among the funniest in the world – such glum Gauleiters always telling us what to write about.
Douglas Livingstone, scientist, poet

If a poet's got any nous at all he struggles with, and is overwhelmed by every facet of his culture.
Douglas Livingstone

Every poet in South Africa is living by the sweat of his or her hands and brow, by his or her brains, and not by poetry.
Douglas Livingstone

One needs literature in one's life, because without it one deteriorates.
Nelson Mandela, President, May 1994-

Many of the books written by Europeans about Africans should be relegated to the dustbin.
Vusamazulu Credo Mutwa, storyteller, sangoma

White writers still write like whites in Africa.
Njabulo Ndebele, academic, writer

The average anti-apartheid novel was unspeakably boring.
Mike Nichol, writer

A kind of taut moral compactness is what I have aimed for, phrases rounded up and cut down to size like blocks of ice.
Lewis Nkosi, writer, academic

It must have been about six o'clock when I reached my room, and I sat down and wrote these words: 'There is a lovely road that runs from Ixopo into the hills. These hills are grass-covered and rolling, and they are lovely beyond any singing of it.'
Alan Paton, writer (on the Norwegian beginning of Cry, the Beloved Country)

If you want to preach you must go to the pulpit, and if you want to teach you must go to the podium, but if you want to tell a story you must go to the desk and obey the rules of the craft.
Alan Paton

Every poem I write is a love poem, because a hatred of inhumanity has got to be inspired by love.
Lesego Rampololeng, author, oral poet

No great book was ever written that did not cost many a sleepless night and many hours of weariness and lassitude.
Olive Schreiner, writer

You cannot be insincere when writing.
Wilbur Smith, writer

Writing is my excuse for living.
Wilbur Smith

If there's one thing that an author must have, it's his originality.
Wilbur Smith

Literature, surely, exists wherever the living word is spoken.
Laurens van der Post, soldier, writer, philosopher

A book about South Africa is a book about race.
Geoffrey Wheatcroft, journalist

Love

Obsessive love is not love.
Anonymous

Romance is always better in the book than between the sheets.
Jani Allan, journalist

We must love God and love our land.
Dane Borrell, schoolboy

I don't believe you need a licence to love.
June Jansen van Vuuren, child minder

Love makes weaklings of us all.
David Lambkin, writer

None of us should be prepared to elevate our love for our community above our loyalty or love for our South African nation.
Nelson Mandela, President, May 1994-

Love at first sight is nothing more than lust with potential.
Jenni Newman, PR

A heart in love is a heart in flight, the body simply follows where passion leads, and a doomed passion is the most dangerous because it is the most powerful of all.
Lewis Nkosi, writer, academic

I have one great fear in my heart, that one day when they are turned to loving, they will find we are turned to hating.
Alan Paton, writer

Love is a word that creates a turmoil of tension that involves you in a tight vice of merciless and idiotic sentiment.
Lin Sampson, journalist

We cannot help love's going, any more than we can help its coming; and when it is gone, it is better to say so.
Olive Schreiner, writer

To be loved, you have to give love first.
Clem Sunter, businessman, scenario strategist

We kill whites not because we hate them but because of love.
Vuma Tikinca, politician

More than most people, I love to be loved. I really do.
Desmond Tutu, cleric, Archbishop of Cape Town

There are no absolutes except those in the Gospel, and the absolutes of truth and love.
Desmond Tutu

Management/Managers

Military management style is the ultimate test, because if you do it badly, you get killed.
Ian Shepherd, businessman

You practise a fervent dedication to detail, coupled with a hands-on management style.
Bill Venter, businessman

Marketing

Targeting an age group as intergenerational as 13-35 is like trying to shoot a moving gerbil from a helicopter: the chances of a direct hit are fairly slender.
Charlotte Bauer, journalist

Marketing is a business art, not a business science, and the chief executive tends to shy away from it, delegating marketing decisions and responsibility.
Darryl Phillips, businessman

If there's no marketing, then you're not going to get your market share.
Bill Venter, businessman

Rapping an advertising exec over the knuckles for using sex to enhance the selling power of their client's product, thereby contributing to the commodification of human life, is like criticising a midget for being short.
Andrea Vinassa, journalist

Marriage

I realised pretty early on that I had made a horrible mistake when, due to boredom, I took up crocheting.
Amanda Forrow, radio and TV presenter

Before I got married I was worried I was going to feel like a mother.
Leleti Khumalo, actress

I see your lovely eyes watering with emotion when you talk about your wife.
Felicia Mabuza-Suttle, businesswoman, TV show presenter, talking to Tokyo Sexwale, politician

The whole purpose of a husband and wife is that when hard times knock at the door you should be able to embrace each other.
Nelson Mandela, President, May 1994-

We find it strange that people should be so amazed that a Zulu marries a Xhosa.
Zindzi Mandela, housewife, daughter of Winnie and Nelson Mandela

A good marriage is the most liberating experience.
Kogila Moodley, academic

How ridiculous it is to call a boat after your wife. Boats last so much longer.
Susie Park, socialite

The institution of marriage has survived despite the arguments of Germaine Greer and the other leftist feminists who saw a capitalist plot in every bridal gift list.
Dene Smuts, politician

Guess who he expects to act as his private secretary now?
Tienie Vorster, wife of John Vorster (1980), when he lost his secretary

Marriage can sometimes be the enemy of friendship.
Sue Williamson, artist

Medicine

I am not against the provision of the necessary medical assistance to Coloureds and natives, because, unless they receive that medical aid, they become a source of danger to the European community.
PW Botha, Prime Minister/State President, 1978-89

The human body, malfunctioning, is a disheartening thing.
Patrick Lee, writer

Sadly, there is no simple, convenient connection between character and health.
Patrick Lee

For those of us who have believed, all these years, that the collective urine of Saxonwold probably contains enough vitamins to supply Soweto, it has been difficult to accept that additional vitamins may indeed prevent serious diseases like cancer.
Pat Sidley, journalist

Men

No man can forgive or forget the fact that, in the beginning, his bottom was wiped by a woman.
Frances Ames, neurologist, psychiatrist

A gentleman never farts in the car, leads when he dances and has true respect for a lady.
John Berks, talk show host

A man is not drunk if he can lie on the floor without holding on.
Garry Brennan, journalist

A man who is isolated and alone can be regarded as a sort of discarded person.
Dinizulu, King of the Zulus

For 20 years, men have been told by women that everything that's wrong on this planet is their fault, thanks to testosterone poisoning, male pattern aggression, the Big Willy syndrome and so on.
Andrew Donaldson, journalist

Men: stuck between a rock and a hard-on.
Andrew Donaldson

We don't want women to assume that we are always horny and unable to refrain from imposing it on them.
Chris du Plessis, journalist

I want a man that wants me to do what he wants me to do to him.
Brenda Fassie, singer

Men are merely desserts.
Amanda Forrow, radio and TV presenter

Men aren't interested in period pains or that now it's seven o'clock and you have to go home and make dinner.
Suzanne Griffiths, lawyer

You don't change a man's heart if you take him out of the community and lock him up.
Johan Heyns, theologian

I think that men are unconcerned about certain things like toilets and their state of cleanliness.
Isabel Jones, cook, consumer journalist

What does society say of the men who bear emotional and physical scars of women who shower them with abuse, boiling oil and water?
Sechaba Khaile

Men are notorious for losing their heads, both of them, in the heat of the moment.
Mike Lipkin, marketer

A man is not whole if he is deprived of participating in some aspects of life; he will grow lopsided.
Albert Luthuli, ANC President General, Nobel Peace Prize

Five orgasms and the man says: 'Nee jong, ek moet slaap.'
Woolf Meyer, sex therapist

The white South African man is totally out of touch with women's needs.
Woolf Meyer

Isolate a man and he begins to die, a little at a time.
Es'kia Mphahlele, academic, writer

Most men, and indeed most people, look awful in a state of undress.
Ken Owen, editor

No man without a loving family, either natural or adopted, can be labelled a total success in life.
Jack Penn, surgeon, philosopher, artist

A man is as good as his genes, and no amount of delusion or pressure – political or practical – can change it.
Jack Penn

If a man has to make up his mind, let it be his own.
Jack Penn

Give them two or three problems at once and all the toys fall out of the cot.
Vanessa Remmington, consultant

Just because he uses a rubber johnny doesn't mean he thinks women are capable of managing companies.
Karen Rutter, journalist

A man with a framed copy of the Desiderata in the lavatory is a man not to be trusted.
Lin Sampson, journalist

A truly honest man is a rare and frightening thing.
Linda Shaw, journalist

Call me a cretin, but there's something about a man in uniform that turns me into a boggle-eyed bimbo.
Penny Stewardson, columnist

New Men want to bond, bond, bond; other men want to bonk, bonk, bonk.
Chris Steyn, journalist, crime novelist

Men only behave badly because women let them.
Marianne Thamm, journalist

If you judge a man by the price of his jacket you are certain to meet some interesting characters.
Mandla Tyala, journalist

The average man is like the average rainfall – it's the one rainfall that never falls.
Laurens van der Post, soldier, writer, philosopher

Like facial hair and Roman noses, veins look infinitely better on men than on women, and a strong arm with a nicely defined contour map of veins is a moving sight.
Annelize Visser, journalist

Migrant Labour

Having lost my cattle there is no tie to keep me here. My home is my work, and I should like to have my wife and children with me at my work.
Anonymous

It was no longer the question of teaching the black man the dignity of labour but of preventing him from competing with the whites on the farms and the whites in the towns.
Anonymous

All the Bantu have their permanent homes in the reserves and their entry into other areas and into the urban centres is merely of a temporary nature and for economic reasons.
WWM Eiselen, Secretary for Native Affairs

They want to walk in Eloff Street, but they don't want to qualify for the post.
Godfrey Moloi, 'godfather' of Soweto

You'd be surprised how many of these blacks prefer migratory work.
Connie Mulder, Minister of Plural Relations (1978)

Tradition has survived the schizophrenia of the migrant labour system.
Mwelo Nonkonyana, chief of the Amabhala, Transkei

Although migrant labour entrenched women's impoverishment and dependence in the rural areas, it also spared them some of the brutalising conditions experienced by their men.
Mamphela Ramphele, academic

It should be a recognised principle of government that natives – men, women and children – should only be permitted within municipal areas in so far and for so long as their presence is demanded by the wants of the white population.
Stallard Commission (1922)

Some semblance of tribal integrity remained in the Reserves, but the migrant labour system made a pretty delinquent bastard out of it.
Can Themba, journalist, writer

They were so bloody successful that now they fear they have drawn too many of us into the fields of urban industry and have sired themselves a problem.
Can Themba

Missionaries

There is often a missionary zeal in foreigners who work here, and we need to be conscious of those ambiguities, of the fact that others before us have come to this continent with both high ideals and base intentions.
Anonymous

My father was a missionary, and he always said the day the white synod sat was the day the prostitutes did their best business.
Chris Barnard, surgeon

It's only the missionaries and relief workers who batten down with the populace through Somalia-type civil wars and Ethiopian-type famines.
Mary Anne Fitzgerald, writer

There's something about South Africa that brings out America's missionary impulse.
Bill Keller, correspondent, New York Times

Among barbarous races a sound missionary method will in every way endeavour to promote civilisation by education and industry, resting on the solid foundation of religious instruction.
James Stewart, missionary

Why do not the missionaries first go to their own countrymen and convert them first?
Dyani Tshatshu, Xhosa chief

Mixed Marriages

We worship together, but never intermarry.
Anonymous woman

Moses had a mixed marriage.
PW Botha, Prime Minister/State President, 1978-89

The people who are opposing the policy of apartheid have not the courage of their convictions. They do not marry non-Europeans.
PW Botha (1948)

If a white man marries a black Transkeian woman, the man will be voting for the white parliament, the black for the Transkei parliament and the children for the Coloured persons' Representative Council. I do not think this makes for a happy family life.
FW de Klerk, State President, 1989-94; Deputy President, 1994-

A man can possibly not afford to marry a White woman, so he says to himself: I must marry the best Coloured woman that I can get because she can live cheaper and work better. We must stop that.
SM Pettersen, politician (1950)

It is in the nature of the Native that when he can have intercourse with the European he prefers it.
JHB Reitz, politician

We will see to it that coffee and milk are never mixed in this country.
CR Swart, politician

Morality

No one is morally debased in what he does in the privacy of his home.
Ralph Boffard, publisher

Morals need to function in the context of what is happening.
Cheryl Carolus, politician

If you hate your oppressor and not his evil deeds, you show yourself as insufficiently developed morally.
Albert Luthuli, ANC President General, Nobel Peace Prize

Is there some great moral purpose in self-destructive obduracy?
Gavin Relly, businessman

Any struggle against evil, in its historical dimension, itself inevitably carries much ugliness in its wake.
Adam Small, writer

Morality comes after you've spoken to the bookkeeper.
Gavin Stewart, academic, editor

Can a state without any powerbase or even sympathy from the majority of the people have a moral right to rule over the majority or even have a moral right to use violence to preserve an intrinsically violent political system?
Buti Thagale, cleric (1986)

Music

Rap's cool, but ragga's icy.
Anonymous partygoer

I like all kinds of music but I will not spend a cent buying 'boere music'.
Benny Alexander, politician

As four-letter words go, jazz is no exception in terms of the varied and sometimes passionate emotions they elicit.
Tebogo Alexander, journalist

Someone with a gun or a knife has no time to sit on street corners and get good at playing their instrument.
Lara Allen, student of kwela's history

There is nothing about an orchestra that commits it to being the prerogative of an elite, playing only the music of an imported, colonial culture.
Christopher Ballantine, academic

A musician is someone with dreams, someone who sits down to write a song out of anger, and winds up writing a song out of hope.
Bizarro Brooks, rapper

If every South African family had just one Shifty Record in their household, South Africa would be a different place.
Danny de Wet, band leader, drummer

I didn't have the temperament or the bovine qualities to become an opera singer.
Patricia Glyn, TV and radio presenter

Big band jazz that permeated the townships in the 1940s, mbaqanga styles that were created out of a mixture of imported swing and local marabi, the distinctive kwela sounds that were created in Alexandra and other working class districts on the East Rand in the 1940s and 1950s: each of these was a creative response by young men and women to the adverse material conditions and political oppression they faced in the townships.
Eddie Koch, journalist

Viva, classical music, viva!
Richard McNeill, journalist

Music taps into a deep seam in all of us, containing as it does the essence of the people from whence it comes.
Michelle Magwood, journalist

It's a world of confusion and there's only one thing you can rely on – that's good music.
Charles Mbele, pop musician

It's a sad commentary on our recent history that musicians have to come back to South Africa from abroad before South Africans get the opportunity to hear a vital part of their musical heritage – but the occasion should be one for celebration, not recrimination, that the music has, at last, come home.
Tony McGregor, music writer

The SABC and the National Party have succeeded in distorting the meaning of our songs.
Peter Mokaba, politician

Rap music is the only form of pop music to achieve a greater degree of mindlessness than Donna Summer and disco music.
Barry Ronge, journalist

Beethoven belongs to everyone.
Albie Sachs, politician

Rock 'n Roll is a filthy business and the filthier the protagonists, the better.
Jeremy Thomas, journalist

Rap is about freedom of speech; the music is geared towards, not the kid with the ghetto blaster, but the kid walking behind him, wanting the ghetto blaster.
Shamiel X, musician

The National Party (NP)

Slovo's slaves.
Anonymous CP MPs

Next thing they'll be telling us apartheid never existed.
ANC election advertisement (1994)

When it's a toss up between 'adapt or die' the Nats adapt.
Chris Barron, journalist

We made a mistake when we came into power in 1948: We concentrated on dismantling certain practices (and) did not concentrate enough on development schemes and that created an unbalanced stage.
PW Botha, Prime Minister/State President, 1978-89

They are also tainted with their record of trampling on human rights, of racism, of the denial of opportunity, of ruining our economy and of massive corruption in the machine of government.
Zach de Beer, politician

Race remains the basis of National Party Policy, and will remain behind lock and key.
FW de Klerk, State President, 1989-94; Deputy President, 1994-

We understand the masses of South Africa.
FW de Klerk

We have become the most representative party in South Africa.
FW de Klerk

From their first days in power the Nationalists had launched a project of social engineering the like of which the world had never seen.
David Harrison, documentary film maker, author

White nationalists in South Africa began nearly 50 years ago with policies of positively exuberant and militant Balkanisation.
Christopher Hope, writer

The Nationalists went on with their laws but they knew that they had a defiant people on their hands.
Patrick 'Terror' Lekota, politician

They've been on more Roads to Damascus than the average Syrian truck-driver.
Tony Leon, lawyer, politician

It took a decade for the National Party to find its way out of the wilderness, but it finally got there.
Rian Malan, writer

Belonging to the NP was like growing up with a mother and father who are alcoholics – you wouldn't disown them.
Wynand Malan, politician (defector from NP to DP)

The verkrampte will steadily and inexorably gnaw the heart out of the Nationalist Party.
Joel Mervis, editor

It has *always* been our policy to allow people to hold mass demonstrations.
Gert Myburgh, Nationalist (1992)

I saw it for what it was, self-centred, intolerant, exclusive.
Alan Paton, writer

The National Party missed the military glory boat when it chose the wrong side in World War 2, and the destabilisation of Third World neighbours has been a shoddy substitute.
Pat Rogers, journalist, businessman

The NP has become a party of kissing (black) girls and garden kaffirs.
Eugene Terre'Blanche, AWB leader

It is too late simply to repair itself, like a self-sealing tube.
Stanley Uys, journalist

The failure of the NP to govern is an appalling inheritance to bequeath a new government.
Phillip van Niekerk, journalist

We get attacked sometimes for being a referee and a player, but we are the party which has had to bring people together.
Olaus van Zyl, politician

Can Mr PW Botha be serious when he asks who will rejoice when the Nationalist government is toppled from power? Surely he knows the answer: The whole bloody world will rejoice.
Donald Woods, editor, author

National Symbols

No, man, it can't flutter lekker because it's too heavy with colours!
Anonymous woman, Cape Town (on the raising of the interim flag)

Our coat of arms could be a comfortable bed in a field of roses in a circle symbolising a yawn.
James Clarke, journalist

National symbols are emotive issues.
Nelson Mandela, President, May 1994-

Flags are just props: the Union Building is the biggest set we have ever had.
Barry Ronge, journalist

For a bit of peace perhaps we should adopt a transparent square for a flag and a minute's silence for the anthem.
Sunday Times

The National flag shall be rectangular in the proportion of two in the width to three to the length; per pall from the hoist, the upper band red (chilli) and the lower band blue, with a black triangle at the hoist; over the partition lines a green pall one fifth the width of the flag, fimbriated white against the red (chilli) and blue, and gold against the black triangle at the hoist of the width of the pall and its fimbriations is one third the width of the flag.
Addendum to Transitional Executive Council (TEC) agenda on the 'interim' flag

What flag? Which flag? The orange white and blue? The gold-black-green? The Vierkleur? The Red Flag? The multi-coloured IFP dreamcloth? A white flag? A peace flag? No flag?
Pieter-Dirk Uys, satirist

If you want to burn the flag, burn it.
Kobus van Rooyen, censor, academic

The only solution for multi-party negotiations is to accept a flag with white and black spots, which reflects the variety of colours in the country, with a Coca-Cola bottle in the middle to symbolise South Africa's status as an American vassal state.
Robert van Tonder, Boerestaat Party leader

Nationalism

If Zulu nationalism is awoken, then the ANC will be eaten for breakfast.
Anonymous

Each and every nation has the right to change its own destiny.
Mangosuthu Buthelezi, IFP leader, politician

Afrikaner Nationalism, impelled by the death wish of its own race mythology, leads the country into a thundering re-enactment of its own history – the struggle of a tiny, White self-righteous people against the evil of Black barbarism.
Laurence Gandar, editor

There is a link between the processes of democratisation and political disintegration – nationalism.
Hermann Giliomee, academic

Like the Jews, what we want is a country in which we can survive as a people, in which we can live our lives, maintain our standards and our Christian way of life.
Tienie Groenewald, soldier, politician

The time has come when South Africa can no longer be ruled by non-Afrikaners, by people who do not have the right love for South Africa.
Barry Hertzog, Prime Minister, 1924-39

South Africa was for the Afrikaner.
Barry Hertzog

Born under the English flag, I have no wish to die under it.
Paul Kruger, President, Transvaal Republic

The Gospel had to encounter the jealousy of a people proud of their nationality, and instinctively feeling, and that not without reason, that it was seriously threatened by the encroachments of the people that were bringing the Gospel to them.
James Laing, missionary

Organisations and individuals need to govern impulse with ethics and to temper self-interest with national interest.
David Lapin, rabbi, academic

The aims of national unity and reconstruction must not be corrupted by actions that are unworthy of their true nobility.
David Lapin

Where attempts are made to order life to put blinkers on people's eyes, the regression and eventual destruction of that nation is engendered.
Albert Luthuli, ANC President General, Nobel Peace Prize

The most striking of all the impressions I have formed since I left London a month ago is of the strength of this African national consciousness. The wind of change is blowing throughout the continent.
Harold Macmillan, Prime Minister (UK)

We do not want a white proletariat in this country.
Alfred Milner, British High Commissioner

It is the insistence of the Whites that they are 'Europeans' which has, in part, inspired such silly slogans as 'Africa for the Africans'.
Nat Nakasa, journalist

It is a very odd thing that one gives this passionate love to a piece of country for the simple reason that one was born there.
Alan Paton, writer

Nations, like large companies, need a guiding vision if they are to succeed in traversing the slippery slope of the future.
Clem Sunter, businessman, scenario strategist

In essence, Afrikaans nationalism was a question of the heart.
FA van Jaarsveld

If I can serve my nation better by democratic action, I will do so, but if I have to choose between Afrikanerdom and democracy, then there is no choice.
Hans van Rensburg, Kommandant-General, Ossewabrandwag

No nation has ever achieved anything without believing in itself, without frantically adhering to its ideals and to its calling in that country.
Koot Vorster, dominee

Nature

Nothing on the face of South African nature is what it seems.
John Black Atkins, war correspondent, Second Anglo-Boer War

Altering the nature of the atmosphere is probably the most foolish and reckless thing we have done.
James Clarke, journalist

Crimes against nature in South Africa have always been politically skewed.
Jane Conyngham, journalist

By rediscovering our love of nature, we can improve the society within which we live quicker and easier than by many other means.
Sam Mhlungu, environmentalist

Wilderness is a place for reflection.
Ian Player, conservationist

For certain people exposure to wilderness is a profound and healing experience.
Sheila Ramsay, clinical psychologist

As all hope in one's personal life dies out, one clings more and more to nature.
Olive Schreiner, writer

Nothing for nothing; the longer I live the more I feel that to be nature's inexorable law.
Olive Schreiner

If nature here wishes to make a mountain, she runs a range for five hundred miles; if a plain, she levels eighty; if a rock, she tilts five thousand feet of strata on end; our skies are higher and more intensely blue; our waves are larger than others; our rivers fiercer.
Olive Schreiner

The emotional appeal of Nature is tremendous, sometimes more than one can bear.
Jan Christian Smuts, Prime Minister, 1919-24 & 1939-48

It's almost as if mankind has reached a comfort zone – have we gone soft, as a species?
Phillip Tobias, academic

Negotiation

Negotiation is rather like playing tennis.
Wynand Malan, politician

Far removed from the petty posturing, hollow sloganeering, and veiled threats of violence that dominate the South African political scene, negotiation offers a frank and convivial environment for grand posturing, loaded sloganeering, and unveiled threats of violence.
Gus Silber, journalist

Negotiation is a delicate, sensitive process of forced interaction between people who would rather not be in the same country, never mind the same room, and it is therefore vital for delegates to observe certain fundamental courtesies when rejecting each other's outrageous demands.
Gus Silber

Negotiation starts where we draw the borders of various regions.
Andries Treurnicht, CP leader

We either negotiate and prosper, or coerce and be doomed.
Hendrik W van der Merwe, academic (1987)

One cannot go into negotiation with a fixed position.
Stoffel van der Merwe, politician

Nightmares

Many age-old nightmares have come to pass since the afternoon Winnie Mandela arrived an hour late to fetch her husband from prison, but none so deep, so Conradian, as the one that has marauding blacks tearing up the garden path to seize the day and the front door keys.
Charlotte Bauer, journalist

Normality

If you're not feeling totally out of control, perplexed and paranoid, you're not normal.
Reg Lascaris, businessman

Opinion Polls

In this country, where black people have never voted before and where authoritarian employers and fearsome security laws have caused blacks to be reluctant to reveal their true political beliefs, opinion polls are notoriously unreliable.
Allister Sparks, journalist

Pan Africanist Congress (PAC)

Two men with a fax machine in Dar es Salaam.
Anonymous

The PAC are committed to peace but there are some bad Aplas in the barrel.
Anonymous

People create the PAC of their own imagination.
Benny Alexander, politician

Our problem with the major powers is that we refused to be their satraps.
Benny Alexander

We, as the PAC, have to employ misfortune to make President de Klerk agree to our demands – just like Moses did to Pharaoh.
Benny Alexander

The policy of the PAC is neither liberal, nor conservative; neither radical, nor reactionary. Essentially it is romantic.
Wessel Ebersohn, journalist

The PAC moves stubbornly, but bravely, on, consumed by principles that allow few compromises, obsessed by the romance of the old Africa and waiting confidently for the moment of vindication.
Wessel Ebersohn

The PAC has made it clear that the first essential is a mental divorce from the pass laws.
Philip Kgosana, activist, 'The Black Messiah'

We believe there is only one race, the human race.
Clarence Makwetu, PAC leader

The PAC is a liberation movement – it is entitled to have a liberation army.
Nelson Mandela, President, May 1994-

There can be little doubt that the organisation's 'One Settler, One Bullet' policy has proved very effective, as there are very few of the original 1652 or 1820 settlers left in the country.
Gus Silber, journalist

Its ambivalence on the issue of violence is deplorable, its failure to dissociate itself from Apla's claimed acts of murder is shameful, and its propagation of racist slogans such as 'one settler, one bullet' and 'kill the Boer, kill the farmer', are criminally inciteful and disgusting.
Allister Sparks, journalist

PAC March on Cape Town (1960)

A wave was breaking over Cape Town, threatening white power at its very base.
Anthony Heard, editor

It seems most likely that this march was not planned as part of the pass campaign – though it became in some way its finest hour.
Anthony Heard

Fifteen thousand marchers behind, walking peacefully; and, in front, this young leader in shorts remonstrating with a man bent on violence.
Anthony Heard

He (Terblanche) fell to his knees in the police station and prayed before embarking on a daring quest for peace – which, without doubt, clashed with the views of the government.
Anthony Heard

The fate of Cape Town, with its hundreds of thousands of lives, lay in the hands of two men: a seasoned police colonel who was the son of a bankrupt ostrich farmer and an African student from Pretoria in short pants.
Anthony Heard

I fear something terrible will happen today.
AC Jordan, academic

We are not going to fight or attempt to fight, insult or attempt to insult, provoke or attempt to provoke the police in their lawful duties.
Philip Kgosana, activist, 'The Black Messiah'

I thought it was not wise to force my way to a Parliament surrounded by troops because otherwise we would have been presented to the racists to shoot, and that was not my purpose.
Philip Kgosana

Let us be silent . . . just like people who are going to a graveyard.
Philip Kgosana

The hour in which the Bastille might have been stormed in South Africa and wasn't.
Joseph Lelyveld, editor (USA)

The moment at which black leaders were finally forced to see the inadequacy of non-violent tactics in the South African context.
Joseph Lelyveld

Come on, Kgosana, you can't see the minister with all these people round you.
Colonel Reay, SAP (the Minister of Justice, FC Erasmus, was at lunch)

There was a powder keg in our midst and I did not want to bring a match near it.
IPS Terblanche, policeman

Mr Kgosana, I speak to you as one gentleman to another.
IPS Terblanche

I am firmly of the opinion that all hell would have broken loose over Cape Town if we had used force that day.
IPS Terblanche

Parliament

All parliamentarians are gays.
Gora Ebrahim, politician

Only *pampoens* end up on parliamentary benches.
Claire Emary, housewife, KISS Party leader

The parliamentary idea is a noble one that binds elected representatives from many countries into one brotherhood.
Ken Owen, editor

If a murderer can sit in Parliament, why can't I?
Eugene Terre'Blanche, AWB leader

Parties

The party's over but the fun's just beginning.
Patrick Lee, writer

Divided we stood, united we jolled.
Rian Malan, writer

If you don't have a gift you shouldn't come to a party.
Nataniel, performer

Charity balls have really turned into a fee for all.
Jenni Newman, PR

South Africans are definitely in favour of the multi-party system – one on Friday and one on Saturday night.
Jenni Newman

As outcasts who are still not quite used to being on the guest list again, we are anxious to know what the others at the party might be saying about us.
John Perlman, journalist

Even recession can be an excuse for a party, if you're far enough removed from the breadline for your laughter not to ring too hollow in your empty stomach.
Hilary Prendini Toffoli, journalist

The party is the world's thyroid gland, regulating temperature and disseminating and reasserting mood.
Lin Sampson, journalist

A party is only as good as the people you invite, no matter how many crayfish are present.
Lin Sampson

White South Africans must learn that what most Africans understand the word 'party' to mean is good music, good food, good company (in no particular order).
Mandla Tyala, journalist

There's nothing a good party can't cure.
Pieter-Dirk Uys, satirist

There are still infinitely more invitations than I have time to accept.
John Vorster, Prime Minister, 1966-78 (1980)

Patriots/Patriotism

If you can do something for your country, then do it.
Naas Botha, rugby player

White patriots sit in jail while Communist terrorists roam the streets, looting and plundering and destroying the country.
Gaye Derby-Lewis, right-winger

There is something sad about patriotism in someone who can't really determine what flag they're waving.
Anthony Hamilton Russell, businessman

I am not embarrassed by patriotism.
Roy Macnab, poet

The most important solvent of all our questions in South Africa will be the spirit of South African patriotism.
Jan Christian Smuts, Prime Minister, 1919-24 & 1939-48

We cry for our beloved country which has been so wanton in its waste of her precious human resources.
Desmond Tutu, cleric, Archbishop of Cape Town (at Steve Biko's funeral, 1977)

It's not necessary for anybody to accept National Party policy to qualify as a patriot.
John Vorster, Prime Minister, 1966-78

You as whites have a vocation to fill in South Africa.
John Vorster (referring to the prospect of a mixed cabinet, 1963)

Peace

Peace is the most ruthless creature in the world.
PW Botha, Prime Minister/State President, 1978-89

Everyone knows that I am committed to peace.
Mangosuthu Buthelezi, IFP leader, politician

It is not possible to have peace in South Africa until we put it in the idiom people understand.
Mvume Dandala, cleric

If I'm to be killed for making peace it's better than being killed without knowing what you are dying for.
Jacob Dlomo, messenger, peacemaker

Like the comrades, I say that while we must encourage peace efforts we must still increase the capacity of the people to defend themselves.
Harry Gwala, politician

It seems to be easier for South Africans to win the Nobel Peace Prize than for Transvaal to win the Currie Cup.
Anton Harber, editor

If you want to live in peace with your enemy then you must come and talk to your enemy with a sword in your hand and then you can attain peace.
Louis le Grange, politician

As a malevolent neutral, I pray hopelessly for peace on earth.
Douglas Livingstone, scientist, poet

To have peace in our land our leaders must have peace in their minds.
Emmanuel Luthuli, schoolboy

There is no such thing as total peace at any given time.
Magnus Malan, soldier, politician

I will go down on my knees to beg those who want to drag our country into bloodshed not to do so.
Nelson Mandela, President, May 1994-

I'd strut naked for peace anytime.
'Baby Jake' Jacob Matlala, boxer

Go out and spread peace, keep it in your hearts and minds and share all the love you have with people of all races in South Africa.
Jacqui Mofokeng, beauty queen

Peace belongs to all of us – it does not belong to a particular party.
Stanley Mogoba, cleric

Fighting for peace is like fucking for charity.
Jenni Newman, PR

You cannot wear a ribbon on your lapel and carry a gun in your pocket.
Tai O'Kill, cleric

Symbols, songs and ribbons are nice, but rigid enforcement of law and justice would more effectively secure peace.
Pat Rogers, journalist, businessman

If we really want peace, perhaps we should get less naive and more angry.
Pat Rogers

Does it take a shooting in a church on a Sunday to wear a white ribbon for peace?
Pieter-Dirk Uys, satirist

I have in my hands here a dove, which I now send out into space as a symbol of peace and prosperity, which we wish all peoples on earth. It will be our messenger of goodwill.
HF Verwoerd, Prime Minister, 1958-66 (the dove was a pigeon, and it fell to the ground) (1960)

People

There are people who have been killed in jail, and killed in exile and in the townships, and we want to know who did it, and you have burnt the files and we want to know why.
Anonymous schoolgirl to Pik Botha

Every mob is composed of individuals with a wish to be liked and a need to be respected.
Denis Beckett, journalist

No matter from which stock we come, whether Dutch or English, we must try our best to become part and parcel of a great African nation.
Louis Botha, Prime Minister, 1910-19

Our (the Nationalist) policy makes provision for this great constellation of different peoples in South Africa in which each can move in its own orbit in this great universe without coming into collision with one another.
MC Botha, politician (1972)

South Africans are not inclined to be threatened – they don't accept it.
PW Botha, Prime Minister/State President, 1978-89

In life, there are things people must struggle for with all they have.
Mangosuthu Buthelezi, IFP leader, politician

Milk chocolate! That's what is needed among all people in Africa generally and South Africa more specifically.
Michael Cassidy, evangelist

You only need one person to start a miracle.
Margaret de Paravicini, journalist

South Africans never give up.
Fanie de Villiers, cricketer

There is a certain courtesy and a good deal of formality observed among the natives which is appreciated by but a few of the white men who come in contact with them.
Percy Fitzpatrick, politician, writer

If you can get people first of all to understand one another and to know the facts, such differences as remain must be either legitimate ones or those which it is past the wit of man to remove.
Percy Fitzpatrick

There's a power and pathos in these people that's frightening.
Nadine Gordimer, writer, Nobel Prize for Literature

I'm a bit flattered because when your enemy rates you as being dangerous, then you get the feeling that you've tried to do your best for the oppressed people.
Chris Hani, Umkhonto we Sizwe chief of staff, SACP general secretary

Each of us, with all of our ethnic nuances, spring from brave, pioneering forebears.
Shaun Johnson, journalist

We all, whites and blacks, think we're entitled to Swedish social security, but with Polish GNP.
John Kane-Berman, businessman

A stroll through central Pretoria and one walk through the Monument's parking lot were enough to see that they're no-account people – dumpy women in white ankle socks and flowerprint sundresses, skinny, quid-spitting men with hair oil on their heads and gun-nut sideburns.
Bill Keller, correspondent, New York Times

Africans and Afrikaners all want representative government, literacy, independent courts, a free press, flushing lavatories, electricity, Coco-Cola, pop music, and American TV.
Andrew Kenny, journalist

South Africa's people are living testimony to the unconquerable spirit of mankind.
Albert Luthuli, ANC President General, Nobel Peace Prize

Nothing brings one back to earth more quickly than encountering Johannesburg's young, rich and trendy en masse.
Richard McNeill, journalist

Bring together those who belong together by inner conviction.
DF Malan, Prime Minister, 1948-54

There were gunfighters from kwaMadala, and I must say they were quite dashing – black leather jackets, trench-coats, guns in socks, shades and a few baseball caps on backwards.
Rian Malan, writer

South Africans develop antibodies to the poison, they grow numb and blind, but if you leave long enough to detoxify and come back with clear eyes, your skull gets fractured.
Rian Malan

People here are so underpowered in skills.
John Matshikiza, actor

The greatness of a nation is not determined by the number of its people but by the quality of their existence.
Nthato Motlana, doctor, businessman

We deal not with each other but with illusions of one another.
Ken Owen, editor

Few things unite us so closely as our greed, our love of wealth and glitter, our perpetual scramble for the products of consumer capitalism.
Ken Owen

They are divided by race and will kill for it.
Edward Pearce, journalist (UK)

Fancy, a whole nation of lower-middle class Philistines, without an aristocracy of blood or intellect or of muscular labourers to save them!
Olive Schreiner, writer

The warmth of country folk and pioneer stock lies only a sip or two beneath the surface.
Allister Sparks, journalist

Man's needs are many; the means to satisfy all these needs are limited; and Man seeks to satisfy as many needs as possible with the limited means at his disposal.
Chris Stals, financier

We are tired of hating and weary of warring with each other.
Peter Storey, cleric

Tragedy in this country serves to bind people together rather than drive them apart.
Clem Sunter, businessman, scenario strategist

While one accepts contact between people as individuals, there is a residual consciousness of race difference, and of concern as to where things are and where they are going.
Andries Treurnicht, CP leader

A people can take only so much and no more.
Desmond Tutu, cleric, Archbishop of Cape Town

Ordinary South Africans, black and white, are more solid than they are often given credit for.
Phillip van Niekerk, journalist

South Africans are trapped in old ideas and bad habits that they have the utmost mental difficulty in surmounting.
Phillip van Niekerk

We have a large element of non-Western people here and they haven't got our age-old tradition of democracy and our old Christian culture.
Robert van Tonder, Boerestaat Party leader

The potential that truly rests in the wider community, the ability to love when the odds are so profoundly against you – and with such integrity and power as I have seen in my people – this indicates to me that the fundamental goodness of ordinary people has not been corrupted.
Paul Verryn, cleric

Perhaps nowhere else in the world have the indigenous people not only survived, but so increased as to become the problem with which the outside world does not have to deal but which is our problem and which we are prepared to solve, but in our way and the only way in which people who are at different stages of civilisation can live together.
HF Verwoerd, Prime Minister, 1958-66

If we, despite our differences and separate identities, lock arms, we will form a chain of iron which no enemy will break.
John Vorster, Prime Minister, 1966-78 (1979)

People don't gossip enough about their neighbours these days.
John Vorster

When people are on the verge of tasting power, they do not mind using measures which were used against them in the past when they were still a liberation movement.
David Welsh, academic

It is well known that perhaps the sole affinity between all the groups that make up South Africa is a love of soap operas.
Peter Wilhelm, editor, poet

The final test of the will of a people will always be found in their ability or inability to resist that which they reject as fundamentally wrong.
Goodwill Zwelithini, King of the Zulus

of Benny Alexander (politician)

The most appealing person in South African politics has been wriggling his way through the year (1992), full of sound and fury, signifying nothing.
Gavin Evans, journalist

of Jani Allan (journalist)

A red-lipped image of feminine seduction... the whole lot topped by a cute soldier's hat.
Anonymous journalist

I want to be known as a writer and not a glamour girl.
Jani Allan (1982)

Men are always asking me to wear something sexy.
Jani Allan

A tart, a liar and £300 000 in debt.
UK tabloid

of Chris Barnard (surgeon)

His life is laid out like a public smorgasbord heaped with unsavoury titbits that leave a foul taste in the mouth.
Caroline Hurry, journalist

of Steve Biko (Black Consciousness leader)

They kept him in chains, naked.
Mrs Biko, mother of Steve Biko

I am not glad and I am not sorry about Mr Biko . . . He leaves me cold.
Jimmy Kruger, Minister of Justice

Biko was the very symbol of a lifeforce: he ate life in shovelfuls.
Es'kia Mphahlele, academic, writer

This was a new breed of South African – the Black Consciousness breed – and I knew immediately that a movement that produced the sort of personality now confronting me had qualities that blacks had been needing in South Africa for three hundred years.
Donald Woods, editor, author

of John Bishop (journalist, TV presenter)

Bishop is a living example of the promethean intellect that can be developed merely by reading SABC news bulletins non-stop for 20 years.
Robert Kirby, satirist

His mind works so fast he gets to the end of an argument before his guests do.
Richard McNeill, journalist

of Elize Botha (housewife, former First Lady)

Koeksister to the People, patron saint of milliners, and first in line for prosecution under the fashion war crimes tribunal.
Arthur Goldstuck, journalist

of Louis Botha (Prime Minister, 1910-19)

He was one of the truly great men of the world.
Winston Churchill, Prime Minister (UK)

The greatest, cleanest, sweetest soul of all the land – of all my days.
Jan Christian Smuts, Prime Minister, 1919-24 & 1939-48

of Naas Botha (rugby player)

Youngsters need heroes. They need figures like Batman, Tarzan or Naas Botha.
Abe Malan, SA rugby manager

When New Zealanders hear the name Naas Botha they subconsciously whisper the opening phrase of their world-famous haka: 'Ka mate, ka mate – it is death, it is death'.
Dan Retief, sportswriter

of Pik Botha (politician)

Sometimes when we have a tough discussion Pik puts on his Batman suit and flies around the room, and we have to wait until he comes down and talks again.
Anonymous American diplomat

Pastimes include poetry, classical music, eastern philosophy, and donnering the bliksem out of anyone who checks him skeef.
Arthur Goldstuck, journalist

He has dominated audiences with his particular blend of charm, righteous wrath, and an aquiline, unblinking gaze that blazes with frankness.
Hugh Murray, publisher

A man fully conscious of being forced into a position in which he had to defend what he knew to be untenable.
Njabulo Ndebele, academic, writer

In the caucus of hard men who run the National Party he is regarded as malleable and ductile.
Ken Owen, editor

The archetypal Afrikaner, to my mind, is Pik Botha who, bristling like a porcupine, draws a fierce line in the sand and dares the world to cross it, meanwhile retreating ferociously to the next line in the sand.
Ken Owen

Much of Pik's huffing and puffing is calculated drama: it rarely gets out of control.
Peter Younghusband, foreign correspondent

of PW Botha (Prime Minister/State President, 1978-89)

The Pangaman.
Anonymous

I never have the nagging doubt of wondering whether perhaps I am wrong.
PW Botha

Although he was the supreme leader of a regional superpower, PW Botha ironically had the mind of an embittered Third World dictator seeking foreign help against local enemies.
Chester Crocker, politician, businessman (USA)

He was a cantankerous old bastard, to be sure, but he'd come a long way against the grain, considering that he'd learned his ideological chops from the master, DF Malan.
Rian Malan, writer

It would be a fool or a liar who discounted as worthless the quantum leap taken by PW Botha in moving social and political reform along.
Hugh Murray, publisher

He is a man who lacks any evident sense of the limits of power.
Ken Owen, editor

If he was female, he would arrive in Parliament on a broomstick.
Helen Suzman, liberal, retired politician

An obnoxious bully.
Helen Suzman

We should give 'Die Groot Krokodil' his due: PW Botha was South Africa's Gorbachev.
David Welsh, academic

He is a modern day Shaka, powerful and totally ruthless.
Peter Younghusband, foreign correspondent

of Breyten Breytenbach (poet, writer)

Prison, in some ways, strengthened what were already my deepest psychological tendencies – a desire to please and at the same time a need to lash out, to say 'Dammit, I'm going to be and do exactly what I want'.
Breyten Breytenbach

Calm, controlled, quiet, he seems temperamentally lean.
James Wood, journalist

of Zola Budd (athlete)

Fast on her feet, slow with her brain – it took her about five years after getting her British citizenship to figure out she didn't like apartheid, but by then she was back in Bloemfontein and it didn't matter anyway.
Arthur Goldstuck, journalist

of Redvers Buller (soldier)

Whatever his own people have to say to his discredit, Sir Redvers Buller had to operate against stronger positions than any other English General in South Africa.
Christiaan de Wet, soldier, Second Anglo-Boer War

of Mangosuthu Buthelezi (IFP leader, politician)

Like Hitler, he does not know he has lost the war.
Anonymous

I am the only major leader who does not own a farm or a big shop.
Mangosuthu Buthelezi

I never pontificate outside the decision-making body of the central committee.
Mangosuthu Buthelezi

I must be the most insane politician.
Mangosuthu Buthelezi

I am just a person who has tried to do what Shakespeare has put into the words of one of his characters: 'No one can do better than his best'.
Mangosuthu Buthelezi

I am not a kaffir – I will never submit to white baasskap.
Mangosuthu Buthelezi

I believe I am in a position to judge what black South Africans really want.
Mangosuthu Buthelezi

With friends like he's chosen, who needs enemies?
Gavin Evans, journalist

Simultaneously a potential threat to the state and indispensable to it.
Shula Marks, historian

His errors were not constitutional, but political.
Ken Owen, editor

He made the wrong move at the wrong time, and handed the making of history to lesser men.
Ken Owen

Mangosuthu Buthelezi stands tall in a storm of his own making.
Hilary Prendini Toffoli & Gus Silber, journalists

Chief Buthelezi defends his turf with his traditional weapons of ire and brimstone.
The Star

He holds the Guinness Book of Records entry for the longest-ever speech, a 400-page effort delivered over five days in the kwaZulu legislative assembly.
Weekly Mail & Guardian

of Sheila Camerer (politician)

I like to believe I transfix voters with my big blue eyes.
Sheila Camerer

of JM Coetzee (writer, academic)

He is a scientist, fascinated with the mechanics of language, yet able to enter the liberating and anarchic realm of writing fiction.
Andrea Vinassa, journalist

of Zach de Beer (politician)

Possesses a certain gravitas which commands respect.
Gavin Evans, journalist

He became the youngest person ever to take his seat on the green leather benches of Parliament.
Peter Fabricius, journalist

of FW de Klerk (State President, 1989-94; Deputy President, 1994-)*

He is a political jellyfish with no backbone.
Mangosuthu Buthelezi, IFP leader, politician

I don't believe that I am irreplaceable.
FW de Klerk

On the major issues and the major decisions, I have no regrets.
FW de Klerk

He is one of the few politicians anywhere to have deliberately put himself out of power and to have taken most of his supporters willingly with him.
The Economist

It seems he is not content with the epitaph of slayer of apartheid on his political gravestone.
Richard Ellis, correspondent, The Sunday Times (UK)

A poor man's Gorbachev – vacillating, scared of his security forces and even more scared of the future.
Gavin Evans, journalist

He, the son and grandson of National Party leaders who helped erect the artifice of apartheid, has travelled further from his heritage than anyone could have predicted.
Paul Gray, correspondent, Time International (USA)

* See also **of Nelson Mandela & FW de Klerk.**

He was a pragmatic politician, eager to press the flesh and do the deal.
Paul Gray

Bland, self-assured, a wily politician who is able to turn opposition weaknesses to NP advantage.
Jean le May, journalist

In spite of my criticism, it must be acknowledged he has made a very important contribution to the transformation of an apartheid state into a non-racial society.
Nelson Mandela, President, May 1994-

I think we can do business with this man.
Nelson Mandela

I was disappointed by him because he did things that I did not expect.
Nelson Mandela

One of the greatest sons of South Africa.
Nelson Mandela (on Inauguration Day, 10 May 1994)

Nominally he presides over a swarm of locusts, an end-of-empire feeding frenzy; in fact he spends his time campaigning for office while the anarchy of the townships, and the brutal conflicts of Natal, spill across the country.
Ken Owen, editor

De Klerk had indeed seen the Damascan light.
Alan Robinson, journalist

He's probably the only conviction politician left in the world today.
Harvey Thomas, election adviser (UK)

He high-jacked the DP platform and so won a Nobel Peace Prize.
Pieter-Dirk Uys, satirist

of Marike de Klerk (housewife, former First Lady)

'n Tawwe antie.
Anonymous

of Clive Derby-Lewis (politician, murderer)

A man whose love for his country is unparalleled.
Gaye Derby-Lewis, right-winger

I think sometimes he became an embarrassment to us.
Gaye Derby-Lewis

of Gaye Derby-Lewis (right-winger)

Our very own Lady Macbeth.
Andrew Donaldson, journalist

of Dingane (King of the Zulus)

Fat, obese, lazy, oversexed, bloodthirsty and treacherous.
Nathaniel Isaacs, trader

Bone-lazy and unable to separate considerations of national policy from his personal affairs.
Donald Morris, writer (USA)

of Percy Fitzpatrick (politician, writer)

Sir Percy had a good South African heart in the right place.
FW Beyers, soldier

A man men could but love.
Inscription on his grave above the Sundays River

of Bruce Fordyce (sportsman)

A raving hedonist with a weakness for red wine, women and rock 'n roll.
Hilary Prendini Toffoli & Gus Silber, journalists

of Richard Goldstone (judge)

He's managed to rile everyone, a good sign.
Gavin Evans, journalist

Judge Richard Goldstone was the official apartheid ghostbuster.
Anton Harber, editor

A man almost unique in senior SA legal circles in his lack of pomposity and sincere desire to hear the opinions of others.
Sunday Times

of Nadine Gordimer (writer, Nobel Prize for Literature)

Nadine Gordimer has the look of a merciless ballet mistress.
Hilary Prendini Toffoli & Gus Silber, journalists

of Chris Hani (Umkhonto we Sizwe chief of staff, SACP general secretary)*

Cheats at Patience.
Arthur Goldstuck, journalist

He was a humble leader with a vision – a man who loved his country and worked for peace.
Mondli Gungubele, ANC peace desk spokesman

of Alan Hendrickse (politician)

Alan Hendrickse, leader of the Labour Party, has moved from being a Cabinet Minister to singing 'We shall overcome' and toi-toi-ing in the parliamentary chamber after losing control to the NP.
Frederik Van Zyl Slabbert, academic

of Sol Kerzner (entrepreneur)

What you dream, he does.
Patrick Lee, writer

However soft and cuddly he may look, he has very sharp teeth.
David Thomas, correspondent, The Daily Telegraph (UK)

of Anneline Kriel Kerzner Tucker (beauty queen, housewife)

She is the Cinderella who never finds the right shoe.
Laurence Ackermann, journalist

* See also **Assassination of Chris Hani**

Anneline Kriel is the Naas Botha of beauty.
Dene Smuts, politician

of Paul Kruger (President, Transvaal Republic)

He had travelled by rail from Pretoria to Bloemfontein; the remaining ninety-six miles of the journey had been accomplished in a horse-waggon – he, whom we all honoured so greatly, had been ready to undergo even this hardship in order to visit us.
Christiaan de Wet, soldier, Second Anglo-Boer War

Only a peasant, but a great peasant whose name history will preserve in honour.
Fremdenblatt

One would have preferred to see him die full of glory amid the din of battles surrounded by his comrades-in-arms, to have seen him linked with his country's fortunes to the last, conquered with her, instead of seeking oblivion in the old world.
L'Independence Belge

The total collapse which characterises the last act in the drama of his life must of necessity prevent his figure from living in the annals of history with that halo of the heroic about it which is readily accorded by posterity to the unfortunate.
The Times

President Kruger cannot be numbered among the most enlightened and progressive rulers of the earth, and he has never shown indications of any feverish ambition to push his country higher up on the scale of civilisation; but he is astute, strong and firm; he has one or two fixed ideas which he never departs from.
Sir Francis Younghusband, journalist, explorer

of Albert Luthuli (ANC President General, Nobel Peace Prize)

To remain neutral in a situation where the laws of the land virtually criticised God for having created men of colour was the sort of thing I could not, as a Christian, tolerate.
Albert Luthuli

The real story of his life is the story of his fortitude.
Alan Paton, writer

of Felicia Mabuza-Suttle (businesswoman, TV show presenter)

I am a crusader; a crusader for change, a crusader for peace.
Felicia Mabuza-Suttle

Talk hostess supreme.
Jon Qwelane, editor

of DF Malan (Prime Minister, 1948-54)

Like most social engineers, he was somehow cold and bloodless, more comfortable with books and theories than human beings.
Rian Malan, writer

of Nelson Mandela (President, 1994-)*

There's something about this man that turns grown men into blithering idiots.
Anonymous

* See also **of Nelson Mandela & FW de Klerk.**

As soon as he renounces violence and undertakes not to start violence in South Africa, government will release him.
PW Botha, Prime Minister/State President, 1978-89 (1988)

He is revered as half George Washington and half Moses.
H Brandt Ayers, editor (USA)

Mandela is a figure of monumental integrity and humanity.
John Carlin, correspondent, The Independent (UK)

He carries around him an aura of African aristocracy and English nobility – and it works.
City Press

South Africa is fortunate to have in Mandela a leader of enormous stature, a man of firm principle and generous spirit, and a better politician than anybody dared hope for.
The Economist

Years of choosing politics over a personal life meant that finally Mandela had no personal life to choose.
Emma Gilbey, author

Far from assuming celestial status, Mr Mandela's quality is, on the contrary, so fully and absolutely that of a man, the essence of a human being in all the term should mean, could mean, but seldom does.
Nadine Gordimer, writer, Nobel Prize for Literature

He is at the epicentre of our time; ours in South Africa, and yours, wherever you are.
Nadine Gordimer

Incommunicado, without the opportunity to speak out on specific issues, Mandela in his silence became South Africa's most persuasive presence: an inspiration to blacks, a recrimination to whites.
Paul Gray, correspondent, Time International (USA)

In a time that has seen dreadful wars, systematic genocide, the disgrace of dictators and presidents, the world's thirst for moral heroism now slakes itself on the resonant presence of Mandela, the man who waited.
Pippa Green, journalist & Peter Wilhelm, editor, poet

Forged in the crucible of time and pain, his credo of faith and forgiveness has moved profoundly the community of nations.
Leadership

Is he a nationalist or is he communist controlled?
Louis le Grange, politician

I don't think there is much history can say about me. I just want to be remembered as part of that collective.
Nelson Mandela

I am a convicted prisoner, serving a sentence of five years for leaving the country without a permit and for inciting people to go on strike at the end of May 1961.
Nelson Mandela (Rivonia Treason Trial, 1964)

His warmth came through the glass separating us.
Zindzi Mandela, housewife, daughter of Winnie & Nelson Mandela

He is a most impressive man – handsome, tall, relaxed, very much in control of himself.
Helen Suzman, liberal, retired politician

This is a man who would be courteous to Adolf Hitler if he ran into him.
Phillip van Niekerk, journalist

Nelson Mandela is the quintessential Georgian gentleman, the freedom fighter with impeccable manners.
Phillip van Niekerk

Anyone who wants to talk to me on the basis that Mandela is the leader of black South Africa can forget it.
John Vorster, Prime Minister, 1966-78 (1975)

of Nelson Mandela (President, 1994-) **& FW de Klerk** (State President, 1989-94; Deputy President, 1994-)*

Brothers in political crime.
Mangosuthu Buthelezi, IFP leader, politician

Both Mandela and De Klerk are remarkable stories and together they are a stern rebuke to the cynics of the world.
Bill Clinton, President (USA)

On major issues such as nation-building, we are finding it possible to work together.
FW de Klerk

Mandela and De Klerk have been forced into a fascinating pas de deux, co-ordinating their steps while not so secretly resenting the necessity of their partnership.
Paul Gray, correspondent, Time International (USA)

We are going to face the problems of this country together.
Nelson Mandela

* See also **FW de Klerk, Nelson Mandela.**

I think we are a shining example to the entire world of people drawn from different racial groups who have a common loyalty, a common love, to their common country.
Nelson Mandela

I am proud to hold your hand and to work together.
Nelson Mandela

Some of our most unpleasant quarrels have been on a one-on-one basis – we've said very cruel things to each other.
Nelson Mandela

Mandela and De Klerk were delivered to each other by history.
Carl Niehaus, politician

The image of partners-in-travail is the one that lingers.
Stanley Uys, journalist

of Winnie Mandela (politician)

The people love Winnie because she's a warlord.
Anonymous

She's a wonderful role model for women.
Julie Belafonte, wife of Harry Belafonte

Mandela herself is a political figure of almost Shakespearean tragic proportions.
Dennis Davis, lawyer

The fire of hatred for the white regime that burned inside her was fed until it raged almost out of control.
Richard Ellis, correspondent, The Sunday Times (UK)

A woman of extraordinary faith and love of God and of country.
Edward Kennedy, politician (USA)

She endured the persecutions heaped upon her by the Government with exemplary fortitude and never wavered from her commitment to the struggle for freedom.
Nelson Mandela, President, May 1994-

I am not Mandela's political creation.
Winnie Mandela

No one is prepared to write her off in South Africa, where the warping effect of apartheid has produced a society marked by large moral grey areas.
Neil McMahon, journalist

Time was when blacks and a large number of whites saw this serenely beautiful woman as a Madonna figure.
Hilary Prendini Toffoli & Gus Silber, journalists

Winnie Mandela is no angel, although she could have been.
Jane Raphaely, editor, publisher

She showed herself on a number of occasions to be a calm, composed, deliberate and unblushing liar.
Michael Stegmann, judge

The undisputed queen of survivors.
Paul Stober & Ferial Haffajee, journalists

She looks excellent in the back seat of a Mercedes Benz – it suits her – that's her style.
Jaco Vandenberg, dress designer

Her statements may be those of an embittered, impassioned and ambitious woman, but her actions are not those of a lunatic.
Andrea Vinassa, journalist

of Lucas Mangope (former president, Bophuthatswana)

Courting him for profit or for votes, or even in the hopes of feeding local residents, is an obscenity that must be ended.
John Seiler, political scientist

of Eugène Marais (writer)

Eugène Marais was a human community in the person of one man.
Robert Ardrey, writer

of Ray McCauley (cleric)

He would have been the Studebaker King in the Sixties and the Hollywood fixit man in the Seventies.
Pnina Fenster, journalist

I'm selling Jesus. It may sound coarse, but I'm selling the Lord. I really believe in the product.
Ray McCauley

Ray is like John the Baptist in a tailor-made suit.
Ron Steele, PR

of Alfred Milner (British High Commissioner)

With his long, thin face and downcast grey-brown eyes, he looked older than his forty-four years, and sadder than a brilliantly successful diplomatist should be.
Thomas Pakenham (Lord Longford), writer

There was a whiff of the Athenaeum and the British Museum about him.
Thomas Pakenham

of Jacqui Mofokeng (beauty queen)

Jacqui is a Mofokeng, the Mmaphoka of her people, which means that she is the 'wind of strength'.
Anonymous

She doesn't drizzle – no, she's all fizz.
Glenn Cowley, journalist

of Nat Nakasa (journalist)

His death must be laid at the door of the people who made him take an exit permit – this government.
Nadine Gordimer, writer, Nobel Prize for Literature

of Beyers Naudé (cleric)

His only tendency I have not been able to like, is his tendency to almost like to be on the losing side.
Harry Oppenheimer, businessman

of Harry Oppenheimer (businessman)

He is deemed to be a safe target.
Ken Owen, editor

of Ken Owen (editor)

Experience and misfortune have made him cynical.
Paul Bell, journalist

It is his fiercest dogma, the liberalism of Ken Owen, and, if at times it is a perplexing one, that must be put down to the ideological ignorance of those who might sit in judgement on him.
David Beresford, correspondent, The Guardian

Who is Ken Owen?
CF Eloff, judge

He looks a little like WC Fields: pliable but pugnacious.
Gus Silber, journalist

The last of the red-hot liberals.
Style

of Alan Paton (writer)

He joined politics and got stuck in an old railway engine at a siding.
Vusamazulu Credo Mutwa, storyteller, sangoma

Alan Paton stood his ground and we are fortunate, in this faithless century, to live in the shadow of such a man.
Ken Owen, editor

I grew up with an abhorrence of authoritarianism, especially the authoritarianism of the State, and a love of liberty, especially liberty within the State.
Alan Paton

of Andries Pretorius (voortrekker)

This man has been sent by God. He will help us take revenge.
Mev. Piet Retief

of Jon Qwelane (editor)

For far too long I have been the native who caused all the trouble and now my position has been a little bit upgraded to becoming the nigger in the woodpile.
Jon Qwelane

of Cyril Ramaphosa (politician)

Comrade Breakthrough.
Anonymous

His smile is small, a careful impassivity hiding whatever he might be feeling.
Wessel Ebersohn, journalist

Ramaphosa combines an outward charm with a ruthless political instinct.
Anton Harber, editor

Being a former township boy, he knows how to hustle.
Bafana Khumalo, journalist

He dismisses political ambitions with an almost languid diffidence.
Peter Wilhelm, editor, poet

of Cecil John Rhodes (Imperialist)

Watch that man: he is the future man of South Africa and possibly of the world.
Saul Solomon, MP (1891)

He is an adventurer of a very magnificent sort.
Transvaal Advertiser (1890)

Rhodes was the worst England had to offer.
WT Tyler, critic

of Jonty Rhodes (cricketer)

The Star of India.
Anonymous

Every time you look up, he's there.
Allan Border, Australian cricketer

The only player in history to build an international career on a flashy run-out and a crooked grin.
Peter Davies, journalist

When he comes before the Great Tallyman in the Sky, he is likely to report a chanceless innings.
Drew Forrest, journalist

His presence on either side of the wicket is positively intimidating for an opposing batsman seeking the quick single.
Ian Hawkey, journalist

He's become as South African a symbol as braaivleis and sunny skies.
Jacqui L'Ange, journalist

It's as if people forget that J Rhodes can bat a little bit too.
Jonty Rhodes

I rise to pressure and I can rise to the big occasion.
Jonty Rhodes

There was never much doubt from the teenies on the terraces about the most important figure in South African cricket.
Jon Swift, journalist

All Rhodes lead to Jonty.
Jon Swift

of John Robbie (talk show host)

He looks like a preposterously fit, attractive, self-assured, energetic, macho 37-year-old, a bit highly strung and excitable maybe, with a touch of tension around the eyes, but that's par for the course nowadays.
Hilary Prendini Toffoli, journalist

of Albie Sachs (politician)

I represent the constituency of the flowers, the mountains and the sea.
Albie Sachs

of Olive Schreiner (writer)

The artist is very strong in her, she looks at things rather than *lives* them.
Elizabeth Cobb, housewife

It was curious to note that she seemed unaware that much of what she said was common knowledge – it all came pouring out interspersed with gems of thought which flashed light amid the commonplace like diamonds in a dust heap.
Emily Hobhouse, humanitarian

She was self-revealing, but she could not reveal all that she mentally was.
Rev Robinson, cleric

I don't know what to make of myself.
Olive Schreiner

of Tokyo Sexwale (politician)

I'm a gladiator for the people.
Tokyo Sexwale

of Shaka (King of the Zulus)

A savage in the truest sense of the word, a monster, a compound of vice and ferocity without one virtue to redeem his name from the infamy to which history will consign it.
Nathaniel Isaacs, trader

of Walter Sisulu (politician)

A dour-looking figure; short, stocky, often hidden in the folds of a wide-lapelled overcoat, bespectacled and with a habit of biting his bottom lip in between making terse polemical statements.
Tom Lodge, writer, academic

of Frederik Van Zyl Slabbert (academic)

He's no Ross Perot dressed in a sexy safari-suit.
Sean Badal, journalist

Not only is every woman in the country in love with him, but men like him for his ruggerbugger slang.
Jane Fraser, journalist (Australian)

His departure was sudden, self-indulgent, politically indefensible – and history will in time deliver its verdict.
Ken Owen, editor (on Van Zyl Slabbert's abrupt resignation from both parliament and as DP leader)

Perhaps I am an Andy Capp liberal: a man with many mistakes, but being wrong is not one of them.
Frederik Van Zyl Slabbert

of Jan Christian Smuts (Prime Minister, 1919-24 & 1939-48)

The Oriental despot.
Anonymous

The handyman of the Empire.
Anonymous

The Father of the RAF.
Anonymous

It was of the greatest value to me to take counsel with a statesman of these rare qualities of vision, wisdom and courage.
Winston Churchill, Prime Minister (UK)

It is wonderful that so clever a man should not be clever enough to be reasonably straight.
Percy Fitzpatrick, politician, writer

His hands dripped with the blood of his own people.
Barry Hertzog, Prime Minister, 1924-39

Smuts was a very clever, a very cunning man.
Henning Klopper, founder of the Broederbond.

He is the greatest traitor this country has ever known.
Arrie Paulus, Mine Workers' Union

He was like an explorer, always peering forward into the uncharted future.
Marquess of Salisbury, politician (UK)

I have neither tact nor patience, and you must take me for what I am worth.
Jan Christian Smuts

A type of Afrikaner who uses every effort to keep the races apart.
The Star (1904)

Such men are rare.
Lord Todd, academic (UK)

of Robert Sobukwe (PAC founding president)

Robert Sobukwe was one of the great, lost leaders of South Africa.
Wessel Ebersohn, journalist

of Helen Suzman (liberal, retired politician)

Hers was a voice of reason amid the dreadful baying of the scum rising around her on those plush parliamentary benches.
Andrew Donaldson, journalist

A bright star in a dark Chamber.
Albert Luthuli, ANC President General, Nobel Peace Prize

PW Botha once called me a vicious little cat and I thought that was very accurate.
Helen Suzman

Mrs Suzman was able to survive, magnificently, for 36 years as an MP because she did not allow herself to be consumed by bitterness and venom, even when surrounded by some of the most awful men it has been anyone's misfortune to encounter.
Stanley Uys, journalist

of Oliver Tambo (ANC President)

The gentlemanly, old-school arch-diplomat was the living embodiment of the ANC-in-exile.
Anton Harber, editor

He was my brother, my comrade, my friend and my colleague.
Nelson Mandela, President, 1994-

Martin Schneider (journalist): If I interviewed Oliver Tambo, if I critically examined him on such issues as Press freedom

under another government, and I then went to the State President (PW Botha) for his comments and I wrote a balanced story, would that be acceptable?
Stoffel Botha (then Minister of Home Affairs and Communications): No, it will not be. It will elevate Tambo to a status he doesn't deserve. *(1987)*

I think he got his first pair of shoes at the age of nine.
Tselane Tambo, actress

of Eugene Terre'Blanche (AWB leader)

Right now I've got to remind myself to breathe. I'm impaled on the blue flames of his blowtorch eyes, you see.
Jani Allan, journalist (1988)

Eugene Terre'Blanche doesn't walk into a room: he takes occupation of it.
Jani Allan

If I had to choose between Terre'Blanche's bottom and a chimp's, I'd take the chimp's.
Jani Allan

The man would have made a fortune in the circus if he could have stayed on his horse.
Breyten Breytenbach, poet, writer

A man still looking into the last century at a time when every thinking Afrikaner is looking into the next century.
Alan Cowell, journalist

Essentially he sees himself as a son, a child of his people, an Afrikaner nationalist first: all else is secondary.
Wessel Ebersohn, journalist

The man in the holey green undies has become a pathetic, quixotic figure.
Gavin Evans, journalist

Well-pickled actor, orator, and comedian, with severe dislike for communists, blondes and horses.
Arthur Goldstuck, journalist

In the glare of television floodlights, he is a razor-fanged silver jackal howling at the moon.
Hilary Prendini Toffoli & Gus Silber, journalists

I am precisely what the Fatherland expects of me.
Eugene Terre'Blanche

I do not fit into little red sports cars.
Eugene Terre'Blanche

of Andries Treurnicht (CP leader)

The world's only fossil with a million followers, yet he can't find his own home.
Arthur Goldstuck, journalist

The truth is that he was a leader who seldom led.
Sunday Times

He had the Afrikaner's unique ability to read the writing on the wall while standing with his back to it.
Stanley Uys, journalist

He was against the tide of a historical saga that is bigger than all of us.
Phillip van Niekerk, journalist

of Steve Tshwete (politician)

He was a sensible man even though he was ANC.
Danie Craven, SA Rugby Board President

Words like charisma and presence will have to suffice.
John Perlman, journalist

of Desmond Tutu (cleric, Archbishop of Cape Town)

A mad baboon with a dress on.
Anonymous CP spokesman

This dynamic, diminutive man has made himself available because others asked that he should, to be a light in the darkness and to help lead us into the dawn of a new day.
Michael Nuttall, cleric (1986)

The archbishop has an unerring instinct for schmaltz, for the tear on the cheek of the child, for the single raindrop in the rose.
Ken Owen, editor

I was this man with the big nose and the easy name who personalised the South African situation.
Desmond Tutu

Please do not be angry with God because of me.
Desmond Tutu

of Shado Twala (disc jockey)

She is, quite simply, too sexy for her shirt.
Andrea Vinassa, journalist

of Gillian van Houten (TV presenter)

She was just sitting there, showing a delicious amount of alabaster cleavage, asking her usual sweetly bland questions and twinkling her amazing black eyes at him, as if she were actually interested in his answers.
Hilary Prendini Toffoli, journalist

of HF Verwoerd (Prime Minister, 1958-66)

No native South African adopted Nationalist ideology with more fervour than this son of a missionary.
David Harrison, documentary film maker, author

Verwoerd dealt only in revealed truth, and although he was undoubtedly a humble and pious Christian by his own lights, he made sure that he did the revealing when it came to matters of black and white in South Africa.
Joseph Lelyveld, editor (USA)

The author of our calamity.
Albert Luthuli, ANC President General, Nobel Peace Prize

Verwoerd never won any black heart that I know of.
Alan Paton, writer

Doubt was unknown to him.
AN Pelzer, academic

Had he lived he would have gone down in history as a reformer.
Oom Koos Potgieter, politician

He rode apartheid too hard in all its pettiness to lend verisimilitude to his larger image.
The Star

It is one of those ironies of our history that Dr HF Verwoerd is nowadays held up as a great oppressor whereas his one aim in life was to lead people to freedom.
Wilhelm Verwoerd, academic (and grandson)

of Constand Viljoen (soldier, politician)

A fitness fanatic, and the sexiest thing the right has to offer (he can see his toes).
Charlotte Bauer, journalist

The only people who care are the people like General Viljoen who have seen war.
Jan Breytenbach, soldier

He may not be astute politically – he is a soldier – but he is a man of integrity.
Nelson Mandela, President, May 1994-

If I can give assistance in peacemaking, in peacekeeping, then this may be a good way of ending off my life.
Constand Viljoen

His generally amiable manner belies his almost mythical warrior image among right-wingers, but occasionally the steel is evident.
Chris Whitfield & John Soderlund, journalists

of John Vorster (Prime Minister, 1966-78)

A great man who missed the chance to be a great statesman.
Mangosuthu Buthelezi, IFP leader, politician

He found himself psychologically impotent to move away from the Afrikaner Nationalist Ideology.
Alan Paton, writer

So extremist were his ideas that not even the nationalist could stomach them at first, in 1946.
Time (1966)

He is never too busy to listen and to help us. But we have to do our own homework.
Pieter Vorster, son of John Vorster (in 1966, when 14 years old)

of Kepler Wessels (cricketer)

A woeful lack of enterprise.
Anonymous

Captain Cautious.
Anonymous

The most unimaginative captain in the history of South African cricket, one who would be happy with 50 draws in a 50-test series as long as he did not lose.
Anonymous cricketer

It is little wonder that he has again been lambasted for his blind negativeness.
Mike Coward, journalist (Australian)

The vivid picture conjured up by many is Wessels standing at first slip, feet crossed, arms folded, a frown creasing his forehead and staring bleakly at the ground while furiously chewing gum.
Jackie McGlew, former cricketer

If conservatism is indeed a national trait, Wessels has been endowed in abundance.
Jon Swift, journalist

Obstinate, unyielding in his approach and unwilling to listen to the advice of others.
Darrell Thomson, journalist

Pets

Give them (dogs) reasonable grub, a few pats and attention, and they'll go through fire for you: that's my idea of a good friend.
Andy Andrews, businessman

It's little they know of life who cannot guess the secret springs of loneliness and love that prompt the keeping of a trifling pet; who do not know what moves a man who daily takes his chances of life and death – man whose 'breath is in his nostrils' – to lay his cheek against the muzzle of his comrade dog, and in the trackless miles of wilderness feel he has a friend.
Percy Fitzpatrick, politician, writer

Even if they have fox terriers, which haven't got the confidence to attack, they want them to learn to bark when someone comes near.
Schalk Jacobs, dog trainer

My horse... look after Somerset.
Dick King, wagon driver (after his epic Durban/Grahamstown ride. Somerset died)

A lot of us are having trouble persuading our Rottweilers to adapt to the new South Africa.
Krisjan Lemmer (columnist, Weekly Mail & Guardian)

The Maltese Poodle, a breed so fierce and loyal that it has been known to carry on barking for up to six hours after being locked in a garden shed by the person who has just ransacked your property.
Gus Silber, journalist

Places

You can't have an airport named after John Vorster, or a railway siding called Kafferstad.
Franco Frescura, academic

I think I can safely say we've eradicated the word 'Kaffir' from all official place names in South Africa.
Elwyn Jenkins, National Place Names Committee

Some Anglo-Saxons simplify a place name such as Mtubatuba to Mtubatwice, but such opportunities are rare.
Graham Linscott, journalist

Names reflect the cultural and linguistic history of everyone in the country.
Peter Raper, toponymist

The history of place names in South Africa is in many ways a history of petty spite, revenge, colonialist arrogance and roughshod trampling on other people's heroes and traditions.
Gus Silber, journalist

of Alexandra

Alexandra is uncomfortably close to white areas. The neat, spacious white homes with their manicured lawns and double garages are little more than a stone's throw from the mean, unmade streets of Alexandra where blacks live up to seven to a room in houses without electricity or water.
Nicholas Ashford, correspondent, The Times

of Bloemfontein

I did not myself consider the place much superior to any other town, and I would not have thought it a matter of any great importance if it had been destroyed.
Christiaan de Wet, soldier, Second Anglo-Boer War

of Cape Town

I love these bold strokes with which the Almighty has separated the dry land from the sea in his chaos. The Bay opens beautifully at the foot of the mountains, while the Hottentot hills at 20 miles distance rise in forms so stupendously eccentric that I look at them with admiration every time I see them.
Lady Anne Barnard, socialite

This Cape is a most stately thing, and the fairest Cape we saw in the whole circumference of the earth.
Chronicler of Sir Francis Drake's voyage (1580)

This city skinders its own
secretions,
its salty masala of sea and
semen.
Lisa Combrinck

The doors of a Bioscope entertainment are open, and the crowd awaiting admission and jostling each other as they get tickets, includes representatives of every colour from the light-haired, fair-complexioned Scandinavian sailor or English workman to the sooty-black of the Shangaan, and if he enters the overcrowded room and braves the foetid atmosphere, he will find no distinction made, all and every colour occupy the same seats, cheek by jowl, and sometimes on each other's knees.
Maurice S Evans, segregationist

Living in a city of no consequence induces a pleasant lethargy and a benign tolerance in even the most sociopathic.
Tony Karon, journalist

It's genteel, elitist and frightfully smug.
Hilary Prendini Toffoli, journalist

A great plaine, pleasant in situation, which, with the fragrant herbs, variety of flowers and flourishing verdure of all things, seems a terrestrial Paradise. It is called the Table of the Cape.
Samuel Purchas, cleric (1611)

Cape Town has always been a bit flaky.
Lin Sampson, journalist

This is a nipped off bit of Africa, stripped and soldered and separate.
Lin Sampson

High up by the lighthouse, watching the seagulls pondering over the waves, I thought of the yearning of those travellers on

the open sea who faced this sandy beach for the first time or further south, where there was nothing human left any more, and had to climb back to the belly of the earth to find a soul, a mind, a heart.
George Seferis, poet, Nobel Prize for Literature (Greece)

A poor, niggery, yellow-faced, half-bred sort of place, with an ugly Dutch flavour about it.
Anthony Trollope, British post office official, novelist

of Cato Manor

The tin shacks of Cato Manor clung precariously as if for dear life to the hillsides and slopes overlooking a stream called Mkhumbane, whose greenish slimy waters flowed eastward and southward on its sluggish journey toward the Indian Ocean, embracing to its already heavily polluted bosom all the scum and filth of innumerable shacks without proper sewage, without proper toilets or plumbing, on hot days as unbearably hot as overheated ovens, on rainy days as leaky as open sieves.
Lewis Nkosi, writer, academic

of District Six

District Six was the symbol of South African evil.
Anthony Heard, editor

of Grahamstown

This great cultural mecca dedicated to the British settlers who brought the civilising influence of newspapers and craftsmanship clearly suffers from historical amnesia.
Heather Robertson, journalist

The population is a strange mixture of lounging officers, idle tradesmen (merchants, I beg their pardon), drunken soldiers, and still more drunken settlers.
Cowper Rose, author

of Hillbrow

The delinquent suburb is asking questions faster than we can supply the answers.
John Michell, editor

While the rest of Johannesburg sleeps, Hillbrow tries to.
Gus Silber, journalist

of Johannesburg

Monte Carlo superimposed on Sodom and Gomorrah.
Anonymous

Manhattan in the Veld.
Anonymous

The financial Gibraltar of South Africa.
Barney Barnato, mining magnate

A mining town whose lode is exhausted.
James Clarke, journalist

Driving around Jo-burg, wander downtown, mooch about the shopping malls in the whites' laager north of the city, and you'll see nerves.
Nick Gordon, journalist

If you don't know how to make Johannesburg, you're unlikely to make it anywhere.
David Kavana, journalist

This is South Africa's racial front line.
Graham Leach, correspondent, BBC Radio

It is the unholy Jerusalem that no one can relinquish, not because of its history or its saints but because of its wealth.
Joseph Lelyveld, editor (USA)

The city has spawned – against all odds – a select group of managers and proprietors who give it class, style and daring without sacrificing a jot of decency or business ethic.
Hugh Murray, publisher

Johannesburg was built by the White technical know-how and enterprise plus the indispensable co-operation of Black labour.
Nat Nakasa, journalist

All roads lead to Johannesburg.
Alan Paton, writer

In Johannesburg, what matters is what you do, how well you do it, and how much money you make.
Hilary Prendini Toffoli, journalist

Do you mean to say that there is not a man in Johannesburg who will get up and lead a revolution and not mind if he's shot?
Cecil John Rhodes, Imperialist (referring to the proposed Jameson Raid)

It has become a hypermarket of the heart.
Lin Sampson, journalist

Hell.
Olive Schreiner, writer

As the train turns there are colours of ripe fruit in the sky.
George Seferis, poet, Nobel Prize for Literature (Greece)

Johannesburg doesn't ask to be liked, it seeks to be served.
Can Themba, journalist, writer

of the Karoo

It is a place where the day starts lightly but by midday there is a hammer of heat.
Lin Sampson, journalist

To the stranger, oppressive, weird, fantastic, it is to the man who has lived with it a scene for the loss of which no other on earth compensates.
Olive Schreiner, writer

of Kimberley

Beneath your feet lies the entirety of the Kimberley mine, so open, so manifest, and so uncovered that if your eyes were good enough you might examine the separate operations of each of the three or four thousand human beings who work down there.
Anthony Trollope, British post office official, novelist

If there be a place on God's earth in which a man can thoroughly make or mar himself within a space of time, it is the town of Kimberley. I know of no spot more odious in every way.
Anthony Trollope

of Knysna

Knysna's greatest asset is the sense of luxurious unreality it evokes.
Marilyn Keegan, journalist

of Natal

The hills were drenched in treachery and blood.
Anthony Heard, editor

Natal whites can be every bit as racist as the most conservative Afrikaners, as anyone who went to school there can confirm.
Anthony Heard

For all too long in its history it tended to be sundered from the rest of South Africa by mutual ignorance and mountains.
Jan Hofmeyr ('Oom Jan'), politician (1931)

I cannot fancy a more charming spot; I think I scarcely ever saw one exceeding it; it really looked like a fairy land, with Arcadian beauties on every side: the scattered huts of the natives – the cattle indulging in the rich pasturage – cultivated patches rising ever and anon on the inequalities of the surface – the adjacent hills towering one above the other in all the magnificence of picturesque form – presented such a combination of objects that we were almost perplexed in admiration of their variety.
Nathaniel Isaacs, trader

Natal boasts a host of laughing streams gurgling between tree-clad hills, so beautiful they make you ache inside.
Aggrey Klaaste, editor

If you grow up in Natal you are liable to experience, from time to time, a nostalgia for lives never lived.
Patrick Lee, writer

The contrast between past glory and present poverty could not be starker.
Shula Marks, historian

On a clear day you could see the white plumes of smoke rising for miles around in a shimmer of brilliant sunshine from the brown clusters of village huts, the broken furrows of red earth marking the dongas where the rain had bitten deeply into the earth.
Lewis Nkosi, writer, academic

These hills are grass-covered and rolling, and they are lovely beyond any singing of it.
Alan Paton, writer

of the Orange Free State

A territory untouched by modern civilisation for thousands of years.
Gus Silber, journalist

of Orania

A self-declared independent homeland for people who find the Orange Free State too exciting.
Gus Silber, journalist

of Pretoria

It's an open city. Open streets, open spaces, open arms, open minds.
Advertisement

May locusts devour their jacaranda trees!
Breyten Breytenbach, poet, writer

It's safer and quieter than Johannesburg, the odd trendy soul does emerge on a winter night and sometimes the odd jacaranda does wiggle its hips a little.
Adam Levin, journalist

It is called the RSA ('die Republiek' for short), and it is a place where nearly everybody dresses in uniform and most things happen in triplicate.
Ivor Powell, journalist

In Pretoria you can walk in the city centre in the evening without your ankle holster.
Hilary Prendini Toffoli, journalist

Sunday in Pretoria – is that what they mean by capital punishment?
Mike Reed, journalist

One has the impression that sleep, a strange god in a white blouse and a spray in its hand, is walking beside every pedestrian, beside every car, every moving thing and spraying it with an odourless drug.
George Seferis, poet, Nobel Prize for Literature (Greece)

of Robben Island

See Robben Island

of Sophiatown

The little Paris of the Transvaal.
Anonymous

She looks like a bombed city.
Benson Dyantyi, journalist

The swarming, cacophonous, strutting, brawling, vibrating life of the Sophiatown that was.
Can Themba, journalist, writer

Some places it was such as dreams are made of.
Can Themba

What people have thought to be the brazenness of Sophiatown has really been its clean-faced frankness.
Can Themba

Soweto*

It's only when you are in Soweto that you experience the dust that the toyi-toyi whips up.
Anonymous

There is actually no life worth living in Soweto.
Solly Madlala, Soweto resident

Soweto was one big apartheid tragedy.
Rian Malan, writer

Take an area like Soweto: we would rather cut it out and accept that this is a black area under its own autonomous government, the form of which is still under discussion, which would be politically linked with other parts of the population, than include those people in any unitary system with whites.
Andries Treurnicht, CP leader

* See also **Soweto 1976.**

Police

When the price of books, or petrol, or electricity goes up by a few cents, the public is furious and we see immediate – and effective – protests. But when policemen are gunned down, we don't hear a peep from the public.
David Bruce, policeman

The police lashed Africans on the streets in unprovoked and indiscriminate fashion.
Anthony Heard, editor

We know the South African Police Force are trying to create a fresh new image, but no one wants a Fairy Squad consisting of gun-bearing ballet dancers and hairdressers to come to the rescue in dangerous situations.
Hustler

It is important for the police themselves and whoever is in government to study the past, so they can best deal with the present and the future.
Aggrey Klaaste, editor

We are the bridge to democracy and to stabilising it thereafter.
Craig Kotze, policeman

The police are the sort of people who wear shorts, who went into action in the Western desert with no shirts on, despite what the rule book said.
Jimmy Kruger, politician, one-time Minister of Police

South African cops are a bit dim-witted and heavy-handed, but they aren't suicidal.
Rian Malan, writer

The South African Police is a very secretive brotherhood of paranoid authoritarians.
Rian Malan

These guys don't read newspapers or understand limp-wristed subtleties like politics or propaganda.
Rian Malan

Every time a policeman looses a round of birdshot, or swings a quirt, he recruits another child to the cause.
Ken Owen, editor

The South African Police would leave no stone unturned to see that nothing disturbed the even terror of their lives.
Tom Sharpe, writer

The time has undoubtedly come for the perception of the police as a single, ravening beast, to be destroyed.
David Strydom, policeman

Traditionally defensive and hostile to critics, the South African Police have been slow to learn that firm policing and the rule of law do not have to mean the sjambok or the jackboot, or that being held accountable for their behaviour is not an attack on the very necessary institution of a police force.
Phillip van Niekerk, journalist

They are dedicated to their task and are prepared to fulfil our motto: We protect you and we serve you.
Adriaan Vlok, politician

Politics/Politicians

During the years, all political parties have come with beautiful promises.
Anonymous

In the end revolution had nothing to do with politics and politics could not tolerate revolution.
Breyten Breytenbach, poet, writer

Politics is the maintenance of power, the administration of power even when it's done by good people.
Breyten Breytenbach

It is only by *klapping* them (politicians) against the *kop* from left and from right that we can help them move down the straight and narrow – without getting their hands jammed in the till.
Breyten Breytenbach

I have no private army and I have never used any form of intimidation as a method of political action.
Mangosuthu Buthelezi, IFP leader, politician

What is there in South Africa, I wonder, that makes blackguards of all who get involved in its politics?
Joseph Chamberlain, Colonial Secretary

Politicians will never admit to anything disadvantageous to themselves, and it is the duty of newspapers to tell people when a politician wishes to remain silent.
William Deedes (Lord Deedes of Aldington), politician, editor (UK)

Politics isn't for sissies. It's robust and I'm not overly sensitive.
FW de Klerk, State President, 1989-94; Deputy President, 1994-

Politicians don't tamper with recipes when they are met with applause.
Willem de Klerk, businessman, academic

Politicians, like clergymen, doctors, economists, and many others, love to mystify their role; it makes them seem important and stops the people 'interfering'.
Cosmas Desmond, cleric

Politicians can be environmentally hazardous, to say the least.
Julienne du Toit, journalist

Politicians don't have sole rights on jargon.
Pnina Fenster, journalist

Political fashions change overnight and today's centrist majority is tomorrow's radical minority.
Chris Gibbons, broadcaster

Don't trust the politicians. I should know – I'm one myself.
Chris Hani, Umkhonto we Sizwe chief of staff, SACP general secretary

Politics remains the backbone of South African reality, even if it feels like a strait-jacket.
Christopher Hope, writer

The South African political problem rates at PhD level – if British or American politicians want to graduate as Masters, they should try operating here, where there are few easy answers.
Derek Keys, businessman, politician

A bucket of pitiless hypocrites.
Robert Kirby, satirist

Every politician knows that you sit opposite your opponents – your enemies are the ones sitting behind you.
Hernus Kriel, politician

Politicians do not risk referendums unless they are sure they can win them.
Patrick Laurence, journalist

Politics for whites is going to be like weather; sometimes pleasant, sometimes infuriating, but beyond the realm of emotional or rational involvement.
Patrick Lee, writer

Politicians are not lovers.
Winnie Mandela, politician

One of the things that makes a good politician is financial independence.
Peter Mokaba, politician

A political stance is a posture and doesn't say much about what you personally believe.
Es'kia Mphahlele, academic, writer

Once you become a politician you become a merchant of hatred, a pedlar of fear, a liar.
Vusamazulu Credo Mutwa, storyteller, sangoma

With all the various parties jostling for position in this land of ours, it's going to take a code of many colours to satisfy all the demands.
Jenni Newman, PR

Politicians think they control everything.
Harry Oppenheimer, businessman

No political movement can survive without a healthy dose of humbug.
Ken Owen, editor

The curse of South African politics has always been the search for thousand-year solutions.
Ken Owen

In politics the emphasis is usually on the next election rather than the next generation.
Jack Penn, surgeon, philosopher, artist

Politicians can buy the votes of the unscrupulous, but they cannot buy gratitude.
Jack Penn

Politics is like a combination of Chinese checkers and Russian roulette – a synthesis of intelligence and chance.
Jack Penn

Let's raise huge echoing jeers to the plague of politicians, the moralising prigs, the scheming weasels on the make, oafs almost all.
John Platter, wine farmer, writer

That feeling of political *déjà-vu* is really just the familiar smell of bad faith.
Ivor Powell, journalist

It is the preserve of politics to promise free lunches.
Reg Rumney, journalist

The mental image of our politicians on their dimpled hands and knees scrabbling for every cent they can wring out of us would be amusing if it were not so sickeningly accurate.
FH Snow

Community politics is what will transform this country.
Clem Sunter, businessman, scenario strategist

Politicians eat and thrive on the freedom of others.
Pieter-Dirk Uys, satirist

Political correctness could become the concrete condom on the weapon of satire.
Pieter-Dirk Uys

In politics, as in romance, never trust a man who says: trust me.
Phillip van Niekerk, journalist

Neither black nor white politicians could plausibly be described as nature's democrats: neither group has the history, culture or traditions which would easily predispose it to democracy.
Patti Waldmeir, correspondent, Financial Times (UK)

There was a time when I used to proclaim as the first principle of South African politics: 'Expect the worst'.
David Welsh, academic

Traditionally our politics has been a zero-sum game: winners take all.
David Welsh

Politics is a game of paradoxes and ironies.
David Welsh

Everybody knew that politics after apartheid would get boring.
Chris Whitfield, journalist

Poverty

Real, spiralling mass poverty is the enemy of democracy.
Mangosuthu Buthelezi, IFP leader, politician

Whereas white South Africans compare the prosperity of South African blacks favourably with Zambian blacks, South African blacks compare their prosperity with South African whites, and therein they see injustice.
Nicholas Fairbairn, politician (UK)

Poverty is not an excuse, all it does is delay the process of reaching one's goals.
Zola Kananda, businesswoman, TV presenter

If you want to continue living in unbridled poverty without clothes and food – then go and drink in the shebeens.
Nelson Mandela, President, May 1994-

There are many kinds of poverty and everyone who lived under apartheid was in some way or other diminished by it.
Jane Raphaely, editor, publisher

The squatter camps of Cape Town are the new face of South African poverty.
Jonathan Steele, journalist (UK)

Poverty is not some morally neutral phenomenon which needs merely to be understood. It is an evil that must be rooted out.
Francis Wilson & Mamphela Ramphele, academics

Power

I believe in the devolution of power.
PW Botha, Prime Minister/State President, 1978-89

We have no intention of handing over power to a bunch of Marxists.
Pik Botha, politician (1986)

The greed for power – the ancient lust for privilege fed on the political pornography of intimidation – has now obscured the vision of a unified democratic state which was to embody and to express our shared South Africanness.
Breyten Breytenbach, poet, writer

Steynberg's overscaled Strijdom head with its sundial shadow must surely be one of the most naked and banal expressions of political power to dominate any public place.
Neville Dubow, artist, academic

Nowhere does the iconography of power emerge in a South African context with greater clarity than in the piazza of the State Theatre in Pretoria.
Neville Dubow

Whoever is in power, they are going to abuse the powerless, so there's always a struggle.
Sheena Duncan, Black Sash, SA Council of Churches

Power must be shared in such a way that domination of any constitutional entity by others is impossible.
Chris Heunis, politician

When a group has entrenched itself in power, then it regards its rights and privileges as sacrosanct.
Robert Mugabe, President (Zimbabwe)

Power is seductive, and the closer powerful men get to renouncing it, the more inventive they become in finding ways to delay elections.
Victor Nell, community psychologist

The powerful people are the politicians.
Harry Oppenheimer, businessman

There is nothing wrong with ambition, and power is necessary in the right hands.
Jack Penn, surgeon, philosopher, artist

In deadlock, power frustrates power.
Frederik Van Zyl Slabbert, academic

A balance needs to be maintained between civil and physical power.
Pierre Steyn, soldier

Physical power is reserved for the state in its role as objective keeper of law and order.
Stoffel van der Merwe, politician

After decades of authoritarian rule, it is chilling to discover how dangerous a power vacuum can be.
Phillip van Niekerk, journalist

Praise

Public praise is very pleasant, and it does not necessarily offend one's desire to remain a private person.
Alan Paton, writer

Popularity with the masses can never be a motive for principled action.
Franklin Sonn, educationist, ambassador

The Press

Sub-editors? I can pick them up in the gutter any time I want them.
Anonymous newspaper manager

The editor's indecision is final.
Anonymous journalist (referring to The Star's stance on the 1983 referendum)

The unprofessionalism of some South African journalists is only matched by their malice.
Jani Allan, journalist

Lurking with the lunatic fringe is what a journalist loves best.
Jani Allan

The news is never the whole truth.
Denis Beckett, journalist

It could almost be characterised as 'frontier journalism': crude, earthy, but somehow more satisfying.
David Beresford, correspondent, The Guardian

The alternative Press is locked into an unending, precarious battle for financial survival – under-capitalised, over-dependent on inexperienced staff and victims of monopoly control of printing and distribution.
David Beresford

Will they (the international press) stand up and say to the outside world there is still a free press in this country?
PW Botha, Prime Minister/State President, 1978-89

Are you in agreement with this? And I say you are. This is why we put a stop to *The World.*
PW Botha (on the banning of The World, 1977)

Press freedom must be earned by an honest Press.
Stoffel Botha, politician

I would like to remind the journalism profession of the accusation that the media have become more than observers of the scene. They have become participants, as someone said – and I quote – 'On the great battlefields of perceptions where modern conflicts rage as much as they do in steamy jungles or shanty towns'. They are the field commanders.
Stoffel Botha

Some journalists and editors tend to lay claim to the sole right to prescribe what people may read and what not, even if it favours self-acknowledged revolutionaries.
Stoffel Botha

They put you on the front page when they do the misquote and when they correct their mistakes they put it on page 99.
Bles Bridges, singer

Journalists are sentimental cynics – unconscious victims of the information age.
Marie Bruyns, TV producer

Journalists are not well paid, so if they have Persian rugs on their walls, they must have other sources of income.
Gaye Derby-Lewis, right-winger

I won't trust a journalist with my wife, my daughter or my money.
PG du Plessis, writer

Ons fade nie. Ons fokof.
Max du Preez, editor (on the closure of Vrye Weekblad, 1994)

Certainly, when a bomb goes off, dismembered body parts take precedence over background analysis.
Mark Gevisser, journalist

A great newsman must have integrity, a profound commitment to truth and an equally profound commitment to freedom of speech.
Chris Gibbons, broadcaster

When a newspaper closes the lament may be fierce but it is transient, and then the waters close and that's that.
Rex Gibson, editor

When one has bad news to tell, it is best to tell it quickly.
Rex Gibson (on the closure of the Rand Daily Mail, April 1985)

I never thought of myself as a journalist – I always thought they were sort of close to God.
Patricia Glyn, TV and radio presenter

Show me a country with no free press and you will be showing me a country where human rights are not respected.
Richard Goldstone, judge

The death of any newspaper, no matter how good or bad, means the death of some ideas, some ideals, the end of an adventure of the mind and spirit.
Dave Hazelhurst, editor

In journalism, the gold rule in a riot situation is check escape routes.
Anthony Heard, editor

The caricature of a bloodthirsty ANC was carefully nurtured by the South African government and its faithful media, the pro-Nationalist press and the South African Broadcasting Corporation.
Anthony Heard

They did it in 48-point capitals and Times Bold.
Anthony Heard (referring to the 'brave' stance of the English press during the apartheid years)

Newspapers may be reminded that, in a volatile situation, they should not cry 'fire' in a crowded theatre.
Hernus Kriel, politician

The Old Nats always prefaced their attacks on press freedom with affirmations of their belief in a free and responsible press.
Patrick Laurence, journalist

Oh how we loved the *Rand Daily Mail*. It provided that essential trace element of guilt in the morning muesli.
Patrick Lee, writer

Next to joining the underground, journalism was the most honourable calling for a white leftist, and besides, there was a certain overlap between the two professions.
Rian Malan, writer

A critical, independent and investigative press is the lifeblood of any democracy.
Nelson Mandela, President, May 1994-

It would not be an interview unless there were some difficult questions.
Nelson Mandela

We're not prophets of a new order or advocates of grand philosophies. We are more in the role of dredging engineers. Our job is simply to keep channels clear.
Tertius Myburgh, editor

I want to put it clearly today: it does not matter whether limitations are imposed on the freedom of the Press; nor does it matter whether there is a degree of control over the Press; nor does it matter whether action is sometimes taken against the Press. The Press is free of principle.
Louis Nel, politician (1981)

I have never thought it could alter things to the extent one is sometimes tempted to think, as one does when one is feeling rather cross about something appearing in the Press one doesn't like.
Harry Oppenheimer, businessman

(The *Rand Daily Mail*) not only gave offence to conservative whites but tended to open up a gap between leaders of black opinion and the businessmen who, partly on moral grounds but also for strong reasons of self-interest, should have been their natural allies.
Harry Oppenheimer (on the closure of the Rand Daily Mail)

If our newspapers are liberal, they are, by and large, the wettest liberals on earth.
Ken Owen, editor

All newspapers have their virtues, and the best South African newspapers are, at their best, a match for any provincial journalism in Britain or the United States.
Ken Owen

If you read it in the newspaper, it's wrong.
Ken Owen (1982)

As a political instrument, the English Press is so discredited, and so bad, that I doubt it has much utility. I doubt anybody cares where the hell it goes.
Ken Owen (1982)

I believe you need to love gossip to be a good journalist.
Debora Patta, journalist

The media has always been the whipping boy of South African politics.
Percy Qoboza, editor

The demise of the *Mail* was a market judgement, however regrettable, and had nothing to do with the quality of its journalism or the values for which the paper stood.
Gavin Relly, businessman (on the closure of the Rand Daily Mail)

It is an unsettling experience to be photographing a dying child with a piece of equipment in your hands which is worth the cost of feeding that child and its family, at Operation Hunger no-profit prices, for about five years.
Struan Robertson, photographer

I would no more sneak into an interview under false pretences than I would willingly watch a festival of Chevy Chase movies.
Barry Ronge, journalist

Who wants to die for a three-minute piece on the evening news?
John Rubython, journalist (on township reporting)

No reporter can be objective, no newspaper can be neutral, and that for newspapers to be acceptable to people, they must reflect their social reality.
Zwelakhe Sisulu, editor, businessman

Pressmen are the plenipotentiaries of the people.
Vere Stent, Reuters correspondent, Second Anglo-Boer War

It is the task of the media to hold up a mirror to society, not to cry peace where there is no peace.
Richard Steyn, editor

Argus and TML must surely have perfected the art of supplanting talent with mediocrity over 20 years.
Style

The press is never neutral.
Clem Sunter, businessman, scenario strategist

The giants have disappeared and haven't really been replaced.
Helen Suzman, liberal, retired politician

Journalists, white or black, are not settlers, let them do their job.
Walters Toboti, politician

The South African press, controlled exclusively by powerful white bosses, had by and large been pandering to white interests at a time when they should have been opening the eyes of the white public to the dangers to which our country was exposed by the iniquitous system of apartheid and its draconian state of emergency measures.
Desmond Tutu, cleric, Archbishop of Cape Town

Numbers of law-abiding newspaper editors, including those of Afrikaans newspapers supporting the government, have criminal records.
Harvey Tyson, editor (on the difficulties of editing under censorship)

If we don't have a public sympathetic to a free press, not only will we not have a free press, we won't have a democracy either.
Harvey Tyson

Even when the press does what it is supposed to do – point out that the emperor's wife has no clothes – somehow it still comes out smelling like the villain.
Phillip van Niekerk, journalist

At the end of the day no constitutional provision for a free press will be worth the paper it is written on unless the press improves the quality of its product and finds its vocation as the voice of the people.
Phillip van Niekerk

You hate me and I hate you.
John Vorster, Prime Minister, 1966-78, to members of the press

In any country the freedom of the press is one of those bastions which cannot be allowed to go without the greatest possible defence.
Gordon Waddell, businessman

I wish to place on record in categorical terms that no credible journalist carries a gun on assignment.
Paul Weinberg, SA Union of Journalists

People who work on newspapers are being pushed and pulled by forces which test their integrity.
David Willers, editor

In Durban an editor of a morning paper, who weekly fences with the local ANC on issues of press freedom, came in one morning to discover a bullet hole in his window in line with where his head might have been.
David Willers

Prison

Every day in here feels like a life.
Anonymous female prisoner

We cannot ignore the peculiar relationship between the South African prison system, with the rope dangling at its core, and the society outside the walls.
Hugh Lewin, author

In prison you learn the value of self-discipline. You stand outside yourself, and see your weaknesses.
Nelson Mandela, President, May 1994-

Now that we have television, and the food is improved, maximum is better than a hostel.
Enoch Mazibuko, criminal

They made sure that there would never be more than four women in any prison because women were considered to be more vicious than the men.
Thandi Modise, politician

Jail is tough and it breaks people.
Carl Niehaus, politician

Prisons are universities of crime.
Ken Owen, editor

Something is wrong somewhere if prison doors are being opened for murderers, terrorists, robbers and rapists, while a journalist is sentenced to a year behind bars for honouring his profession.
Hennie van Deventer, businessman (on the prison sentence for Beeld reporter Andries Cornelissen, 1993)

Professionalism

Part of professionalism is knowing the price.
Lin Sampson, journalist

Promises

Making promises is easy – especially during election campaigns – but carrying them out as a government is very much more difficult.
ANC's Reconstruction & Development Programme (1994)

Beware the promises of lover, drunk, migrant and literary patriot.
Christopher Hope, writer

Propaganda

The propagandists just stand on the corpses and make speeches.
Rian Malan, writer

This should be a war, an effort, a programme in which no rules or regulations would inhibit us.
Eschel Rhoodie, propagandist

With propaganda you never let up.
Alexander Steward, political commentator, SABC

Protest

Although marching in the street is the most common form of public protest in the New South Africa, the man in the street is often reluctant to join in because of the lengthy distances involved – up to three city blocks in some cases – and the fact that you can never find parking before the march.
Gus Silber, journalist

Punishment

If we want the natives to be law-abiding, let us speak to them in the language they understand: the language of the sjambok, administered frequently and with vigour.
Anonymous

I don't carry my sjambok in the bakkie any more: it is only a temptation. It's like trying to stop smoking while you carry cigarettes with you.
Anonymous bushveld farmer (1990)

Man, I'm bleeding, I'm bleeding.
Pik Botha, politician (after being told off by PW Botha for saying there would be a black state president, 1986)

Hanging is a barbaric way of punishing people that does not resolve anything.
Jeremy Cronin, politician

There is something blood-curdling about the way in which capital punishment is invariably used as a law and order stick by conservatives who discard rationality for emotion and prejudice.
Dennis Davis, lawyer

For murder, execution on the turn; for theft, cut off one hand, and for rape, cut off the offending appendage.
Basil Goldstone

I want to feel that I am part of some sort of endeavour, the object of which would be not to punish whites for apartheid or any of that old stuff, but to build something new.
Rian Malan, writer

Some people need a good clout to knock sense into them.
Winnie Mandela, politician

Punishment is no proper treatment for erring children, nor is it the proper treatment for erring countries.
Alan Paton, writer

Killers of innocent people and vulnerable children, rapists and child molesters are among the kind of barbarians that deserve nothing less than the gallows.
Jac Rabie, politician

A kid can't reason, but if he gets a smack and he's got a sore bum, it makes him think about having a sore backside because he did whatever, so it doesn't pay to do it, it hurts.
Clive Rice, cricketer

The end of hangings in a nation where apartheid had been enforced at the end of a rope was an important symbol of the government's willingness to change itself.
Franklin Zimring, academic

Race/Racism

That this property shall not be let or occupied or be transferred or in any manner assigned or disposed of to any Jew, Asiatic, African, Native, Cape Malay or any person who is manifestly a coloured person.
Anonymous (title deed for the Cloete home, Alphen, 1947)

One of the realities about South Africa is that race matters.
Floyd Abrams, jurist

I want to see other skin-coloured people rule.
Frank Arendse, businessman

In the South African context, racism and gender oppression are integral, permanent and virtually indestructible components of our society.
Kader Asmal, academic, politician

In South Africa, decades, nay, centuries, of the institutional thuggery of a system based shamelessly on race and class have taken a heavy toll.
Christopher Ballantine, academic

In the wink of history's eyelid, race has receded from be-all-and-end-all to a spook that creeps in and out of issues so subtly that you don't know when it is there and when not.
Denis Beckett, journalist

This nagging fixation on race, race, race, is becoming a thing that all of us, surely, and not only the high priests of the non-racial democracy, have to rise above.
Denis Beckett

We were all racists, one way or another. The ANC too.
Denis Beckett

These methods have been reported in Johannesburg as being used by the Race Classification Boards to determine whether a man was Native or Coloured: A soccer player is a Native, a rugby player is a Coloured. A high bed is Coloured, a low bed Native.
Cape Times (1956)

Racism is a problem and you can only get it out of the hearts of people by talking to them.
FW de Klerk, State President, 1989-94; Deputy President, 1994-

Institutionalised racism screwed up this country; the unscrewing is going to have to involve a measure of institutionalised racism.
Andrew Donaldson, journalist

To be a white African you have to throw in your lot with the black majority.
Nadine Gordimer, writer, Nobel Prize for Literature

A white cannot exist on a native wage scale, because this means that he has to give up his own standard of living and take on the standard of living of the native.
Barry Hertzog, Prime Minister, 1924-39

Is there no higher aspiration for the Sons and Daughters of South Africa, no nobler task than that of racial strife and dissension?
Barry Hertzog

Ethnic hygiene is where, with the support of most white South Africans, we most emphatically began.
Christopher Hope, writer

There is a soul under every colour which represents God.
Kenneth Kaunda, President (Zambia)

Our people justifiably felt that they were dealing with slippery thieves, and the Europeans thought of Africans as uncultured barbarians who could not honour their word.
Patrick 'Terror' Lekota, politician

Race, or colour, is neither a natural divider nor a natural unifier of men.
Patrick 'Terror' Lekota

In critical moments of history the bonds of class have often proved to be stronger than those of race.
Patrick 'Terror' Lekota

I am just not a tribesman, whether I like it or not. I am, inescapably, a part of the city slums, the factory machines and our beloved shebeens.
Nat Nakasa, journalist

Racism lies not in telling the truth but in hiding it.
Jane Raphaely, editor, publisher

A total of one hundred and one Coloured people became white; one Chinese became white; two whites received Coloured classification; six whites became Chinese; two whites became Indians; ten Coloured people became Indians; ten Malays became Indians; eleven Indians became Coloured; four Indians became Malays; three Coloured people became Chinese while two Chinese were reclassified as Coloured people.
Alwyn Schlebusch, politician (1980)

What can we do about it when God Himself created colour?
Jan Christian Smuts, Prime Minister, 1919-24 & 1939-48

For your own sakes never appear ashamed that your father was a Kafir, and that you inherited some African blood.
Tiyo Soga, missionary, writer

We must not be so starry-eyed about the non-racial dream that when this day arrives the only thing that would have changed is the colour of the skin of the oppressor.
Franklin Sonn, educationist, ambassador

The Grail of brotherhood across lines of race and ethnicity, however earnestly sought, is extremely hard to find.
Clem Sunter, businessman, scenario strategist

The only pressing needs of a savage are those of food and sex, and the conditions of native life in Africa are such that these are as a rule easily supplied.
Transvaal Labour Commission, 1904

If loyalty to and love for one's own people and culture and language, if that is racism, then there are a lot of racists in this country.
Andries Treurnicht, CP leader

We in South Africa are not at all obsessed with race.
NF Treurnicht, politician

Racism fought with racism leads to more racism, just as violence fought with violence leads to the edge of the abyss.
Pieter-Dirk Uys, satirist

Radio

I have never understood why it is that South African broadcasting is so reactive to the whims of those poor tortured souls who do not like what they hear, yet somehow cannot avoid listening.
Will Bernard, actor, broadcaster

Broadcasting should be governed by such concepts as decency and good taste. But don't forget that one man's decency is another man's perversion.
Will Bernard

There was a time when I regarded Radio 702 as part of the enemy press. They were quite vicious against us at one stage.
FW de Klerk, State President, 1989-94; Deputy President, 1994-

The Days of His Master's Voice are over.
Barney Desai, politician (on the draft Independent Broadcasting Authorities Bill)

Radio presenters need personalities first: a good voice is secondary.
Chris Gibbons, broadcaster

Radio is ephemeral; ask any broadcaster who faces the microphone about those words and ideas which float out into the ether and are gone for ever.
Ian Gray, journalist

Talk radio is so compelling because it works on a one-on-one communication level.
Stan Katz, disc jockey, businessman

When all you do is talk radio, you cannot bullshit people.
Stan Katz

Broadcasting's future should be determined through democratic process which is transparent and accessible to all especially the traditionally disadvantaged.
Ivy Matsepe-Casaburri, academic, businesswoman

Radio is simply another word for service.
Malcolm Russell, broadcaster

There is nothing more savage than a wounded white female pensioner let loose on the airwaves.
Style

The hissing dowagers, berserk zealots, trainee dictators and frustrated housewives who phone talk shows to air the contents of their uncluttered minds must surely constitute some sort of pollution against which steps will ultimately have to be taken.
Style

The best form of mass communication in South Africa will remain the radio.
Clem Sunter, businessman, scenario strategist

Public broadcasting as opposed to state broadcasting is an ethos, an ethic honed out of democracy.
Peta Thorneycroft, journalist

Rape

As a cultural phenomenon, date rape is a spurious fiction, a capricious bit of giddiness from the politically correct; it is the mewling runt of the feminist litter.
Andrew Donaldson, journalist

Rape is determinedly deviant behaviour – a function of people exerting what little power they have over the powerless.
Mike Muller, academic, writer

Rape is a concrete expression of the power men have over women in society, and pornography adds to that power.
Alex Schoeman, student

Date rape is replacing dating as a 'legitimate' activity among young men.
Clem Sunter, businessman, scenario strategist

If anything is crucified in a rape case it is the survivor's credibility.
M van Sittert

Reform

Because reform is being carried out for other people, and not with them, one is brought to the conclusion that reform does not address the real issues, which are the questions of equal opportunity and equal justice.
Wynand Malan, politician (1987)

Reform is a tightrope business.
Stoffel van der Merwe, politician

Regrets

If something was dealt with inadequately or with ineptitude it is better to admit it, express regret and then state the intention to rectify matters.
Pik Botha, politician

I have said time and again, 'We are sorry that that happened.'
FW de Klerk, State President, 1989-94; Deputy President, 1994- (referring to apartheid)

I feel very sorry for people. Especially when I'm walking all over them.
Susie Jordan, editor

While I say I'm remorseful and sorry and pained about what happened – and I've said it over and over again – I am also very sorry for the thousands of black people killed by a brutal and iniquitous system.
Robert McBride, politician (and Magoo's Bar assassin, 1986)

It has never been my intention to offend farmers and Afrikaners.
Peter Mokaba, politician

The Nationalist Party stood accused in the court of its own conscience and returned a verdict of guilty against itself.
RJ Mokotja, politician

I think to discuss how sorry you are or not is a perfectly idle pursuit.
Harry Oppenheimer, businessman

In '48 we started wrongly. If only we could have started without discrimination and domination, but our history is past.
Oom Koos Potgieter, politician

I'm not sorry. I have no regrets. I have no remorse. If I have to, I will murder again.
Barend Strydom, murderer

Retreat

To flee – what could be more bitter than that?
Christiaan de Wet, soldier, Second Anglo-Boer War

Revenge

In a country where life is cheap, to seek revenge is a normal reflex.
Anonymous

Vengeance or witch-hunts should have no place in an orderly transition.
Kader Asmal, academic, politician

You must not, in revenge, destroy a nation.
Louis Botha, Prime Minister, 1910-19

In a country where there have been thousands of deaths from political violence, where the state routinely tortured people to death or had them cold-bloodedly executed by hit squads, to fight back and kill can sometimes be a badge of political correctness.
Richard Ellis, correspondent, The Sunday Times (UK)

Feelings of revenge and retribution can easily cloud a debate which should not be driven by primordial reflexes.
Peter Gastrow, politician

We can't base our lives on revenge.
Nyameka Goniwe, housewife, widow of Matthew Goniwe

Now we're suffering the revenge and hatred of the people our government regarded as inferior.
Lee Larkins, housewife

An eye for an eye won't build us.
Emmanuel Luthuli, schoolboy

A racially motivated revenge is pushing our country into a race war.
Moses J Masilela, academic

When the people of this country have begun the process of constructing a new society then we can forgive, but not without atonement.
Nchaupe Mokoape, activist

I believe that in the end this country has to forgive, but forgiveness can't precede the surrender of the evil man.
Nchaupe Mokoape

The evil that goes before and that must be expunged from the social fabric apparently can be expunged only by way of much that is itself evil.
Adam Small, writer

The desire for vengeance can drive one as hard as ambition.
Phillip van Niekerk, journalist

Revolution

The stench of politics tends to drive away the perfume of revolution, and we must be perpetually fighting this.
Breyten Breytenbach, poet, writer

In the turmoil of revolution, the basis for peace and brotherhood in Africa is being restored by the resurrection of national sovereignty and independence of equality, and the dignity of man.
Albert Luthuli, ANC President General, Nobel Peace Prize

Revolutions don't break out in times of intense oppression.
Rian Malan, writer

Revolutionaries shouldn't divorce themselves from the masses under the guise of maintaining their purity.
Maxwell Nemadzivhenani, politician

The truth is that few revolutionaries can sustain their fervour beyond victory
Ken Owen, editor

No revolution of this sort happens without the mark of blood on people's hands.
Adam Small, writer

The journey to revolution may be a much protracted affair.
Adam Small

One of the most important principles of counter-revolutionary action is that unity of purpose within the framework of a co-ordinated plan is essential.
Leon Wessels, politician

The goal of revolutionaries in South Africa is to obtain power, to seize the state.
Craig Williamson, spy

Rights

Human rights: the democratic right of all persons, regardless of age, citizenship, language, national origin, race, religion or sex, to eat junk food, get cosmetic surgery and drop litter in ugly buildings.
Anonymous

The expression 'human rights' is both tautologous and a little obscure.
Laurie Ackermann, judge, academic

Let us say to the black man, you have rights, and we recognise those rights.
PW Botha, Prime Minister/State President, 1978-89

You're entitled to your own opinion but not your own facts.
Dennis Davis, lawyer

Easy access to good ice cream is a basic human right.
Carol Gale, journalist

The first real recognition of black rights to political decision-making can be attributed to Dr Verwoerd's acceptance of a black nation's right voluntarily to secede into full political independence if it so desired.
Chris Heunis, politician (1985)

If we have learnt nothing else from our messy, painful history, we should at least have realised by now that human rights selectively applied are not secure rights at all.
Shaun Johnson, journalist

It will be your right, under the new constitution, to enjoy whatever you manage to keep for yourself without a moment's pause re what Nadine Gordimer would think of you.
Patrick Lee, writer

We have no designs to elbow anyone out of South Africa, but equally we have no intention whatsoever of abandoning our divine right, of ourselves determining our destiny according to the holy and perfect plan of our Creator.
Albert Luthuli, ANC President General, Nobel Peace Prize

We should never abdicate our human rights to our oppressors, nor should we trade these rights for a mess of pottage.
Albert Luthuli

If you deny human rights you are bound to have conflict.
Thabo Mbeki, Deputy President, 1994-

Human rights go hand in hand with human duties.
Ina Perlman, charity worker

With rights comes responsibility, and when you have rights it does not mean you can violate and impose on other people's rights, because then you don't have the right.
Nazeer Suliman, student

Rights are passive in that they stress what a person should receive and how he or she should be treated.
Clem Sunter, businessman, scenario strategist

Rights! Rights! Rights! No! Obligations! Obligations! Obligations!
Clem Sunter

The best way to guarantee rights is to have a situation in which guarantees are written in the hearts of people and not only in the constitution.
Stoffel van der Merwe, politician

Robben Island

The men who were on Robben Island are very great men.
Anonymous

One of the things the prison guards believed in the early days was that they could bury us alive and they thought no one would hear about it.
Anonymous detainee

It was an enriching experience in that one finds that in the face of such adversity human beings who believe in a certain cause are able to endure all the disadvantages, all the hardships.
Achmad Kathrada, politician

On this island we abound in hope.
Nelson Mandela, President, May 1994-

You will be surprised to know the friendships, the strong friendships, which were built between black prisoners and white warders.
Nelson Mandela

We came out of prison with the idea that not every white man, and especially every Afrikaner, hates blacks.
Nelson Mandela

I couldn't feel the pain when I was going through it.
James Mange, politician

When we came in there, young as we were, the welcome we received and the leadership training we received kept us very strong.
Seth Mazibuko, politician

Robben Island is part of our history; it is part of our future and if you take it and belittle it you are insulting the people who suffered on it.
Thandi Modise, politician

My worst experience was watching a man I had loved and worshipped being arrested inside the prison and being stripped naked and put on a wooden horse and walloped by the warders there.
Mike Mohohlo, businessman

We understood that Robben Island was just another terrain of struggle.
Nchaupe Mokoape, activist

It was glorious because some of the greatest freedom fighters this country has known were on Robben Island: it was a privilege.
Dikgang Moseneke, advocate, IEC deputy chairman

The most vicious element was the attempt to make us accept the status quo and morally it was quite devastating.
Solomon 'Sticks' Mrewa, politician

The truth of Robben Island can't be concealed as a tourist attraction – its history is an integral part of the history of South Africa, and it must be preserved for the sake of the future.
Solomon 'Sticks' Mrewa

It must be remembered as the symbol of the triumph of good over evil.
Solomon 'Sticks' Mrewa

There's no doubt prison has not broken their spirits.
Helen Suzman, liberal, retired politician

It never featured on Lifestyles of the Rich and Famous, but some of its inhabitants became known around the globe.
Oliver Thom, journalist

This island represents more completely than any other patch of South African earth that which has been unspeakable (in both senses of the word) in the last three centuries and more of the country's history.
Stephen Watson, poet, teacher

Robben Island is one of those patches of earth invested with a significance literally unfathomable because it is the actual site of a human suffering that, to most of us, borders on the inhuman.
Stephen Watson

Rugby

It's naturally assumed in some rugby circles that whenever a rugby player is injured either falling off a scrumming machine or cutting his finger opening a can of beer that Uli is to blame.
Anonymous

Before our international rehabilitation, provincial rugby was brutal beyond description.
Luke Alfred, journalist

It may not be politically correct, but the sight of green and gold jerseys on a rugby field is immensely stirring.
Colin Bryden, journalist

To the Afrikaner rugby audiences the singing of *Die Stem* is a commitment, a chosen battlefield gesture of collective self-assertion against a hostile world. It is a rally cry and a call to arms, it is the initiation into manhood. It is a sacred covenant.
Bryce Courtenay, writer

They do the hard things brilliantly and the easy things they fuck up.
Paul Dalton, former Australian coach (on the Springboks)

The most crucial period of a rugby game is the last 10 minutes.
FW de Klerk, State President, 1989-94; Deputy President, 1994-

Rugby must be seen for what it is: it is a wonderful form of recreation which is excellent for building camaraderie and discipline.
Morné du Plessis, sportsman

The sight of 30 boys thundering down a hill, their hearts set on victory, their faces golden in the afternoon sun, is enough to bring tears to one's eyes – and at least the odd shudder to one's groin.
Pnina Fenster, journalist (on the annual Michaelhouse v Hilton College rugby match)

If the only South African male capable of making a decent pass holds a rugby ball in his hands, most girls are going to find themselves caught between a rock and a hard on.
Caroline Hurry, journalist

I can't stop them singing, whether it is Die Stem, Ave Maria or even God Save the Queen.
Abe Malan, SA rugby manager (re his team and the national anthem)

The belief in an enduring superiority, which had sustained SA rugby through the years of isolation, turned out to be false – a myth which did not survive the test of reality.
Dan Retief, sportswriter

Rugby stadiums throughout the world have become like Colosseums of old where the rich and famous are entertained by gladiators fighting for little or no reward.
Dan Retief

In the greater scheme of things, any rugby tour is unimportant.
Peter Robinson, journalist

There is something about rugby that is both sacrosanct and defensive.
Lin Sampson, journalist

I want them to know that I would die for my country on the rugby field.
James Small, rugby player

Rugby is a game for hooligans, played by hooligans. I tell you, we're beasts.
Balie Swart, rugby player

Referees elsewhere in the rugby-playing world do not take lightly to having their integrity queried, their legitimate parentage questioned or the anatomy of their manhood challenged.
Jon Swift, journalist

SABC

Since the reign of the Boere Messiah, Hendrik Verwoerd, almost every member of the SABC has been a Nat supporter; a member of the secret Afrikaner Broederbond; almost exclusively Afrikaans-speaking.
Anonymous

The SABC is no Mickey Mouse outfit.
Arrie de Beer, academic

It is a supposed public broadcaster that depends on commercial programming for its livelihood.
Mark Gevisser, journalist

All noble intentions to enhance art, culture, language preferences, education (and other matters) through the SABC's transmitters would come to nothing if the concept of affordability were not always kept in mind.
Wynand Harmse, businessman

We (the SABC) always had a news code but there was never a political policy.
Wynand Harmse

Our broadcasting authority should have three aims: to inform, to entertain and to use every minute of spare capacity during the day for educational programmes designed to help eliminate the disparities of apartheid schooling as soon as possible.
Jenny Hobbs, writer

The one thing the SABC could never deliver was provocative radio.
Stan Katz, disc jockey, businessman

Anyone who has had to deal with the SABC knows the bureaucratic tribal dance one has to perform before getting business done.
Bafana Khumalo, journalist

How many times have you watched Wielie Walie while the country was burning, in the hope that there would be a news update?
Bafana Khumalo

What is deeply sincere and looks like a cross between the Social Welfare Department and the Legal Aid Bureau? Why, it's the All-New SABC Board – and it's all we've got.
Robert Kirby, satirist

The people there don't even read newspapers, which I find scary.
Charles Leonard, journalist

To call the SABC opaque is an understatement.
Ivy Matsepe-Casaburri, academic, businesswoman

It is intolerable in a Third World country that there should be one medium of influence and profit run by the wealthy for the wealthy.
Wilf Nussey, journalist

There is a long-established belief that among television services SATV contrives to be worse than most.
Peter Robinson, journalist

People who miss the smell of napalm in the morning could probably better explain the SABC's enduring romance with our most violent legends.
Pat Rogers, journalist, businessman

We have some brilliant people in TV at the SABC; I think they should all be fired on Friday – and rehired on Monday with a new value system.
Dali Tambo, TV chat show host

The SABC radio service not only helped keep white support behind the NP, it also tried, albeit to a large extent unsuccessfully, to keep blacks in check.
Mathatha Tsedu, journalist

The SABC must move closer to society ... for society will not move closer to the SABC.
Carel van der Merwe, businessman

The SABC is an organisation rather like that of The Party in George Orwell's *1984,* capable of completely rewriting history to suit the political line of the day.
Peter Wilhelm, editor, poet

Sacrifice

Everything has been sacrificed – cattle, goods, money, wife, and child.
Koos de la Rey, soldier, Second Anglo-Boer War

What right do I have to hold back, to rest, to preserve my health, to have time with my family, when there are other people who are no longer alive – when they have sacrificed what is precious, namely life itself?
Chris Hani, Umkhonto we Sizwe chief of staff, SACP general secretary

If we have to sacrifice ourselves, our cause is just.
Constand Viljoen, soldier, politician

Sculpture

It's like sado-masochism in sex – you enter the character, you get into this uniform and you go wherever it takes you.
Geoffrey Armstrong, sculptor

Sex

The extent of purity one aspires to is closely linked with one's capacity for depravity.
Anonymous male prostitute

Cruising is not just a deed, it's a place where you exist in limbo.
Anonymous gay cruiser

It's silly to ban a safe-sex video for being sexy.
MF Blatchford

In this country anything slightly off the gender-defined straight and narrow is suspect and anything feminine expressed within the male is attacked, denigrated.
Jeremy Crutchley, actor

Men are becoming very tired of being treated like sex objects by women who immediately assume we want to sleep with them, when all we want to do is have a chat or maybe borrow money for a beer.
Chris du Plessis, journalist

I sing when I make love... I sing for them.
Brenda Fassie, singer

It's just as ludicrous to ban pornography and expect that people won't use it, as it was to criminalise homosexuality and imagine we were all missionary-position heterosexual die-hards.
Joanne Fedler, academic

The ultimate sexual experience with women isn't penetration.
Pnina Fenster, journalist

What is known in porn parlance as girl-on-girl action is a classic male fantasy, one even older than the obsession with garters and seamed stockings or women in business suits but no underwear.
Pnina Fenster

Suburban husbands, taking a black 'maid' home, would frequently place her alone in the back of the car and drive on like a cab to the drab townships, hoping for the best.
Anthony Heard, editor (referring to the Immorality Act)

I find it very difficult to imagine a more important factor in the destruction of human relations between White and Brown than in fact sexual intercourse over the colour line.
Chris Heunis, politician (1971)

The South African consumer is still very conscious about having a pack of condoms in the basket at the check-out counter.
Etienne Human, businessman

Too much sex with the wrong people is like saying one word over and over again: eventually it becomes absurd.
David Lambkin, writer

Monkeys are far more adept at figuring out when a woman is hot to trot than most men are.
Mike Lipkin, marketer

One thing is certain to precipitate faked orgasm and that's for men to commit the cardinal carnal error: asking a woman whether she's come.
Mike Lipkin

I believe we all deserve a good lay in South Africa.
Thandi Modise, politician

A man sees a pretty woman and wants to have her, while women want to live and love.
Gordana Morsdorf, hunter

With her wide painted, half-open mouth she formed the shape of an egg, a zero, an omega.
Lewis Nkosi, writer, academic

Sleeping with what used to be the enemy is proof that reconciliation has really succeeded.
Hilary Prendini Toffoli & Carolyn Sacks, journalists

The day when sex was shrouded from head to toe might have made the female more intriguing but I wouldn't like to know what the boys were thinking as they stole glances at the provocative upholstery.
Molly Reinhardt, columnist

He had a practised knowledge of when and with whom it was permissible to pass on from discussing the Batavian Fruit Bat to discussing Buggery.
Lin Sampson, journalist

Sex is daemonic, a far darker power than most people admit.
Lin Sampson

Making your body do something it would rather not – such as preserving a hymen – is a Muslim tradition.
Christina Scott, journalist

I saw a large white bottom rising up and down between Miss Allan's knees, I assumed they were having sex.
Linda Shaw, journalist (on Jani Allan's affair with Eugene Terre'Blanche)

This law belongs to the days of witch burning.
Helen Suzman, liberal, retired politician (referring to the Immorality Act)

Is it honestly true that we don't want to have affairs with white girls? What kind of white supremacy is this that cannot stand fair competition?
Can Themba, journalist, writer

I'm all for letting it all hang out, but I'm really disappointed to find out that the hump at the end of the rainbow is actually only a rump.
Andrea Vinassa, journalist

I am the author of the saying that every man kisses his wife in a different way.
John Vorster, Prime Minister, 1966-78

Sex at its best is a mystical experience but you have to have about 1 000 partners to find out.
Jeff Zerbst, academic, journalist

Sex is so important – it's one of the few truly ecstatic states available to us.
Jeff Zerbst

Sharpeville (21 March 1960)

Afrika! We will not carry passes from today.
Anonymous PAC chant

Afrika Izwe Lethu (Africa Our Land).
Anonymous chant

I wish to surrender myself. I and my people don't want passes.
Anonymous protester to police

They bared their chests and shouted, 'Shoot us, shoot us.'
Anonymous policeman

I could tell by his attitude he was going to throw the stone at me. So I raised my rifle, aimed and fired. He fell.
Anonymous policeman

They are shooting our people.
Anonymous protester

Africans are unpredictable.
Anonymous policeman, Security Branch

Dead and battered bodies lay sprawled all over the place. It was like another Vietnam.
Anonymous protester (1983)

Soon they were routed. They fled so quickly that hundreds of shoes, trousers, jackets – and even chairs – were left behind.
Anonymous police officer

Did shout at, jeer, swear at, and jibe members of the SAP.
Charge, Court Entry

The echo of gunfire which rang out on that shameful day of March 21 1960 still reverberates in the consciousness of that nation.
Julian Drew, journalist

The government admits that the condemnation of South Africa by the civilised world was just.
Albert Luthuli, ANC President General, Nobel Peace Prize

As I turned my back a bullet hit me in the left knee, from the back.
Adam Malefane, Sharpeville victim

We are here lest we forget, the torch of freedom burns on.
Lillian Ngoyi, politician (at the 1974 Sharpeville commemoration)

The natives were working themselves into a frenzy.
Lt Col Pienaar (in charge of the police station)

I cannot see how I could have acted differently.
Lt Col Pienaar

Western peoples did not appreciate that riots among semi-developed Natives could not be equated to an uprising among Western people.
Jan Sadie, academic

We offer you, God, those who have died so that we could be free.
Desmond Tutu, cleric, Archbishop of Cape Town (at the 1980 Sharpeville commemoration)

When the shooting started it did not stop until there was no living thing in the huge compound in front of the police station.
Humphrey Tyler, journalist

The groups of people seeking their own gain are small and they make use of mass psychology at mass gatherings, and by threats and other means are sometimes the cause of trouble.
HF Verwoerd, Prime Minister, 1958-66

Shopping

Going shopping is good therapy for depression because it shifts the depression on to inanimate objects that you know you will never be able to afford.
Jani Allan, journalist

A friend with a compatible shopping style is worth her weight in gold.
Cosmopolitan

'Born to Shop' is not a bumper sticker – it's a sign of breeding.
Fair Lady

Sociologists have yet to explain why anybody would voluntarily take out a second bond on the house in order to afford clothes emblazoned with somebody else's name.
Pnina Fenster, journalist

Shopping mania is a spiritual calling, an eternal search for the ultimate little black dress and the last word in bathroom fittings.
Pnina Fenster

When I get depressed I go shoe shopping, although unfortunately it's not a cheap thrill any more.
Anneline Kriel Kerzner Tucker, beauty queen, housewife

Rule Number One is to shop still wearing the tennis outfit... it indicates the family is so well-off the wife does not have to work and provides an opportunity for exhibiting well-tanned legs and arms, not to mention expensive jewellery.
Graham Leach, correspondent, BBC Radio

I want to die rich... no, I want to die shopping.
Nataniel, entertainer

I don't think anybody goes into shops and buys things without thinking what they cost.
Harry Oppenheimer, businessman

We are what we buy.
Lin Sampson, journalist

In a society devoid not only of faith, but of hope and charity, shopping has become the last true religious experience.
Gus Silber, journalist

If someone is seeking love and fulfilment in a shopping mall then something is wrong.
Marianne Thamm, journalist

Silence

When you have a critical mass screaming *Vark! Hond!* and *Weg!*, silence becomes conspicuous and opposition foolhardy.
Denis Beckett, journalist

Something is always happening that makes a sound.
John Cage, composer

Only in silence can we hear the voice of the soul – when we're talking, or preparing to talk, we're deaf to the songs within us.
Sally Wendkos Olds, journalist

Nothing is ever quiet, except for fools.
Alan Paton, writer

You have to keep quiet, you have to go in, you have to listen and then your life will tell you what's really happening in it.
Karel Schoeman, writer

When I'm silent, I get clarity.
Mickey Stern, feminist

I cannot help it when I see injustice, I cannot keep quiet, I will not keep quiet, for, as Jeremiah says, when I try to keep quiet, God's word burns like a fire in my breast.
Desmond Tutu, cleric, Archbishop of Cape Town

Slogans

If I advance, follow me.
If I retreat, shoot me.
If I die, avenge me.
So help me God.
Stormjaers' oath, World War Two

War against the enemy, peace among Africans.
Anonymous PAC slogan

One settler, one bullet.
PAC

One bomb, many kaffirs.
Anonymous

Liberation first, education later.
Anonymous

Strike the woman, you strike the rock.
Anonymous

Freedom and Bread.
Anonymous

Disease knows no colour bar.
Anonymous (1945)

Workers of the World Unite and Fight for a White South Africa.
Anonymous (1922 strike)

Die kaffer op sy plek, en die koelie uit die land.
Anonymous National Party election slogan (1948)

White leadership with justice.
Anonymous United Party slogan (1959)

Afrikaans is a tribal language.
Anonymous (Soweto, June 1976)

Parents don't mourn: mobilise.
Anonymous (Soweto, 1976)

Render South Africa ungovernable.
Anonymous ANC slogan (1985)

Amandla Awethu (Power is ours).
Anonymous ANC slogan

Viva Boks – Vat hom Danie Gerber.
Anonymous (Nyanga, 1992)

Each bullet takes us forward.
Apla (1993)

One president, one Mandela.
Anonymous (on Chris Hani Day of Remembrance, 1993)

Communism is Jewish.
Anonymous AWB slogan (1993)

Eie Volk, Eie Land.
Anonymous AWB slogan (1993)

One white child, one squatter camp.
Anonymous AWB slogan (1993)

Buy now while shops last.
Anonymous (election, 1994)

We shall overcome.
We have overcome.
I am overcome.
Anonymous (Inauguration Day, Pretoria, 10 May 1994)

Shine, South Africa, shine!
Anonymous (Inauguration Day, Pretoria, 10 May 1994)

The country is running the Comrades and the comrades are running the country.
Anonymous (Comrades Marathon, 1994)

Adapt or die.
PW Botha, Prime Minister/State President, 1978-89

If the slogans are repeated often enough and those who believe them see no change, they are plunged into despair and fall prey to new rhetoric.
Saths Cooper, academic, businessman

The effect of sloganeering, on those chanting the slogans and on their targets, is utterly destructive.
Wessel Ebersohn, journalist

Ultimately the degree of outrage felt at a slogan, song or speech depends on one's own political views.
Wessel Ebersohn

You mustn't judge the slogan of a particular organisation without reading that organisation's literature.
Gora Ebrahim, politician

South Africa First.
Barry Hertzog, Prime Minister, 1924-39

Kill a Boer: kill a farmer.
Peter Mokaba & Winnie Mandela, politicians

People who shout slogans are too lazy to think independently, or think things through without having to lean on supporting noises.
Es'kia Mphahlele, academic, writer

You can't eat slogans.
Monise Ponoane, chairman, Pan African Students Organisation

Black Man, you are on your own.
Abraham Ongopotse Tiro, activist

Society

Haunting songs fill the air and there is the hunger of the zealot for a total and cleansing transformation of society into a new and just order.
Don Beck, conflict resolution specialist

I'm no longer attached to the social stigma of being white.
Tonie Botha, farmer, politician

Being non-sexist and non-racist is, in any society, almost impossible, but it is especially so in societies where there are girls and different coloured people.
James Clarke, journalist

We have constructed a society in which neither blacks nor whites are completely themselves.
Wessel Ebersohn, journalist

African society has been destroyed and is yet to be replaced by anything acceptable to its peoples.
Wessel Ebersohn

Only a society in crisis regards all strangers as potential criminals.
Mary Anne Fitzgerald, writer

When the very survival of society is in question you need free speech more than you need satire.
David Frost, TV interviewer (UK)

South Africa has been and will probably continue to be a doff-your-cap-and-touch-your-forelock society.
Robert Greig, journalist

If an order is repugnant to the morals and good order of society, you have a right to refuse to carry it out.
Harry Gwala, politician

Ethnic conflict can only occur in multi-ethnic societies.
Hernus Kriel, politician

The essence of our society is that it is a bivouac, away from the centre of the civilisation, run under martial conditions.
Patrick Lee, writer

In the absence of real change, we remain an imprisoned society.
Hugh Lewin, author

In South Africa, getting through the day, let alone through one's life, has become the greatest challenge.
Mike Lipkin, marketer

We live in a society which does not recognise the value of the knowledge within our community.
Ivy Matsepe-Casaburri, academic, businesswoman

It is expected that moving upwards means becoming as white as possible.
Eric Miyeni, comedian

In free societies individuals are encouraged to seek their own ends in the belief that society itself is the principal benefactor of personal success.
Stephen Mulholland, publisher

A democratic government must be accountable to civil society, and civil society must be involved in decision-making.
Jay Naidoo, politician

Society as a whole is hostile to free speech and open debate.
Ken Owen, editor

Neither intellectual enlightenment nor a change in institutions could save society and man without a change of will.
Alan Paton, writer

The synthetic notion of a multi-ethnic society is the sort of paper dream which the people on the ground will not, cannot conform.
Edward Pearce, journalist (UK)

Cut the flab, trim the fat, munch the crackling and you'll find that society pared to the bone is no more than a lot of symbols stuck together.
Lin Sampson, journalist

The real broth of society is the people.
Lin Sampson

If you are politically involved, you understand the dynamics of society better than someone who is not.
Zwelakhe Sisulu, editor, businessman

Tribal societies have their customs, their way of jumping from boyhood to manhood but the white male stays a kid for ever.
Paul Slabolepzy, playwright, actor

Social sang-froid in the new South Africa will require more than a commitment to reconscientising your Rottweiler or forsaking aerobics and learning to toyi-toyi.
Jessica Smith, journalist

Without the familial web, society becomes a jungle in which no amount of laws and police can control the uncared-for and undisciplined youth.
Clem Sunter, businessman, scenario strategist

It is a myth to believe that a healthy society should display complete unity.
Clem Sunter

When you are not part of the mainstream of society, when you have no say in how its affairs will be directed, the notion of utterly transforming it through revolution appears attractive.
Clem Sunter

The traditional rules of social order that have so structured some of us to do the right thing for when things go wrong have also killed our sense of adventure, just because to take a chance today might remove a choice tomorrow.
Pieter-Dirk Uys, satirist

South Africa

From afar, South Africa was fascinating when it was a morality play.
Anonymous

This is a Third World country with a débutante's appetite.
Anonymous

South Africa has developed a strapping body but lacks a soul.
Jim Bailey, publisher (1985)

The downside in South Africa is so bad that a dole queue in Bradford would seem like heaven in comparison.
David Barritt, editor

We are basically a country of minorities.
PW Botha, Prime Minister/State President, 1978-89

South Africa has the potential to alter the world trend towards greater ethnic division and establish a powerful model for democratic reform and national reconciliation.
Bill Clinton, President (USA)

As a white-ruled nation, South Africa is doomed.
Richard Cohen, critic

Too many South Africans have exaggerated our importance in the world, whether as an indispensable strategic stronghold or the focus of a cosmic moral crusade.
Desmond Colborne, businessman

South Africa has always been a bobby-socked meisie from the platteland.
Michelle Constant, journalist

This place is a microcosm of all the great struggles and hopes and aspirations of all history.
Chester Crocker, politician, businessman (USA)

It's an intellectual dorp.
Geoff Durrant, academic

In South Africa's wilderness of mirrors, the only sure things are death and uncertainty.
Richard Ellis, correspondent, The Sunday Times (UK)

Because of apartheid, South Africa still does funny things to well-educated, reasonable people.
Richard Ellis

An overwhelming force bearing down on an unyielding object.
Laurence Gandar, editor

The world's opinion on South Africa is likely to be one of boredom.
Chris Gibbons, broadcaster

South Africa is the graveyard of political predictions.
Hermann Giliomee, academic

South Africa couldn't organise a bonk in a brothel.
Gwen Gill, journalist

Given the challenge it faces, South Africa's most vital national resource may be optimism.
Joshua Hammer, correspondent, Newsweek

It was a country where the lunatic fringe was in the centre of politics.
Anthony Heard, editor

In South Africa there is never a night of storm not followed by a day of sunshine.
Barry Hertzog, Prime Minister, 1924-39

This is a land where euphemism has long been, like war, an extension of policy by other means.
Christopher Hope, writer

South Africa is the most fascinating laboratory in the world.
Adam Klein, businessman

Although South Africans' biggest worry is escalating crime and lawlessness, there is a hunger for national pride.
Reg Lascaris, businessman

Fatigue is the national plague.
Reg Lascaris

South Africa's aesthetic underbelly is quite possibly the bad taste capital of the world.
Adam Levin, journalist

South Africa is an issue-driven society.
Mike Lipkin, marketer

South Africa is a museum piece in our time, a hangover from the dark past of mankind, a relic of an age which everywhere else is dead or dying.
Albert Luthuli, ANC President General (on receiving the Nobel Peace Prize, 1961)

This is South Africa, where nothing can be taken for granted, even if you see it with your own eyes.
Rian Malan, writer

It has a way of making your brain seethe and your blood boil.
Rian Malan

South Africa holds the souls of its sons and daughters in an almost inescapable grasp.
Rian Malan

This country is teeming with luminously decent black people, men and women who just want justice and dignity, a better life for themselves, and a shot at glory for their children.
Rian Malan

There's something to be said for living on the edge, in a country where rival kingdoms of consciousness overlap and interact in strange and intoxicating ways.
Rian Malan

If you have a heart for South Africa, you are African.
Londi Mncube, schoolgirl

In South Africa we do not have a nation, we have factions.
Joe Modise, politician

Every damn issue of our epoch, black, white, north, south, is somehow represented in the crucible we live in.
Tertius Myburgh, editor

When the Europeans came to South Africa it was in a state of wild barbarism, but after 300 years and particularly after 100 years of close contact, what do we find in South Africa today? We find a half-civilised barbarism and a half-civilised barbarism is more dangerous than wild barbarism.
MC De Wet Nel, politician (1951)

Whatever we achieve in the new South Africa will have been built at the cost of so many lives, most of them unknown, humble people.
Ron Nicolson, cleric

A strange land. There's a beat that runs through her body; sometimes, if you listen carefully, you can hear the spirits of the Abadala.
Obie Oberholzer, photographer

In the new South Africa, change is the only certainty.
Ken Owen, editor

Cry, the beloved country, for the unborn child that is the inheritor of our fear.
Alan Paton, writer

Alas my country! Thou wilt have no need of enemy to bring thee to thy doom.
Sol Plaatje, SAANC general secretary, writer

The trickiest part is to stay alive in this brand-new old South Africa.
Jon Qwelane, editor

The spoilt and unrepentant nature of racist white South Africa wrenches the soul.
Jon Qwelane

The magnetic quality of this land is strong.
Anton Rupert, businessman

There is nothing measured, small nor pretty in South Africa.
Olive Schreiner, writer

The sad side of our life in South Africa is our native question.
Olive Schreiner

South Africa, as the name suggests, is the vast tract of land that keeps the rest of the African continent from sliding into the ocean as it makes its way towards the South Pole.
Gus Silber, journalist

It is a country with a heartbeat as strong as a jackhammer.
Jessica Smith, journalist

More than any other country in the world, South Africa is a great human laboratory where experiments in racial co-operation are essential to our future success.
Jan Christian Smuts, Prime Minister, 1919-24 & 1939-48

A country where people occupy the same space but live in separate time frames, so that they do not see one another and perceive different realities.
Allister Sparks, journalist

As a nation, we have given the lie to the gloomiest predictions.
Sunday Times

This country has the potential to astonish the world.
Clem Sunter, businessman, scenario strategist

After a quarter of a century of writhing about in guilt and anguish about one's mother country, it is a great relief even to be able to acknowledge one's origins to the likes of taxi drivers.
Janet Suzman, actress

In South Africa, when we want to make a point, we take a sledgehammer to it.
Stanley Uys, journalist

This new South Africa is not as fragile as we think.
Phillip van Niekerk, journalist

The irony of the new South Africa is that democratisation is itself impeding growth: ending apartheid has meant unprecedented social turmoil, as the battle for power pits black political groups against one another, police against township residents, organised labour against the government.
Patti Waldmeir, correspondent, Financial Times (UK)

The trouble with the South African jigsaw was that even when they were forced together the pieces did not fit.
Geoffrey Wheatcroft, journalist

Soweto 1976

It was horrible, terrifying. I will never forget it as long as I live.
Anonymous

Education is not the business of politicians.
Anonymous

The minority group cannot force their language down our throats.
Anonymous

The thugs have taken over.
Anonymous

Why kill kids for Afrikaans?
Anonymous placard

If it had not been the school issue, there would have been another.
Anonymous journalist

Another Sharpeville.
Anonymous policeman (17 June 1976)

I saw one boy hit in the temple and he fell to the ground and I started running.
Anonymous schoolboy (17 June 1976)

An orgy of arson and pillage.
Anonymous journalist (17 June 1976)

It has revealed the depth of Black desperation and anger, as Sharpeville did not do.
Anonymous journalist (20 June 1976)

It has become too much to bear.
Anonymous journalist (20 June 1976)

Rather kill three now than two next week.
Anonymous policeman (20 June 1976)

Driving home from Soweto last night was worse than a nightmare.
Anonymous journalist

They say we are members of the 'Ja, Ja Madam' generation.
Anonymous woman (20 June 1976)

It's a cold-blooded, ideological regulation which could not do more to downgrade Black education if it were designed for that purpose.
Anonymous journalist (referring to compulsory Afrikaans, 20 May 1994)

They ignored us and thought, as usual, they would get away with it.
Mangosuthu Buthelezi, IFP leader, politician

The Africans gave the black power salute yesterday. Is this significant?
Californian radio host speaking to a local journalist

Having endured a baptism of fire, they will return (to school) as seasoned revolutionaries.
Caroline Clark, journalist (20 June 1976)

As far as I'm concerned, the pupils are at school.
MC de Beer, civil servant (1 600 pupils were on strike, 22 May 1976)

We thought that if we sat it out, the strikes would peter out.
Thys de Beer, school inspector

Soweto is slowly awakening to unity.
Tony Duigan, journalist

The children have shown us all the inevitable consequences if this government continues to display the insane arrogance and power satiated pride which is rapidly bringing us to disaster.
Sheena Duncan, Black Sash, SA Council of Churches (17 June 1976)

My wife is hysterical. There are five of us trying to hold her down. She mustn't scream or they'll know we are here.
José Fernandez, businessman (in a telephone conversation to the police during a riot)

I can't fathom their way of thinking.
WF Kotze, policeman

From now on it will snowball.
Sonny Leon, politician

Everything is in such upheaval here, I don't really know what is going on.
R le Roux, policeman (directing police operations in Soweto, 16 June 1976)

The blood was streaming, but he just ran.
Solly Liefman, photographer

I saw Nunu crawl on all fours, and then drop to the ground.
Madoda (16)

Parents of Soweto, unite.
Winnie Mandela, politician (12 June 1976)

Our children are likely to spit on our graves because we have let them down.
Winnie Mandela (12 June 1976)

I have the highest admiration for the patience they (the police) showed in not trying to shoot their way through.
Manie Mulder, civil servant

This was simply because it was white man's property.
Manie Mulder (referring to the burning of a bank and a library)

Nunu dropped after he had been hit by three bullets – two in his chest and one in his back. His friends carried him home dead.
Mike Ndlalazi, journalist

Just as we put Hector in the car, the man who was carrying him said, 'He has gone.' That is when he died, though at the time we didn't believe it.
Antoinette Petersen (sister of Hector Petersen)

In Soweto now, a white skin is a death warrant.
Kevin Stocks, journalist

We have the right to determine the teaching language.
Andries Treurnicht, CP leader (then Deputy Minister of Bantu Education)

My patience is at an end.
JF Visser, policeman

From now on we will use tougher methods.
JF Visser

Sport

Q: Do you think you're longer than Fred Couples? *(Anonymous interviewer to golfer Ernie Els)*
A: I don't know, I've never showered next to him.

In sport, like everything else in this country, you get talkers and you get doers, you get foundations and you get frills.
Anonymous

What Ali Bacher and his merry men on the United Cricket Board of South Africa have done in bridging gaps, forging trust

and turning world views upside down has provided a beacon of hope for the country as a whole, in the same way that the manner in which the rugby authorities have gone about their business has offered a warning of the dangers that loom.
John Carlin, correspondent, The Independent (UK)

One of the wonderful things about athletics is that the stopwatch is brutally honest.
Bruce Fordyce, sportsman

When you're out there, wearing the green and gold, representing South Africa, with the eyes of the world on you, you finish. You crawl, bleeding, over the line, but you finish.
Bruce Fordyce

We want jukskei to become a sport and not stay a cultural event like volkspele.
George Hambidge, SA Jukskei Council

Sport was the jugular, the vulnerable spot, in early international campaigns for pressure.
Anthony Heard, editor

The trout stream has always been a metaphor for the idyllic, and the presence in our waters of this elegant fish was, in many ways, a cultural gain.
Robert Kirby, satirist

Boxing – blood sport to some, battle of the gladiators to others – is still a mirror of societies divided.
Stephen Laufer, journalist

If there are some things that tradition still embellishes, horse racing is one of them.
Patrick Lee, writer

July fever is probably the country's healthiest disease.
Patrick Lee

We did it for Africa.
Elana Meyer, sportswoman, on winning an Olympic silver medal

If I knew yesterday what I know today, I would have handled it better.
Elana Meyer (on dropping out of the 10 000 metres at the World Championships, Stuttgart, 1993)

I feel like I've done nothing wrong and I've been bitten by a giant snake and I'm dying.
Nick Price, golfer (disqualified from the Million Dollar Golf Challenge, 1992)

In the overall context of sport and life, victory is far more important than Baron de Coubertin's dictum that taking part is good enough.
Jon Swift, journalist

It's all a matter of geometry, Pythagoras and theorems.
Louis Tshoakane, PRO (on Kaizer Chiefs)

Our teams will be non-racial even if they are all-white.
Steve Tshwete, politician

If I must wear a pink ballet dress and run through Johannesburg streets to play for SA I would do it.
Garth Wright, rugby player

Like theology, horse racing is a whole system of thought.
Jeff Zerbst, academic, journalist

Stress

The most effective antidote to anxiety is at least knowing what the devil's going to look like before you see him.
Reg Lascaris, businessman

Stupidity

Stupidity will find its own course and often its due reward.
Obie Oberholzer, photographer

Style

In some deft and unknowable way style is congenital and it is hard to escape.
Anonymous

Style will not disappear with the new dispensation.
Patrick Lee, writer

If South Africa is a sinking ship, I want to go down First Class.
Alexandra Levin, copywriter

You don't have to be rich to have style, but you have to have courage.
Anthula Markowitz, dress designer

I have seen him march around the lounge rearranging cushions that had been coyly set in triangles and ruthlessly pulling pink gladioli from a vase.
Lin Sampson, journalist

People with duvets have matching accessories and Laura Ashley wedding dresses, Liebermann pottery and name tiles on the front gate, houses called Costa del Sol, striped awnings and problems with premature ejaculation.
Lin Sampson

Life is a cabriolet.
Style

Style is individuality plus nerve plus humour plus timing.
Style

You got No Style: you got No Influence.
Jonathan Taylor, photographer

Style is understated good taste in clothes, a healthy disregard for social pretence, turning down patronising invitations to Northern Suburbs dinner parties and, most of all, wanting the best of everything.
Hellouise Truswell, journalist

White style compared to that of blacks is so subdued it borders on paralysis.
Hellouise Truswell

Success

It isn't easy to win if you don't start off on the right side of the field.
Pnina Fenster, journalist

At the rendezvous of victory there is room for all.
Nadine Gordimer, writer, Nobel Prize for Literature

It doesn't matter if you win or lose until you lose.
Hilton College sanatorium sign

Victors can afford to be generous.
Jan (Onze Jan) Hofmeyr, politician

Anybody who's successful is always a bitch.
Susie Jordan, editor

The key to success lies less with finding the 'right' shape, than how that shape is found.
Ron Kraybill, conflict mediator (USA)

Perseverance is the mother of success.
'Baby Jake' Jacob Matlala, boxer

All recipes for success in life depend ultimately on enthusiasm.
Ernest J Mchunu, author

If you accept challenges, believe in yourself and in God, you will make a success of your career.
Georg Meiring, soldier

The stairways to success are entwined with snakes and adders.
John Michell, editor

It is often not having a ruthless way that enables you to win.
Harry Oppenheimer, businessman

Anybody can deal with success; the real test is defeat.
Ken Owen, editor

If you go on whether you win or lose, then you have something more than success or failure. You keep your own soul.
Alan Paton, writer

The wavy path to success, like a road through the mountains, may be more difficult and slower than a straight road – but the scenery on the way is more interesting.
Jack Penn, surgeon, philosopher, artist

Short cuts never lead to success, the only roads leading to that being generally hard and steep and often full of pitfalls.
Cecil John Rhodes, Imperialist

It's having that extra sense which pushes you to get that other guy out and make conditions so tough that he doesn't want to be part of it. When that happens, you've won.
Clive Rice, cricketer

In order to win, one must turn others into winners too.
Clem Sunter, businessman, scenario strategist

Sun City

It's not like anywhere else on the planet.
Julia Beffon, journalist

Cynics maintain that Sun City is a figment of its own imagination.
Peter Devereux, gourmet, businessman

It has its own wild flavour, its own barbarian grandeur and its own sensual perversity.
Andrew Donaldson, journalist

Ritz, glitz and tits.
Huffty, journalist (UK)

Even the manhole covers are beautifully moulded, for heaven's sake.
Sabine Jones, journalist

It has advanced from being simply a lavish and rather gaudy space machine languishing in the hills to a lavish and gaudy space machine with a reputation.
Patrick Lee, writer

This place reminds me of Jurassic Park or something from one of my past lives.
Shirley MacLaine, actress

My first impression was that a designer, stoned on magic mushrooms and borrowed from the setting of a film called 'Tarzan and the Aztecs' had been let loose and told to forget the axiom less is more.
Linda Stafford, journalist

It is an astounding creation whose wild Afro-baroque style – half Bernini, half Indiana Jones – exceeds the wildest hyperbole.
David Thomas, correspondent, The Daily Telegraph (UK)

Surrender

If you can't beat 'em, join 'em.
Adolph Gysbert (Sailor) Malan, pilot, farmer (on joining the Royal Air Force)

I am glad to see you. You have made a gallant defence, sir.
Lord Roberts to Piet Cronje (Paardeberg)

Talent

I have blown my mind at the amount of raw talent which exists in our country.
Welcome Msomi, playwright

It is an illuminating truth that being nice, normal and human tarnishes talent and talent, like Medea, will kill its infants, but will serve them up in an exquisite feast.
Barry Ronge, journalist

Taxation

We have to find the money and a reconstruction levy or a swimming pool tax is one idea. If you don't like that, you'd better emigrate.
Jayendra Naidoo, politician

Television

Sometimes the kindest thing one can say about South African TV is that it's in colour.
David Barritt, editor

Whoever dresses the hosts should be shot for gross violation of their human rights.
Bafana Khumalo, journalist

The sooner South African television stops pandering to the tastes of the militant Philistines of the South African lower middle class, the better.
Robert Kirby, satirist

Every time I tune to TV1, my border collie immediately trots over to the set and tries to lift his leg on the screen.
Robert Kirby

Let us, in our new, open South Africa, celebrate the establishment of an independent TV by rolling in the cameras at 'Beverly Hills', so that we can have the shit and blood and twitching bodies brought to us in full colour over breakfast.
Hugh Lewin, author

By far the best value for money on TV is the advertising.
Pat Sidley, journalist

Despite the fact that millions of people across the country do not pay their television licence, there has been no noticeable improvement in the quality of programming or the hairstyles of some of the newsreaders.
Gus Silber, journalist

Television is going to be the primary medium for reinventing South Africa.
Style

Terrorism

Terrorism is felt everywhere, and its methods have become increasingly sophisticated.
William Deedes (Lord Deedes of Aldington), politician, editor (UK)

It is the policy of the South African government to combat terror, wherever it may occur. The action was like a surgeon's incision against the ANC, using minimum force to achieve maximum advantage.
Magnus Malan, soldier, politician (on an SADF cross-border raid, 1988)

To be politically effective, terrorism must have the capacity to galvanise the mass of the population into rebellion or resistance, and in South Africa the right-wing minority can never aspire to mass support.
Ken Owen, editor

Threats

All along it has only been the black mothers who have been mourning. Now the time has come that all of us must mourn, white families must also wear black costumes.
ANC broadcast, Radio Freedom, Addis Ababa (1985)

Before a black puts a foot into our council chamber we'll bulldoze the civic centre, wipe out our businesses and burn down our homes.
Anonymous Delmas resident

Kill us, we are already dead.
Anonymous

Rise up against the blood-sucking white soldier farmers.
ANC policy speech (1986)

Every African must carry a gun and identify the enemy and form defensive community forces.
Benny Alexander, politician

I do not reject any kind of freedom fighting.
Carel Boshoff, secessionist; chairman, Afrikaner Volkswag

Those who will be with me will be with me and those who move to oppose me will be against me.
Mangosuthu Buthelezi, IFP leader, politician

Kill the wizards!
Dingane, King of the Zulus (instigating the assassination of Piet Retief and his followers, February 1838)

The war will come to the AWB when savages come running through the streets, damaging property and attacking whites, that is the form of war we will fight.
Eddie Gagiano, Ystergarde colonel

We don't have grand visions of victory, but we didn't think that either when we had to fight Britain.
Tienie Groenewald, soldier, politician

We are not going cap in hand to the boers.
Harry Gwala, politician

We will burn this country to the ground.
Fanie Jacobs, politician

How long shall we be a rightless, voteless and voiceless majority in our fatherland?
Philip Kgosana, activist, 'The Black Messiah'

What we have not lost is our will to return to the field and do battle.
Patrick 'Terror' Lekota, politician

I fight one war and I fight it hard, and I make sure that I win.
Felicia Mabuza-Suttle, businesswoman, TV show presenter

The time to think and to act is now and we dare neglect neither the spade nor the sword.
Magnus Malan, soldier, politician (1977)

The time will come when I will call on you to defend yourselves with the same might that Pretoria is unleashing against people.
Winnie Mandela, politician

We will not bow to your threats and demands... we invite you to do your damnedest.
Les Manley, diplomat (to the UN, 1988)

Shall we abandon the bullets before the ballot is secured?
Johnson Mlambo, politician

A serious war is coming where no one will sleep.
Albert Mncwango, commander, Inala regiment, IFP

When we ask for ballots, they give us bullets, we will reply with bullets as well.
Peter Mokaba, politician

Kill the farmer, kill the Boer, shoot to kill, shoot the Boer.
Peter Mokaba

We are passing the stage of violence; we are going into war now.
Wami Nhlopo, activist

The SAP and SADF are armed enemy organs and, because the regime relies on them for its perpetual stay in power, they should be wiped out of existence.
Sabelo Phama, Apla defence chief

Even if we lose 5 million out of the 30 million, we must make sure that the other 25 million will be free. Then it will be a sacrifice worth making.
Sabelo Phama

If it comes to shooting, the mask will be torn from the face of democracy and peace.
Willem Ratte, right-wing militia leader

If the Government capitulates, we will take South Africa back with violence.
Eugene Terre'Blanche, AWB leader

We will level you with the stones.
Eugene Terre'Blanche

Arm your women. Steal guns if you must. We will make your women soldiers in the name of God and for the freedom of our fatherland.
Eugene Terre'Blanche

I cannot be declared an immigrant in the land of my birth.
Steve Tshwete, politician

We must keep our military might but we must also put on the armour of God. The same God of Blood River and Majuba will be with us now and if we feel weak we must put our hand in His.
Constand Viljoen, soldier, politician

Not only reason must speak, but blood as well.
John Vorster, Prime Minister, 1966-78 (1963)

Time/Timing

In turbulent times, not only do ills become exaggerated, so do antidotes.
Denis Beckett, journalist

If there is no doubt that we will be hampered for a long time to come by our imprisonment in the roles of the past – the mentality of the master race; the mentality of the victim – we may yet demonstrate, if we are truly serious about it, that we have all gained, at a terrible price, something from it as well.
André Brink, writer, academic

Tomorrow is always more interesting than yesterday.
William Deedes (Lord Deedes of Aldington), politician, editor (UK)

Time, the priest, absolves us all.
Damon Galgut, writer

The daylight is there to be used.
Paul Kruger, President, Transvaal Republic

First lesson in the art of Visibility is to make a point of appearing late – especially if you've gone to a deal of trouble with your outfit.
Wilma Lawson Turnbull, PR

Here, unless there's a gardener and a maid at home, some people can't even manage a job.
Paul Levin, marketing specialist

In life, as in art, as in TV scheduling, timing is everything.
Richard McNeill, journalist

We can talk of geological ages and describe the conditions of the epochs but we cannot conceive of those prehistoric skies: of how they were washed at sunset or how they shone at dawn.
Mike Nichol, writer

When time is limited only the proper priorities can make full use of its qualities.
Jack Penn, surgeon, philosopher, artist

Sitting back in the same old spot, or remaining dug in the old trenches against the march of time is silly and dangerous.
Jon Qwelane, editor

So much to do, so little time.
Cecil John Rhodes, Imperialist

In the huge pile of time, the hours on hours, days on days, years on years, that constitute the past, time warp is simply the subtle pulling of a few threads.
Lin Sampson, journalist

Punctuality is the soul of business and time is money.
Clem Sunter, businessman, scenario strategist

If you integrate the day, the night will take care of itself.
Dali Tambo, TV chat show host

Looking after tomorrow has become such a full-time job that when tomorrow comes, you're too damn tired to be bothered enjoying it.
Pieter-Dirk Uys, satirist

To go slowly is one of the great needs in life.
Laurens van der Post, soldier, writer, philosopher

Tourism

You don't spot lions any more, you spot brakelights.
Denis Beckett, journalist

All the assurances in the world won't convince anyone that we offer Holidays in Heaven.
Garry Brennan, journalist

In South Africa, isolated for so many years while other countries have courted the tourism market, willingness is a rare commodity.
Colin Bryden, journalist

The lions and leopards of the Kruger Park hold fewer terrors than empty beaches, isolated rural retreats and the centre of Johannesburg, where diplomats and UN observers have been among the muggers' prey in recent weeks.
John Carlin, correspondent, The Independent (UK)

Every now and then a doughty German tourist will step out of the firing squad (of photographers) and pose with the dancers: a snapshot of her brush with primitivism to place next to the images of lions and elephants in the photo-album.
Mark Gevisser, journalist

'Coming to South Africa without seeing Apartheid is like going to New York without getting mugged', is a comment frequently overheard by muggers waiting outside some of South Africa's top tourist resorts.
Gus Silber, journalist

Townships

It is an offence to climb on to, under, over or through a gate or fence, wall or railing in or around the township; or to enter or leave the township otherwise than through some authorised means of ingress or egress; to sink any well, make any excavation, or dig any hole without the permission of the superintendent, except for bona fide gardening purpose; to deface, obliterate or destroy any number painted, inscribed or affixed on the premises, to incorporate in any dwelling, building, fence or outbuilding any material which has not received the prior approval of the superintendent; to fail to furnish one's full name, identity number and address or proof of the right to be in a black residential area as may be required by an authorised officer of the administration board or council; to convene or address a public meeting or assembly or to use a loudspeaker in the township without the written permission of the location superintendent; to permit a public meeting or entertainment in the location to continue later than midnight without the approval of the location superintendent; to collect any money for any purpose other than bona fide church purposes at a public meeting or assembly without the written approval of the location superintendent; or to use a dwelling mentioned in the site permit, residential permit, or certificate of occupation for any purpose other than that authorised under the regulations.

Arthur Chaskalson, lawyer, & Sheena Duncan, Black Sash (Second Carnegie Commission into Poverty & Development, 1984/85)

Despite the sordid meritriciousness of the neighbourhood, there was a great supportive energy to the way the sweaty streets felt, the people dawdling on the pavements, the children scampering behind the grey iron shacks, the old men and women shuffling belatedly into front rooms, pausing to peer

with incredulous wonder at the bright carnival of summer being endlessly enacted on the streets.
Lewis Nkosi, writer, academic

In the townships, divorcing your husband usually means divorcing your accommodation as well.
Mamphela Ramphele, academic

Transport

Following the repeal of Apartheid legislation, minibus taxis are open to all races, the majority of which take place at 140 km/h between red robots on Commissioner Street.
Gus Silber, journalist

Travel

The dust lay inches deep on the one worn veld road, and the long strings of oxen toiling along kicked up suffocating clouds of fine dust which there was seldom any breeze to carry off: it powdered white man and black to an equal level of yellowy red.
Percy Fitzpatrick, politician, writer

The ox-wagon creaks slowly along the sandy road in the dark, the driver walks beside it and calls at intervals to his tired oxen; you look out across the wagon-chest, and, as the wagon moves along, the dark outlines of the bushes on either side seem to move too; now a great clump comes nearer and nearer like a vast animal; then as you peer into the dark, they seem like great ruined castles coming to topple over you; and you creep closer down behind the wagon-chest.
Olive Schreiner, writer

Whether you're a first-time visitor, a returning exile, a coastal holiday-maker, a suburban commuter, an eminent person, an imminent emigrant, or someone who has never been outside the borders of the Orange Free State, finding your way around the New South Africa should not be any more difficult than finding your way around the old South Africa.
Gus Silber, journalist

Trends

Couturiers know this: anything that smells like hot teen spirit also smells like cold green cash.
Andrew Donaldson, journalist

On the face of it, grunge certainly appears decadent, if not a little *gamey*.
Andrew Donaldson

Objects are not simply bad taste any more, they are Fifties, Sixties, Boere-kitsch, Latin-divine, trash, ugly and more.
Adam Levin, journalist

Bad taste is a way of life, not just a fashion fad.
Petra Mason, businesswoman

New speak identifies the cerebrally deficient as being two sandwiches short of a picnic or missing the ace of spades.
Jenni Newman, PR

As soon as one becomes upwardly mobile, one moves to white suburbs.
Ndo Nyembezi, businesswoman

Why does schlock always stick?
Sheila Roberts, writer

Grunge is the way stupid, poor people have always dressed.
Barry Ronge, journalist

If bisexuality is a Nineties trend, it's a trend which helps break down old stereotypes.
Nicci Stein, counsellor

Truth & Lies

For poignancy, truth can relegate screenplay to the little league.
Denis Beckett, journalist

I don't think it's lying or falsifying to present a positive side of a situation.
Reeva Forman, businesswoman

I shall conquer untruth with truth, and in resisting untruth I shall put up with all suffering.
Mahatma Gandhi, activist (India)

No matter how hard its adversary – falsehood – may try to overwhelm it, truth refuses to yield.
Nelson Mandela, President, May 1994-

We all tell each other countless lies in this country – across the colour line.
Es'kia Mphahlele, academic, writer

Truth has become our cheapest national commodity.
Allister Sparks, journalist

All evidence is a blatant lie.
Eugene Terre'Blanche, AWB leader (on the Jani Allan trial, London, 1992)

The public is entitled to know what is happening around it, but at the same time it is equally entitled to the truth.
Adriaan Vlok, politician

Umkhonto we Sizwe (MK)

There was a lot of romance in MK.
Anonymous MK soldier

They thought they would come back in camouflage uniforms, marching through the streets of Pretoria with their heads held high.
Anonymous MK soldier

It takes a particular kind of consciousness to say 'I'm prepared to die'.
Anonymous MK soldier

They expected to return to South Africa as heroes and found only poverty and loneliness.
Jacklyn Cock, academic

Rated the second least effective guerrilla army in history, but that's only because the Manchester United Supporters' Club was also counted.
Arthur Goldstuck, journalist

The aim of Umkhonto was to engage in various acts of sabotage, with great care being taken not to cause any injury or loss of life.
David Kitson, engineer, activist

We are going to keep to non-violence, but we give you permission to go and start the organisation to embark on armed actions.
Albert Luthuli, ANC President General, Nobel Peace Prize

Militarily, MK was a laugh.
Ken Owen, editor

MK has committed itself to ensuring peace and democracy in our country and will continue to conduct itself in a manner which will contribute to the establishment of peace and democracy.
Umkhonto we Sizwe statement

Unrest

We despair of saving this country from the potential threat posed by the seditious and dishonest behaviour of vagrants, who have been allowed to spread over all parts of the country; nor do we see any prospects of peace or contentment for our children in a country in which internal dissension is so rife.
Piet Retief, Voortrekker leader

We have to start inculcating a culture of tolerance, and we can't do that as we chant *Aluta Continua!*, shout 'one settler, one bullet' and fire AKs into the air at funerals.
Allister Sparks, journalist

Much of South Africa's menacing ultra-right is the product of a highly combustible mixture of political uncertainty and deepening economic distress.
David Welsh, academic

Violence

The colour of the finger upon the trigger is irrelevant.
Anonymous

It is all right to kill an impi because you are looking for him and you are ready to die and he is looking for you and he is ready to die.
Anonymous Msinga induna (1988)

There is a frontier of rough country that divides war from murder, and faction fights lie along that frontier, in thickets that are unexplored.
Creina Alcock, journalist

The death toll headlines go on and on until you don't want to read anything but Enid Blyton.
Denis Beckett, journalist

The propensity for violence is like a shadow darkening the horizon.
Breyten Breytenbach, poet, writer

Bugger up the ANC, they are going to bugger up you and your future.
Mangosuthu Buthelezi, IFP leader, politician

If white South Africans had the black opposition party they deserved or, to be less uncharitable, a black opposition party that offered a response commensurate with the crime systematically imposed on the black population all these years, then the terrors that lurk today in white hearts would indeed be justified; then indeed would black youths be running riot, lynching every white person that came their way.
John Carlin, correspondent, The Independent (UK)

Whenever we got instructions with phrases such as 'remove permanently from society' or 'take out' activists, we knew they meant one thing only – kill.
Dirk Coetzee, policeman, assassin

If all of us imagined violence as violence against ourselves, perhaps we would have peace.
JM Coetzee, writer, academic

The only thing to come out of a head that's being continually bashed is blood.
Steven Cohen, artist

What kind of inhumanity is it that allows its most important asset, its people, to be terrorised by random and wanton killing, and then frantically seeks to evade its responsibility and culpability?
Saths Cooper, academic, businessman

The world will not succeed in pushing South Africa off its feet by stimulating insurrection.
William Deedes (Lord Deedes of Aldington), politician, editor (UK)

Any insinuation that the cabinet or State Security Council planned or approved murder or any other crime at any stage is devoid of all truth.
FW de Klerk, State President, 1989-94; Deputy President, 1994-

We believe every man is made in the image of God and we do not want to brutalise that body by pumping 1 000 bullets into it.
Phillip Dlamini, PAC

Even Woody Woodpecker is pretty violent these days.
Gora Ebrahim, politician

Coping with violence in a society so blighted by its many forms has become an all-important life skill for too many women.
Pippa Green, journalist

Officialdom tells us that 33 times more people are murdered every year in South Africa than in Britain which has a population twice the size of ours.
Shaun Johnson, journalist

Victims of domestic violence move like ghosts through society, their bruises covered up and their broken bones explained away with excuses.
Jacqui L'Ange, journalist

Exhortations to kill, whether from the ANC Youth League or the Pan Africanist Congress – whose battle cry 'One settler, one bullet' echoes around the townships on every political occasion – create a psychological milieu which legitimates murder as part of 'the struggle' and elevates plunder to a patriotic duty.
Patrick Laurence, journalist

The suburbs are a rolling gunfight.
Patrick Lee, writer

No one can blame brave, just men for seeking justice by the use of violent methods, nor can they be blamed if they try to create an organised force in order ultimately to establish peace and racial harmony.
Albert Luthuli, ANC President General, Nobel Peace Prize (1964)

I had so many killings already, a whole suitcase full of them, adding up to next to nothing.
Rian Malan, writer

Massacres in South Africa date back decades.
Nelson Mandela, President, May 1994-

For how long do ordinary, decent South Africans tolerate the barbarous savagery, bloodshed, intimidation, fascist intolerance and destruction of property that the ANC and IFP excuse, defend, connive at and encourage?
Graham McIntosh, farmer

No act of violence can be condoned, whoever the perpetrator.
Stanley Mogoba, cleric

I'm prepared to go out of my way to save the life of a farmer who is being robbed or killed.
Peter Mokaba, politician

If one were to isolate a single image that gave white South Africans a sense of moral failure – of having believed the impossible or advocated liberalism from a position of luxury and plenitude – it would be that of children shot dead.
Hugh Murray, publisher & Peter Wilhelm, editor, poet

It is evident that violence is an integral part of the majority of South Africans' historical baggage, imbibed in the womb and passed on from one angry generation to another.
Charmain Naidoo, journalist

By killing people you are killing the community.
Wami Nhlopo, activist

If my son's death could be a turning point in the history of South Africa, in terms of people realising the stupidity of violence, then I'll thank God for it.
Tai O'Kill, cleric (on the St James Church, Kenilworth, massacre)

We murder each other at 10 times the rate of the violence-prone Americans whom so many of our people affect to despise, louts command the streets at night, and striplings rape women old enough to be their grandmothers.
Ken Owen, editor

Few people feel the need to make war while they're spreading the gravy.
Ken Owen

The difficulty is to persuade a nation bred on violence, and indoctrinated with hate, to beat its swords into ploughshares.
Ken Owen

People who have been massacred take against it, and people who have done the massacring feel inclined to give it another go rather than be massacred themselves next time.
Edward Pearce, journalist (UK)

It would be a crying shame if the blissful hush of peace fell upon this land only to be broken by the thuds of someone breaking his wife's jaw or the crack of a stick raising weals on the legs of a child in school.
Jane Raphaely, editor, publisher

It's not the killing, it's the ongoing mutilations of the dead.
Heidi Rincke, foreign correspondent

You cannot expect non-violence from others or put them behind bars when you allow mass murderers to walk.
Pat Rogers, journalist, businessman

We have so many death squads of different hues and assorted ideologies running around that we could easily stage an international Death Squad Olympiad, a week-long gladiatorial in the old Roman style, with crowds enthusiastically cheering on the team of their choice.
Barry Ronge, journalist

The traffic department situation report notes over the next half hour the arrests of two taxi drivers, the impounding of 59 taxis, five roads blocked by taxis, two shooting incidents in which four people are injured, a sniper shooting at police and roads barricaded with cement refuse drums.
Charlene Smith, journalist (with reference to the taxi blockades, Johannesburg, February 1993)

The only people who will benefit from violence are the government and the police.
Robert Mangaliso Sobukwe, PAC founding president

This one black guy continued to smile and munched a hamburger after I shot him once, so I had to pull the trigger again to make sure.
Barend Strydom, murderer

It is incumbent on the adult fraternity to address more seriously the challenge of providing alternative heroes and heroines for kids to emulate, and to show up violence for what it really is – sickening, gross and to be avoided at all costs.
Clem Sunter, businessman, scenario strategist

Once right-wingers embark on something vaguely criminal, the reality of the violence and of being hunted soon jars with the initial romanticism.
Jan Taljaard, journalist

What the white community perceives as unrest, as a sheer display of savagery when persons associated with apartheid are burned to death wearing the necklace, the burning tyre, the black community interprets as a protest.
Buti Thagale, cleric

The government has moulded a genre of so-called 'terrorists' who will be suicidal, like the Arabs in the Middle East conflict.
Derrick Thema, journalist

I am writing to you, Sir, because I have a growing nightmarish fear that unless something drastic is done very soon, then bloodshed and violence are going to happen in South Africa almost inevitably.
Desmond Tutu, cleric, Archbishop of Cape Town (in an open letter to Prime Minister John Vorster, May 1976)

The violence of humour is as shocking as the grenade.
Pieter-Dirk Uys, satirist

While violence is usually abhorred in public rhetoric, all politicians, and virtually the entire Christian church, believes that violence in its most destructive form, warfare, can be justified under certain conditions.
Hendrik W van der Merwe, academic

It is as if there is the smell of a rotting carcass in our nostrils and we've gone out of control.
Paul Verryn, cleric

Before I commit myself to violence I must be able to stand before God, sure that I have tried all other options.
Constand Viljoen, soldier, politician

The violent repression that served to sustain apartheid and the wider programme of political subjugation and economic privilege that apartheid involved, have spawned hatred and violence not only between white and black South Africans but also within the black community.
Lloyd Vogelman, academic

For the forgotten and the marginalised, violence is a way of ensuring that society does not ignore the pain and loss they have endured.
Lloyd Vogelman

Voortrekkers

Some people gradually became accustomed to the migratory way of life, to the laagers, so that for years afterwards they were still wandering around from one place to another. And this way of life had its own peculiar attractions.
LC de Klerk, voortrekker

The Great Trek might come to be seen as an over-extension of Afrikaner resources made possible only by a temporary setback in African fortunes as a result of the Difaqane.
Hermann Giliomee, academic

If their departure was a bid for self-sufficiency, it was self-sufficiency of a peculiarly South African kind, for they were all but outnumbered by the servants and former slaves they took along.
Joseph Lelyveld, editor (USA)

The Voortrekkers drove into the heart of the Dark Continent, where no light penetrated at all, and there, on conquered land, they set up Boer republics in which blacks were ruled in accordance with the Dopper principle.
Rian Malan, writer

The Voortrekkers quarrelled among themselves, but shared one article of faith: to deny political rights to Africans and Coloured people of mixed race.
Thomas Pakenham (Lord Longford), writer

There were many causes of the Trek, but the prime cause was the desire of the Boers to get away from this new idea of racial equality which to them was abhorrent.
Alan Paton, writer

Imagine a lurching ox wagon, passing through a sea of savages, and under these circumstances the boer wife must lie down and give birth.
Eugene Terre'Blanche, AWB leader

Guns in one hand, Bibles in the other, singing their sombre battle hymns, they penetrated deeply into the interior and took this nightmare of tribal warfare, like a bridal opportunity, into their arms.
Laurens van der Post, soldier, writer, philosopher

The Vote/Voters

I would not give a vote to my three-year-old child, or to any five-year-old child, and it is nonsense to recommend that we should give votes to child-like Natives.
Miles Cadman, politician

The experience of countries like England and America indicates that women do not use their vote less wisely than men do, even if they do not use it better.
Cape Times (1930)

No vote can bring us solace.
Sandile Dikeni, columnist, poet

I don't believe it is possible to have a one-man-one-vote system in South Africa and still maintain democracy.
Chris Heunis, politician (1988)

As regards the extension of the franchise to Kaffirs in the Transvaal and Orange River Colony, it is not the intention of His Majesty's Government to give such franchise before representative Government is granted to those Colonies, and if then given it will be so limited as to secure the just predominance of the white race.
Lord Kitchener, soldier (UK) (1902)

You can't eat a vote, or use it to clothe your children.
Rian Malan, writer

No true Christian will ever vote for witchdoctors to rule this country.
Peter Mokaba, politician

Electioneering is perfectly democratic – until it uses criminality to achieve its ends.
Victor Nell, community psychologist

Most voters seem to prefer lusty sinners to pious goody two-shoes.
Ken Owen, editor

Cape Coloureds can no longer vote for the madam in England.

John Vorster, Prime Minister, 1966-78 (on the removal of the Coloureds from the Voters' Roll. The statement was made in 1961, and later denied)

War

There is war coming and it is the ANC who will start.
Anonymous Zulu (1994)

One of the standard spoils of war is the victor's prerogative to reinvent the past.
Dave Basckin, journalist

It's very easy to cry war, but it's something else to leave everyone behind and go fight.
Kobus Botha, lawyer, politician

Say what we will, a more valiant enemy is never seen than the one with whom we have the misfortune to be now at war.
Cape Times (of the Battle of Majuba, First Anglo-Boer War, 1881)

I don't believe that our solution can come from war.
FW de Klerk, State President, 1989-94; Deputy President, 1994-

If you really want to see a war, try to reintroduce racial discrimination in South Africa.
FW de Klerk (1994)

As a first rule of thumb, you can tell a true war story by its absolute and uncompromising allegiance to obscenity and evil.
Andrew Donaldson, journalist

What is needed is not more military conflict, but a war on poverty.
Richard Ellis, correspondent, The Sunday Times (UK)

If Churchill talked the British people through World War II, then history will record that (Harry) Gwala did likewise for so many communities in the Natal Midlands.
Rob Haswell, politician

You go to the limit of trying to avoid a war, but then your country becomes involved in war and in that situation one would have to come to the defence of the country which stands for the values which it upholds.
Albert Luthuli, ANC President General, Nobel Peace Prize

There is only one war here, you see, the war that was and is and yet will be.
Rian Malan, writer

It is a proposition gravely disturbing to earnest souls that war and participation in war are totally irreconcilable with a Christian morality.
Alan Paton, writer

The greatest revenge and triumph for any soldier is to win the war and then win the peace.
Kathy Poulter

War is no easy jive.
Clem Sunter, businessman, scenario strategist

You can suffer war psychosis living 20 minutes from the city centre of Johannesburg.
Phillip van Niekerk, journalist

The impi starts from the ash-heap.
Zulu proverb

Wealth

Brains are the ultimate source of wealth.
Jim Bailey, publisher

A millionaire – suspense, anxiety all day long.
Alfred Beit, mining magnate

The rich walk slowly.
Denise Bjorkman, consultant

Every nation's wealth lies ultimately in the imagination of its people.
Peter Brinson, dance educationist, writer

I used to read about Player and Nicklaus saying they just wanted to win and that the money did not matter; now I know what they meant.
Ernie Els, golfer

When you are rich, you're emotionally more inclined to share than when you are poor and threatened.
Chris Heunis, politician

Even if you're rich you can't do exactly as you wish unless you sleep all day, party all night and always wear shoes.
Sabine Jones, journalist

Actual wealth has not been important to me for some years now.
Sol Kerzner, entrepreneur

Wealth, in spite of holding all the power, has found no means of repelling the invasion of poverty.
Patrick Lee, writer

The material accoutrements of affluence, like big motor cars and mansions, have become an extreme health hazard in an increasingly lawless society.
Mike Lipkin, marketer

Wealth does not at all enable a people to be recognised politically.
Albert Luthuli, ANC President General, Nobel Peace Prize

Financial independence is only realised when you earn enough from your investments to live without the need to work.
Jack Milne, businessman

I love talking about money.
Nataniel, performer

I think it would be affected to say one would rather be poor.
Harry Oppenheimer, businessman

Wealth takes away the extreme worry carried by the vast bulk of the population – that is, where the next meal is coming from.
Harry Oppenheimer

It is not everything; it is not the most important thing.
Harry Oppenheimer

Prosperity has to be created before it can be shared.
Anton Rupert, businessman

I don't owe any person or individual a cent.
Eugene Terre'Blanche, AWB leader

After a lifetime in politics, my total wealth consists of this home and the flat in Port Elizabeth.
John Vorster, Prime Minister, 1966-78 (1980)

I have always liked Old Money, the tweedy, rich tobacco, Victorian stuffed sofa smell of it, the oak-shaded coolness of it and the frequent eccentricity.
Peter Younghusband, foreign correspondent

Old money does not mess around with helicopters.
Peter Younghusband

Weapons

Even if you go to visit your girlfriend or go shopping with your wife, you carry a traditional weapon because there is nothing so disgraceful in Zulu culture as to be unable to defend your wife and children.
BF Bhengu, chief, Ngcolosi clan

A dump of death.
David Breier, political correspondent (on SA's uranium stockpile)

South Africa's nuclear weapons programme was the greatest threat to this country's security in its history.
Keith Campbell, producer, reporter

It was never the intention to use the devices, and from the outset the emphasis was on deterrence.
FW de Klerk, State President, 1989-94; Deputy President, 1994-

Allegations of South Africa's ability to manufacture nuclear weapons can be viewed as nothing more than an academic exercise.
Wynand de Villiers, president, Atomic Energy Board

We're involved in a domestic arms race.
Nick Haysom, academic

What were we going to do – defend apartheid with an atomic bomb?
Roger Hulley, politician

There is no weapon stronger than organisation.
Patrick 'Terror' Lekota, politician

Unless people here in this country lay down their firearms, there'll be no end to it.
Tai O'Kill, cleric

If I could make a plea it would be simply this – for someone to start by putting their firearm down on the ground and walking away from it, and for others to follow.
Mary O'Kill, housewife

The AK-47 and the necklace have become the everyday working tools of barbarians and street thugs.
Ken Owen, editor

When every other person has a Maxim gun, or at least an AK-47, militarism holds no advantages for a minority.
Ken Owen

Since 1978 and the beginning of a process of privatising the covert arms of the security forces, enough loose cannons – in the form of private front companies linked to the covert arms

of the intelligence networks – have been unleashed to guarantee instability in South Africa for years to come.
Ivor Powell, journalist

What the development of the A-bombs really reveals is not, as one Armscor technician enthused, that South Africa made itself one of the top seven nations of the world, but the extent of the paranoia which gripped our rulers at that time.
Allister Sparks, journalist

The purchase of a gun may be regarded as a rational reaction to the threats around us, but it merely ratchets up the potential for violence.
Clem Sunter, businessman, scenario strategist

An unarmed white man in Africa is a dead man.
Eugene Terre'Blanche, AWB leader

AK-47s: cheaper to buy today than the latest Wilbur Smith novel.
Pieter-Dirk Uys, satirist

A sense of humour is the last truly democratic weapon in the hands of each person.
Pieter-Dirk Uys

South Africa does not have and does not intend to develop nuclear explosive devices for any purpose, either peaceful or as a weapon.
John Vorster, Prime Minister, 1966-78

Men with guns are rarely innocents.
Tony Weaver, journalist

Weight

I've always thought fiscal drag was a weight problem people in Sandton suffer from.
Bafana Khumalo, journalist

Fat has taken on a moral paradigm.
Hedi Lampert-Kemper, journalist

Slimness, no matter what the cost, denotes goodness, achievement and mastery.
Hedi Lampert-Kemper

Our cities are studded with aerobics academies and our countryside with fat farms, all united in a war against cellulite so ferocious it makes the battle on our borders look like a cub-scout jamboree.
Barry Ronge, journalist (1987)

Rich equates with thin.
Hellouise Truswell, journalist

Whites

There are good whites but we can't tell them apart from the bad ones.
Anonymous

If you want to be a white man in Africa, it is always easier if you have had a bit to drink.
Anonymous (1994)

White South Africa has got to get streetwise.
David Barritt, editor

We do not need a white population wilting under the weight of the idea that they are unwittingly complicit in a vast and venal conspiracy.
Denis Beckett, journalist

The white people who came here lived at a very much higher standard than the indigenous peoples, and with a very rich tradition which they brought with them from Europe.
PW Botha, Prime Minister/State President, 1978-89

The Afrikaner people and other minority groups known as English-speaking South Africans – and there are many of them; I have referred to them in this Parliament; the Portuguese-speaking South African, the large number of Italian-speaking South Africans, the Greeks and Jewish South Africans and others, who pass as English-speaking South Africans – stand for the preservation of civilised Christian standards and norms in this country.
PW Botha (1983)

Why do the white people start at nothing?
Cetshwayo, King of the Zulus (1876)

We are visitors in our own houses: the jetsam of the colonial era.
Mary Anne Fitzgerald, writer

For our tribe, to live in black Africa is to plant trees knowing that your children might never sit in the shade of their branches.
Mary Anne Fitzgerald

Whites carried with them the subtle bruises of unjust privilege.
Anthony Heard, editor

We will be many, and we will be forever, one shade in the people's rainbow that makes up Africa's most unusual country.
Shaun Johnson, journalist

A white was described as a person who 'in appearance obviously is, or is generally accepted as, a white person but does not include a person who, although in appearance obviously a white person, is generally accepted as a coloured person'.
Graham Leach, correspondent, BBC Radio

White South Africans have a right to contribute to the task of achieving national freedom, justice, reconciliation and peace.
Patrick 'Terror' Lekota, politician

Imagine the consternation of the Africans when suddenly they were confronted by scores of albino-like beings dressed in unfamiliar and, to them, funny clothes.
Patrick 'Terror' Lekota

We knew there would come a moment when lightning cracked and thunder rolled and the world as we had known it disintegrated.
Rian Malan, writer

I am no longer prepared to waste my time on white people.
Winnie Mandela, politician (1987)

There must be humans on the other side of the fence; it's only we haven't learned how to talk.
Nat Nakasa, journalist

White people should accept that they are not the universal point of reference.
Njabulo Ndebele, academic, writer

What is being asked of the white man is not just a political or an economic decision: it is a decision in faith in which there are no final guarantees.
Franklin Sonn, educationist, ambassador

Our population is a heterogeneous population with the white race divided into practically three groups, the Afrikaans-speaking, the English-speaking and the Jewish sections.
JH Viljoen, politician (1950)

Wildlife

I fell to the ground as his mighty trunk hit me on the back. I just kept rolling and all I remember was his huge tusks coming for my face.
Daryl Balfour, wildlife photographer (on his rumble in the jungle)

If you claim a rhino at 20 metres and your neighbour had a leopard peer through the window, there's no doubt about who's the better man.
Denis Beckett, journalist

It's difficult to get into the mind of a whale.
Peter Best, academic

A wounded buffalo in thick bush is considered to be about as nasty a customer as anyone may desire to tackle; for its vindictive indomitable courage and extraordinary cunning are a very formidable combination, as a long list of fatalities bears witness.
Percy Fitzpatrick, politician, writer

The spectacle of two lions roaring at each other, literally yards away from our open Jeep, was one of such primal power and immediacy as to defy adequate description.
Philip Gawith, journalist

I lived among a troop of wild baboons for three years; I followed them on their daily excursions; slept among them; fed them night and morning on mealies; learned to know each one individually; taught them to trust and to love me – and also to hate me so vehemently that my life was several times in danger.
Eugène Marais, writer

The South African baboon in captivity is singularly like the Bushman in its predilection for tobacco and alcohol.
Eugène Marais

There he was – antediluvian, massive and dangerous looking, rising suspiciously to his feet in a cloud of disturbed flies – a solitary mud-plastered black rhino bull, as compact and uncompromising as a battering ram.
Margaret Reardon, naturalist, writer

We live in a vicious, physical country and we're used to lions and the roughness of the bush.
Leon Schuster, actor

The howl of the African hyena is about the most mournful and weird-like sound in nature, being a sort of prolonged groan, rising in cadence till it ends in a shriek; they only laugh when enjoying a good feed.
Frederick Courteney Selous, hunter

Though it is now the fashion to depreciate the courage of the lion, the power of his voice, and everything else concerning him, yet it is a fact that, under such circumstances, several of them roaring in unison will make the whole air in their immediate vicinity vibrate and tremble, and I know of nothing in nature more awe-inspiring on a dark night, more calculated to make a man feel nervous.
Frederick Courteney Selous

The best time to see these animals is five o'clock in the morning, when teeming collective nouns of antelope, zebra, wildebeest, giraffe, lion, elephant, rhinoceros, warthog, hyena, vervet monkeys and dung-beetles rise before the crack of dawn to escape tourists in Landrovers.
Gus Silber, journalist

Wine

For a country that has been the skunk of the world these last 20 years, South Africa's wines are generally in remarkably good shape – modern, well-made, and full of interesting quirks.
Tim Atkin, wine writer (UK)

People ooh and ah about anything that comes out of a French bottle – even if it's *chevaux lait* – and when, next day, their heads split open and they find their socks have rotted off, they never suspect it might be the wine they drank.
James Clarke, journalist

Wine is all about mouthfeel.
Peter Finlayson, wine farmer

A cellar without food is like a library without books.
Edo Folli, businessman

A study of economics shows that the best time to buy any wine is last year.
Jenni Newman, PR

It is terribly important to know where the taxi is going before you can choose a suitable Champagne.
Peter Noel-Barham, gourmet

We live in stirring, even perilous, times in South Africa, times more than ever for wines of warmth, generosity and maturity, civilised wines with backbone embodying the pride of honest craftsmanship.
John Platter, wine farmer, writer

The optimism and enthusiasm and the new names and fresh techniques which are transforming so completely the face and quality of Cape wine have stood in marked contrast to the political landscape of the recent past.
John Platter

Cape wine was, and by a number still is, branded as a product of cheap labour, of the Dop system, of prison labour, the 'grapes of wrath'.
John Platter

Cape wine has the colour of French wine, yet tastes a little of the fennel which is used to scour the vats.
Abraham van Riebeeck, son of Jan van Riebeeck

Today, praise be to God, wine was pressed for the first time from Cape grapes.
Jan van Riebeeck, coloniser (1659)

If we can make great wine, people will buy it. And if they don't we'll drink it ourselves.
Achim von Arnim, wine farmer

Women

It's customary for a woman to have a lasting love affair with her face.
Anonymous

As women restrict each other's choices we come very close to feminist fascism.
Shona Bagley, journalist

A lady always makes sure that her man is comfortable, and she never blows on some other guy's dice.
John Berks, talk show host

There is nothing that works more on my nerves than a woman who continually interrupts me.
PW Botha, Prime Minister/State President, 1978-89

Good girls are feminine. Bad girls are women.
Suzy Brokensha, journalist

A woman must go where her husband goes.
Sheila Camerer, politician

The concept of the New Age woman has always suggested to me the image of an alligator-wrestling Amazon with a dominant libido who is capable of balancing her cheque book unaided.
Alastair Campbell, student

Although she is not out to get one's balls in a pair of pliers, so to speak, she invariably does.
Alastair Campbell

When one is painting a nude woman the power-game of sex is totally suspended.
Jeff Chandler, artist

I am filled with respect and admiration for all of womankind as well as for little doggies and pandas and whales and things like that.
James Clarke, journalist

What is a man at a dinner party expected to say to a woman who announces she is a housewife?
James Clarke

To have girls running around when one is seriously trying to track something or trying to light a fire with only two matches is intolerable.
James Clarke

A woman should be soft, soft by nature, soft by word of mouth. If they are not soft they simply do not have an influence over a man.
Danie Craven, SA Rugby Board President

Until they get to the altar, some women become the men they want to marry.
Andrew Donaldson, journalist

I know lots and lots of man-haters, the majority of whom are women.
Chris du Plessis, journalist

Though I have been scared of women all my life, I now fear them more than ever.
Chris du Plessis

Blondes are the Rolls-Royce, the French Champagne, the Beluga caviar of the female species.
Peta Eggierth-Symes, businesswoman

Have Nineties women become the men they always wanted to marry?
Pnina Fenster, journalist

Women are sometimes the best soldiers because they are merciless.
Andrew Ford, leader, Boer Resistance Movement

It is through feminist efforts that the old gender stereotypes are being stripped to the bone and that women are no longer perceived simply as passive homebodies, saints, hostesses or whores.
Hazel Friedman, art historian

In a patriarchal society women have no control over their lives, their bodies, their destinies or their reproduction.
Nomboniso Gasa, activist

The post-feminist's strong survival instincts ensure that she will still be around tormenting little grey people well into the 21st century, thank God.
Kendell Geers, artist

Together, no government, no political party, no liberation movement, no group of patriarchal men can stand in our way.
Frene Ginwala, politician

For the past three decades women have trivialised their fight for a seat in the boardroom by striving for the right to open car doors themselves and for the abolishment of words like girlfriend and man-hole.
Arthur Goldstuck, journalist

There is something immediately attractive about a women-only political party.
Lauren Jacobson, attorney

Women are brought together by the common factor of womanhood.
Anne Letsebe, Women's National Coalition

They love a lover with a slow touch.
Mike Lipkin, marketer

Women concern themselves, by and large, with fundamentals.
Albert Luthuli, ANC President General, Nobel Peace Prize

There is no feminist movement that is rooted in Africa that can relate to the African women and their culture.
Linda Mampinga, feminist

Women are people who will pick a flower and stroke it and talk to it as if it were a person. But once you become a fighter, you forget about flowers.
Faith Mashiloane, activist

I resist the notion that women should be defined by their marital status, the number of children they have or their appearance, whereas, in the case of men, the focus is on how well they do the job.
Ivy Matsepe-Casaburri, academic, businesswoman

In the South African context there is still a whole lot more that divides women than what unites them.
Dorothy Mokgalo, activist

It is useless to pretend that issues important to women are also important to men, or that men as a group accept the right of women to make their needs heard.
Gill Noero, consultant

In South Africa, traditionally women are not seen as fighters but peacemakers.
Lt Talita Nothard, SADF

Young women in South Africa have always been more mature than their opposite numbers in other countries because this country is a crucible and those of us who survive and thrive here emerge as tempered steel.
Jane Raphaely, editor, publisher

The unbearable slightness of being nobody is something most women experience at one time or another, but not usually at the hands of another woman.
Jane Raphaely

What women have in common (mainly the huge sense of frustration at the discrimination experienced) can at times override other differences; women are not so locked in power struggles that they lose sight of common purpose; and women have an ability to operate on the basis of tolerance and a will to reach consensus.
Bea Roberts, Idasa

On the brink of the 21st century, the irony is that the only place in which women are allowed to break traditional and political barriers is at a beauty pageant, a contest historically to do with physical beauty.
Nina Romm, artist

She came in slouching towards Rockey Street, but turned at the last moment and sat facing Bryanston.
Hilton Rudnick, psychometrist, composer

There is one beautiful thing with daughters, that their hearts always come nearer and nearer to their mother's as they grow older, and the real weight of a woman's lot begins to fall on them, and they know all it means.
Olive Schreiner, writer

Intelligence, humour, an independence of spirit; I like women who won't be cowed.
Wilbur Smith, writer

While the third wave of feminism rolls on, you can bet your Jockey cuts that most South African women will be making hair appointments, filling in sex quizzes in women's magazines, updating their wardrobes.
Marianne Thamm, journalist

The reality is that a dog that is chained and beaten will probably be removed to a safer environment sooner than a battered woman.
Marianne Thamm

Women have kept life on earth.
Laurens van der Post, soldier, writer, philosopher

The world has been dominated by the spirit of man, and woman has never had the right to give what a woman can give beyond her role as a mother.
Laurens van der Post

We need to break out of our Calvinist strait-jacket, get sensual, get turned on, get satisfied.
Andrea Vinassa, journalist

How better for a woman to assert her unique, individual femininity than to take off her clothes?
Martin Welz, editor

Words

If words, the very materials out of which poems are made, are products of dynamic social changes, works of art made up of words must also be seen as such.
Guy Butler, writer, academic

Relevance is one of those loaded words that are meaningless without a context.
Neville Dubow, artist, academic

There's too much woolly-minded thinking in the suburbs these days, too much guff spoken about win/win situations and similar figments of the anxious white imagination.
Rian Malan, writer

Words, cleverly used, are the ultimate power play.
Barry Ronge, journalist

Many words have had cordons of barbed wire flung around them because they are politically incorrect.
Barry Ronge

If fine words buttered parsnips, social investment reporting would be a cholesterol hazard.
Reg Rumney, journalist

Surely it is not beyond the wit of man to produce a form of words which for the first time clearly demonstrates that white and black South Africans really need each other.
Clem Sunter, businessman, scenario strategist

Youth

Not all youth is interested in never-ending meetings, workshops and toyi-toying.
Anonymous ANC Youth League leader

Youth must be permitted big dreams.
Jim Bailey, publisher

Having rejected the tribal rites of passage and control by their elders in the previous order, they seek unbridled freedom, power and pleasure.
Don Beck, conflict resolution specialist

We are not saying black youths should rob and attack whites, neither are we saying they should not attack the white oppressors.
George Biya, Azayo president

No individual, let alone a generation, should ever be considered lost or forgotten.
FW de Klerk, State President, 1989-94; Deputy President, 1994-

The knowledge of this generation of African children extends no further than the laws of urban survival that govern life on the township streets.
Wessel Ebersohn, journalist

They have stepped into a world where economies teeter and anarchy stalks the streets.
Marilyn Hattingh, editor

In the new age, youth and enthusiasm will always bear out age and experience.
Mike Lipkin, marketer

There is a rawness to being twenty-something and living on the edge of apocalypse.
Mike Lipkin

The English of 'youth' is harmless in itself, but in South Africa the Youth are black and bad, while 'teenagers' are normal white kids.
Mzwanele Mayekiso, author

They are coming – hopefully, fearfully and inevitably – to town, for there is nowhere else for them to go.
Mike Muller, academic, writer

Teenager is a term devoid of political meaning; youth is laden with it.
Jeremy Seekings, academic

Young people are going through trauma – they are falling through the cracks.
Sheila Sisulu, educationist, Woman of the Year 1993

We've been bred on the whiteness of our skin and find ourselves unequipped to deal with reality.
Anne Store, honours degree graduate

When I hear youngsters laugh, I hear a new South Africa.
Pieter-Dirk Uys, satirist

Zulus

You white men have encircled us; but perhaps the day may come when you will allow us to pass through your country, and remind those nobody's people that the Zulus are still on the face of the earth.
Anonymous (after the Battle of Ulundi, 1879)

We are always prepared for war: we are Zulus.
Anonymous (1994)

No men ever fought more pluckily than the Zulus – they are brave men indeed.
Alfred Blaine, soldier (1879)

I have the right and duty to speak for the Zulu people which no power on earth will ever take away from me.
Mangosuthu Buthelezi, IFP leader, politician

Zulus are a nation – just like Lesotho or Swaziland – what is so strange about that?
Mangosuthu Buthelezi

We will not again be conquered and we will not again be subjugated.
Mangosuthu Buthelezi

I shall not agree to any laws or rules from Natal, and by so doing throw the great kraal which I govern into the water.
Cetshwayo, King of the Zulus (1876)

It seems that anyone can say what they like about the Zulu past and Zulu affairs, make wild generalisations, create stereotypes about Zulu militarism, and prognosticate about civil war, all without challenge.
Jeff Guy, historian

We feel it is physically impossible for anybody at whatever level to prevent the Zulu people from carrying the cultural accoutrements, inasmuch as it would be impossible for anybody to stop a white man from wearing a tie.
Frank Mdlalose, politician

There are two major types of Zulus: postcard Zulus and the type of Zulu who is running away from the postcard.
Khaba Mkhize, journalist

When God created the Zulus, there were no whites, no roads, no tractors. The Zulus still lived.
David Ntombela, IFP warlord

Nice people must take it into their heads to understand that in the early 19th century, the Zulus killed everybody who got in their way (a minimum of a million without guns), and bossed the eastern part of Southern Africa in a fashion which might be called decisive.
Edward Pearce, journalist (UK)

Zulus mean never, either in pride or for safety, to submit to the rule of what must be Xhosa domination.
Edward Pearce

The Zulu constitution is essentially military; every man is a soldier, in whose eyes manual labour, except for military purposes, is degrading.
Theophilus Shepstone, Administrator of the Transvaal (1878)

Nothing is as likely to stir the Zulu heart as an appeal to the national hero Shaka, the one symbol which all acknowledge, whether they be Christian or pagan, urban or rural, traditional or modern.
Patti Waldmeir, correspondent, Financial Times (UK)

Restless and teeming, violent and divided, the Zulus are about to reclaim Natal.
David Willers, editor

They are different people with a different history and they don't shy away from a fight.
Jacob Zuma, politician

Loyalty to kwaZulu is the very first requirement in the demonstration of Zuluness.
Goodwill Zwelithini, King of the Zulus

Until we get what is justly ours, there can be no rest for any true Zulu.
Goodwill Zwelithini

A Zulu king is not just another black leader who should be approachable by just anybody.
Goodwill Zwelithini

Index